P9-AQF-541

THE CHIEF RABBI, THE POPE, AND THE HOLOCAUST

THE CHIEF RABBI, THE POPE, AND THE HOLOCAUST

An Era in Vatican-Jewish Relations

Robert G. Weisbord

Wallace P. Sillanpoa

Transaction Publishers
New Brunswick (U.S.A.) and London (U.K.)

Library of Congress Catalog Number: 90-22530
ISBN: 0-88738-416-1
Printed in the United States of America

Library of Congress Cataloging-in-Publication Data

Sillanpoa, Wallace P., 1946-
The Chief Rabbi, the Pope, and the Holocaust : an era in Vatican—Jewish relations / Wallace P. Sillanpoa and Robert G. Weisbord.
p. cm.
Includes bibliographical references.
ISBN 0-88738-416-1
1. Judaism—Relations—Catholic Church. 2. Catholic Church—Relations—Judaism. 3. Holocaust, Jewish (1939-1945) 4. Pius XII, Pope, 1876-1958—Relations with Jews. 5. Zolli. Eugenio, 1881-1956. 6. Rabbis—Italy—Biography. 7. Converts from Judaism—Biography. I. Weisbord, Robert G. II. Title.
BM535.S46 1991
261.2′6′0945632—dc20 90-22530
CIP

To our mothers, Grace Sillanpoa and Rose Weisbord
and
to those of all faiths or none who risked their lives in responding
to the catastrophe of the Holocaust.

. . . for in converting Jews to Christians, you raise the price of pork.

—The Merchant of Venice, *act III, scene V*

Lo sapevi, peccare non significa fare il male:
non fare il bene, questo significa peccare.
Quanto bene tu potevi fare! E non l'hai fatto:
non c'è stato un peccatore più grande di te.
—Pier Paolo Pasolini, A un papa

Contents

Acknowledgments

In the preparation of this work we have incurred numerous debts. We are most grateful to our colleagues in the University of Rhode Island Library: to Andrew Turyn and Gordon Stein and to Vicky Burnett and Marie Rudd for their extraordinary diligence and good humor. A special note of thanks is due Elaine Wills for her secretarial talents and her forbearance and to Louise Hilliard as well. Phyllis Winkler, Judy Testa, Bruce Kupelnick, Dr. Danilo Bracchetti of the United States Embassy in Rome, colleagues Mariano Diaz-Miranda, Mario Trubiano, Shmuel Mardix, Hannelore Crossgrove, Karen Heinze, and Richard Neuse were also most helpful. We are further indebted to Rabbi Elio Toaff in Rome and Rabbi Elia Ricchetti of Trieste who were most kind in making available materials on Rabbi Israele Zolli contained in synagogue files. Judith Berman, the widow of Rabbi Meyer Berman, and Dr. Mary Hochman, the daughter of Rabbi Jacob Hochman, shared personal letters and other documents which were most useful. Lastly, without the financial assistance of William Frost of the Lucius N. Littauer Foundation, this book would not have been possible.

1

Introduction

In December 1939, Israele Zolli, who had been a spiritual leader of Trieste's Jews for some twenty-eight years, officially assumed his duties as the Chief Rabbi of Rome's ancient Jewish community. In March 1939, the Vatican Secretary of State, Eugenio Cardinal Pacelli, scion of an aristocratic Roman family, had been elected Pope in the briefest conclave in church history: one day and three ballots. The new supreme pontiff assumed the name of Pius XII. Six months after Pacelli's election, Adolph Hitler began World War II by sending his army into neighboring Poland, Zolli's native land. Before the fighting ended in 1945, approximately six million Jews, including three million from Poland and more than fifteen hundred from Rome, were to lose their lives, martyrs to Hitler's insane racial theories. Both Zolli and Pacelli were to emerge from the Holocaust surrounded by controversy over their conduct during that darkest of eras in Jewish history.

Before he was offered and accepted the prestigious post in Rome, Zolli visited the eternal city where he found much cordiality and warmth among his future congregants. Writing to his Roman flock in September 1939, Zolli assured them that they were all in his heart and promised to include them in his prayers as long as he lived. He exhorted his brothers to be faithful to God and to Israel as well as to their beloved fatherland, Italy.[1] Five and a half years later those words would have a hollow ring, for in February 1945, Israele Zolli shocked his coreligionists in Rome and throughout the Jewish world by converting to Catholicism and taking as his baptismal name, Eugenio, to honor the Pope for what Zolli saw as his great humanitarianism toward Jews during the Holocaust.

Almost half a century after his conversion to Roman Catholicism, Zolli, who died in 1956, still evokes anger and/or embarrassment. As the major rabbinical *meshummad* (voluntary apostate) in modern history, Zolli's name is anathema to Rome's Jewish community. When visitors to the Italian capital broach the subject of Zolli—Roman Jews almost never do—he is often referred to as *innominabile* (unmentionable). Residents of the old ghetto, which harks back to the sixteenth century, emotionally describe him with course epithets.

His is a saga that a contemporary rabbi labelled "one of the strangest stories of modern Jewish life . . . a unique event in Jewish history."[2] Jews, even rabbis, had converted to Roman Catholicism over the centuries.[3] But, in 1945, Cecil Roth, the esteemed historian, could not recall when he had been more profoundly distressed, for here was no "catchpenny, titular Synagogal dignitary . . . but the spiritual head of the oldest Jewish community of Europe who has disgraced the superb tradition of this office and proved false to his flock at their hour of greatest need."[4] Zolli, it must be remembered, was a prolific biblical scholar of some note as well as a Chief Rabbi.

Because of its highly sensitive nature, Zolli's story has never been adequately told. A book on the conversion, which was rushed into print in 1945, is accurate on many key points but is highly polemical, indeed vituperative, and undocumented in many places.[5] Even brief published references to Zolli are often incorrect and reflect the emotional nature of the scandal that his conversion spawned. For example, a book about the Palestinian Jewish Brigade that fought in World War II and written by one of its officers, mistakenly attributes Zolli's resignation as Chief Rabbi to a dispute over the apportionment of funds raised overseas for communal purposes. Moreover, the book suggests that Zolli became a Roman Catholic priest after his conversion.[6]

Even today in the United States, there are discomfited Jews who prefer to suppress the story. A Jewish navy veteran of World War II asks, "why we don't leave [sic] sleeping dogs lie, after 44 years of unpleasant memories."[7]

In general, the Zolli affair has been treated as a "hot potato" by academics.[8] Back in 1945, his conversion was widely discussed in Jewish circles, but nowadays most Jews, including many who are knowledgeable about twentieth-century Jewish history, do not even recognize Zolli's name. One Jewish scholar wrote the following shortly after Zolli's death.

> Whether Jews like him or not, he cannot be casually dismissed. Whatever his neuroses, derelictions, or incompetencies, he was the guardian of the intellectual and spiritual life of one of the most ancient of Jewish centers. When such a man leaves Israel and embraces Roman Catholicism, his defection cannot help but become a cause célèbre, and by that fact, most pressing of assessment.[9]

We hope to provide that long overdue assessment.

In the Catholic world, Zolli has also attracted little attention since the 1950s. His conversion was described in one Catholic journal in 1954 as "humanly speaking, the most important Jewish conversion in many decades."[10] Yet no Catholic scholar or popular writer has dealt with Zolli in any depth. Mention of his name, even in highly educated circles, is likely to evoke blank stares. Zolli and his tale of tribulations deserve better.

Armchair psychoanalysis of the Chief Rabbi will be kept to a minimum in this volume. Penetrating the Byzantine labyrinth of Zolli's mind is a daunting prospect indeed. Detailed information about his formative years is scarce. This is reason enough to deter a leap into the quicksand of psychiatry. Which factor or factors induced Zolli to embrace Catholic teachings as early as 1938, possibly even earlier, will probably never be known. Nevertheless, the authors believe that by dint of painstaking scholarly detective work they have succeeded in explaining why Zolli left the Jewish fold in February 1945, and why he formally joined the Catholic Church at that juncture.

Zolli's career, especially the events that occurred during the critical years of 1943 to 1945, can aid those who would understand the horrors of Fascism in Italy. It can also illuminate Catholic-Jewish relations in general, and Vatican-Jewish relations in particular, during the Holocaust. Needless to say, there is no consensus among historians on these thorny subjects.

Conor Cruise O'Brien, the Irish diplomat and scholar, recently described the Third Reich as "the greatest concentration of murderous hatred ever attained on earth."[11] Some three weeks after the Third Reich capitulated to the Allies, Pope Pius XII talked to the Sacred College of Cardinals about the "satanic specter" raised by National

Socialism.[12] He solemnly reviewed the sorrowful passion of the Roman Catholic Church under the Nazis and asserted that no one could charge the Church with not having exposed the true nature of Nazism. But many have done precisely that and by concentrating mainly on the manner in which the pontiff dealt with the Jews when their very existence as a people hung in the balance.

During and right after the war, negative commentary on Pius XII for his public timidity in the face of Hitler's "Final Solution" to the Jewish question was almost always voiced privately. The conventional wisdom was that the pope had been fervently committed to an Allied triumph and that he did all that was humanly possible for the victims of Fascism, including Jews.

Then, in 1949, Avro Manhattan's *The Vatican World of Politics* appeared in print.[13] Manhattan argued that the highest spiritual authority in the West had actually preferred Germany to Communist Russia in the recent war. True, Manhattan said very little about Pius XII and the Jews per se, but he was openly belligerent toward the Roman Catholic Church. As might have been expected, reviews in church publications excoriated the author and his book.

Not until the publication and performance in the early 1960s of Rolf Hochhuth's play, *The Deputy, (Der Stellvertreter*) did the emotionally charged issue of the Holy See and the "Chosen People" become the full-blown controversy that it remains to this day. Hochhuth, a young Swiss Protestant, partly attributed the Holy Father's padlocked lips to his pro-German bias that blinded him to the fact that the Nazis were not "The Germans but the despoilers, the perverters of Germany, as well as of everything else."[14] Hochhuth did not ascribe Pacelli's public fence-straddling to anti-Semitism or to any pecuniary consideration of the Vatican. Rather, his errors of omission where Jews were concerned were due in large measure to his character flaws and to his preoccupation with the afterlife and his corresponding devaluation of the importance of earthly suffering. The playwright was of the opinion that for the Roman church, in the divine scheme of things, the wholesale loss of human life was attenuated by the preservation of millions of souls who were with God.[15]

European performances of Hochhuth's *Der Stellvertreter* were accompanied by violence in a number of capitals on the continent. When it was brought to New York City, the play triggered picketing and unleashed a cataract of vitriol. Not only was it flayed by Catholics, but it was disavowed by several Jewish spokesmen and by groups such as the Jewish War Veterans. Worried about the deleterious effect the play could have on the brittle Catholic-Jewish entente, the National Conference of Catholics and Jews called Hochhuth's treatment of the subject slanted.[16] It is important to recall that *The Deputy* was produced at the time of Vatican II when the Roman Catholic Church was redefining its relationship with the world's other major faiths.

Stung by Hochhuth's strong censure of Piux XII, Vatican spokesmen have rarely missed an opportunity over the past quarter of a century to pay tribute to the venerated memory of that pontiff. Typical was the letter sent by Giovanni Cardinal Montini, Archbishop of Milan, almost on the eve of his 1963 election as Pope Paul VI. Montini, who worked side by side with Pacelli during the war, saw *The Deputy* not as history but as ''artificial manipulation of facts to fit a preconceived idea.'' History, he prophesied, ''will show how vigilant, persistent, disinterested and courageous [Pius's] conduct must be judged to have been, when viewed in its true context, in the concrete conditions of that time.''[17] Hochhuth's characterization of the wartime pontiff was false, he wrote. Pacelli was not cowardly or heartless, nor was he a calculating political opportunist. Rather, ''he was a man of exquisite sensibility and the most delicate human sympathies.''[18]

Paul VI never wavered in his devotion. In March 1974, on the thirty-fifth anniversary of Pacelli's election as pope, the ailing Montini used his traditional Sunday blessing to declare that Pius XII had done everything feasible to alleviate suffering and to impede inhuman deeds.[19]

Opinion about Pius's performance during the Holocaust does not correlate with religious background or affiliations. True, for the past quarter of a century Jewish writers have in general castigated the Pope for not doing or saying enough for their coreligionists.[20] However, there are several Jews who have rallied to the Pope's defense: Pinchas Lapide, Joseph Lichten, Meir Michaelis, and, at least initially, Leon Poliakov, to mention just a few.[21]

After the liberation of Italy, Pius XII won encomiums from several Jewish quarters. For example, in the fall of 1945 he received representatives of refugees who had survived various Nazi concentration and death camps. Accompanied by officials of the Roman branch of the

Knights of Columbus and the Pallottine Fathers,[22] the group thanked the pontiff for the generosity he had manifested during the terrible period of Nazi fascism. In response, the Holy Father stated that their visit demonstrated how the Roman Catholic Church transcends narrow limits created by human selfishness and racist passions. He then added a paradoxical observation to the effect that the Church concerns itself with religious questions and maintains a wide reserve in the face of questions that are of a purely political and territorial nature.[23] Whether it was possible to separate religious or moral concerns from political issues would go the very heart of the dispute over the Pope's policies vis-à-vis the Jews.

In March 1946, delegates from the Italian Jewish communities meeting in Rome for the first time since the Nazi withdrawal, paid homage to the pope and expressed their deepest gratitude for the brotherhood evinced by the Church during the years of persecution. Speaking for all Jews, the delegates took note of the many times priests had suffered imprisonment and even death for assisting Jews. Their goodness helped to mitigate the enormous Jewish losses. Jews would always recall just how much had been done for them through the actions of the "Popes."[24]

When, in October 1958, the 261st Pope expired due to a stroke at the age of eighty-two, the announcement of his passing elicited messages of condolence and eulogies from a myriad of Jewish leaders, rabbinical and other. Pius XII, said Rabbi William Rosenblum of New York's Temple Israel, "made it possible for thousands of Jewish victims of nazism and fascism to be hidden away in the monasteries and convents of various Catholic orders and for Jewish children to be taken into their orphanages."[25] His efforts to rescue Jews during the Holocaust were also lauded by Rabbi Joachim Prinz, a German-born refugee from Nazi persecution who was president of the American Jewish Congress.[26] The pontiff's "wartime activities in saving Jewish children from the hands of the Fascist butchers" were recollected by the Jewish Labor Committee.[27] His saintly virtues were compared with those of Albert Schweitzer. There is good reason to believe that the foregoing panegyrics were heartfelt and did not spring from the concept of *de mortuis nil nisi bonum*. Of course, this was in the pre-Hochhuth era before scholars undertook to reassess Pius XII.

For decades, Catholic commentators, with a few exceptions, have been sympathetic to Pius XII because of the delicate diplomatic position in which he found himself and the excruciating choices he had to make. One notable exception is Father John Morley who has emerged as a severe critic of the Vatican's role from 1939 to 1943.[28]

Edward H. Flannery, another American priest and a pioneer in promoting Jewish-Catholic amity, understands the position of papal detractors who have taken Pacelli to task for his silence. On the other hand, he believes that to some extent, the Pope has been a scapegoat. Virtually every Western government was guilty of inaction and complicity. Why single out the Pope?[29]

In actuality, an extensive bibliography has been developed faulting a score of countries including the United States for being less than hospitable when confronted by the Jewish refugee crisis. The moral failure of Roosevelt and Churchill to bomb Auschwitz or the rail lines leading to it has been repeatedly highlighted by historians.[30] Some Jews have also cast a cold eye on what they retrospectively regard as an anemic response by Jewish organizations in the United States and Palestine to the martyrdom of their brethren.[31]

There is more than enough guilt to go around. Protestantism too is culpable. However, Albert Schweitzer, in his preface to Hochhuth's *The Deputy*, was on target when he wrote, "The Catholic Church bears the greater guilt for it was an organized, supra-national power in a position to do something . . ."[32]

Moreover, in some respects, the pope is *sui generis*. Although governments are often characterized by moral pretensions and self-righteousness, the papacy trumpets the fact that it is a two thousand year-old divine institution. Popes profess to be the vicars of Christ on earth. As such they enjoy prestige and moral standing almost never approached by secular leaders. Popes speak in God's name and their pronouncements as heads of the Catholic Church on matters of faith and morals are advertised as unerring. In view of this, it is not surprising that their behavior is often closely scrutinized and they are usually held to a higher ethical standard than presidents and prime ministers. Such is the case with Pius XII.

Because of his wide-ranging biblical scholarship, Zolli was not an unfamiliar figure at the Vatican before the Nazi occupation of Rome. But there is no evidence that he and Pacelli were more than slight acquaintances. Even after Zolli's baptism, notwithstanding occasional audiences with the pontiff, there was little personal interaction between the two men. Their lives ran in parallel orbits, crossing rarely. Still, like Zolli's rabbinical career, Pius XII's long pontificate tells us much about the Church of Rome and its relationship to the Jewish people, with particular reference to the issue of conversion that forms such an important part of this book. Pius XII's comportment will be evaluated to determine if Zolli accurately gauged the pope's efforts to save Jews. Did the Holy Father truly deserve to have a Jew or ex-Jew such as Zolli name himself Eugenio?

Before proceeding to discuss the two Eugenios, Zolli and Pacelli, in the context of the Holocaust nightmare, a cursory survey of the historical encounters between the papacy and the Jews is in order.

Notes

1. *Tempio Maggiore*, Rome, Modern Archives, Israele Zolli File, Message from Zolli in Trieste, 13 September 1939.
2. Meyer Berman Papers, letter from Rabbi Meyer Berman to Judith Berman, 18 February 1945.
3. For instance, in 1735 in Ancona, a rabbi by the name of Sabbato Nachamu had been converted to Catholicism by a priest, Paolo Medici. In the seventeenth century a rabbi by the name of Mosé da Cave had been converted to Catholicism in Italy. See the epilogue on recent controversy spawned by that conversion.
4. *Jewish Chronicle*, 23 February 1945.
5. Louis I. Newman, *A "Chief Rabbi" of Rome Becomes a Catholic: A Study in Fright and Spite* (New York: The Renascence Press, 1945). Also see chapter 5 of Morris N. Kertzer, *With an H on my Dog Tag* (New York: Behrman House, 1947), the reminiscences of a Jewish chaplain who was with the Allied armies that liberated Rome.
6. Wellesley Aron, *Wheels In the Storm: The Genesis of the Israeli Defence Forces* (Canberra: Roebuck Society Publication No. 13, 1974): pp. 176–177.
7. Letter from Julius Frank to the editor of *Judaism*, 15 June 1989 in response to the authors' articles on Zolli in that quarterly.
8. For example, Zolli is scarcely mentioned in Susan Zuccotti's *The Italians and the Holocaust: Persecution, Rescue and Survival* (New York: Basic Books, Inc. Publishers, 1987). Zolli has received more attention from popular writers. See Robert Katz, *Black Sabbath: A Journey Through a Crime Against Humanity*. (Toronto: The Macmillan Co., 1969); Dan Kurzman, *The Race for Rome* (Garden City, N.Y.: Doubleday, 1975); and chapter 41 of Sam Waagenaar, *The Pope's Jews* (Open Court, La Salle, Illinois: A Library Press Book, 1974.)
9. Arthur A. Cohen. *The Myth of the Judeo-Christian Tradition* (New York and Evanston: Harper and Row, Publishers, 1957), p. 105.
10. Michael David, "Great Jewish Convert," *Integrity*, 8 (June 1954), p. 47.

11. Conor Cruise O'Brien, "A Lost Chance to Save the Jews," *The New York Review of Books*, 27 April 1989, p. 27.
12. *New York Times*, 3 June 1945.
13. Avro Manhattan, *The Vatican in World Politics* (New York: Gaer Associates, 1949). Also see Judah L. Graubart, "The Vatican and the Jews: Cynicism and Indifference." *Judaism* 24 No. 2 (Spring 1975): 168–180.
14. Patricia Marx, "An Interview With Rolf Hochhuth," *Partisan Review*, 31 No. 3 (Summer 1964), p. 368.
15. *Ibid.*, pp. 369–371.
16. Andre Ungar, "The Deputy," *Conservative Judaism*, XVIII No. 4 (Summer 1964), pp. 60–62.
17. Giovanni Montini, "Pius XII And The Jews," *The Tablet* [London] (29 June 1963).
18. Ibid.
19. *New York Times*, 11 March 1974.
20. For examples, see Guenter Lewy, *The Catholic Church and Nazi Germany* (New York: McGraw Hill, 1964); Saul Friedlander, *Pius XII and the Third Reich*, trans. by Charles Fullman (New York: Alfred A. Knopf, 1966); Barry Dov Schwartz, "The Vatican And The Holocaust," *Conservative Judaism*, XVIII No. 4 (Summer 1964): 27–50; Judah L. Graubart, "The Vatican and the Jews: Cynicism and Indifference," *Judaism*, 24 No. 2 (Spring 1975): 168–186.
21. Pinchas Lapide, *The Last Three Popes And the Jews* (London: Souvenir Press, 1967); Joseph L. Lichten, "Pius XII and the Jews," *The Catholic Mind* 57 No. 1142 (March-April 1959): 159–162; Meir Michaelis, *Mussolini and the Jews: German-Italian Relations and the Jewish Question in Italy 1922–1945* (New York:, Oxford University Press, 1978); L. Poliakov, "The Vatican And The 'Jewish Question', " *Commentary* (November 1950): 439–449.
22. The Pallottine Society, which consists of lay brothers and clerics, was established in Rome in 1835 by St. Vincent Pallotti.
23. This reception was described in *L'Osservatore Romano*, 30 November 1945, which Harold Tittman enclosed in his dispatch of the same date to the State Department. National Archives, Microfilm 1284–61. Records of the Department of State Relating to the Problems of Relief and Refugees in Europe Arising from World War II and its Aftermath, 1938–49.
24. Trieste Synagogue Files, Resolution of the Union of Italian Jewish Communities, 27 March 1946. The use of the plural "Popes" is significant here. It may signify gratitude toward Pius XI also.
25. *New York Times*, 12 October 1958.
26. Ibid., 10 October 1958.
27. Ibid., 11 October 1958.
28. John F. Morley, *Vatican Diplomacy And The Jews During The Holocaust 1939-1943* (New York: KTAV Publishing House, Inc., 1980).
29. Edward H. Flannery, *The Anguish of the Jews: Twenty-Three Centuries of Anti-Semitism* (New York: Paulist Press, 1985), p. 225.
30. See Chapter 15, "The Bombing of Auschwitz," in David S. Wyman, *The Abandonment Of The Jews: America And The Holocaust 1941–1945* (New York: Pantheon Books, 1984) and Chapter 31 "Bombing Auschwitz: 'Cost . . . to no purpose' " in Martin Gilbert, *Auschwitz And The Allies* (New York: Holt,

Rinehart and Winston, 1982). On the refugee question see Arthur D. Morse, *While Six Million Died: A Chronicle of American Apathy* (New York: Random House, 1968) and Henry L. Feingold, *The Politics of Rescue: The Roosevelt Administration and the Holocaust* (New Brunswick, NJ: Rutgers University Press, 1970) and David S. Wyman, *Paper Walls: America and the Refugee Crisis* 1938–1941 (Amherst: University of Massachusetts Press, 1968).

31. Bitter controversy surrounded a commission of Jews established in the early 1980's to evaluate efforts made by American Jewry to save European Jewry from annihilation at the time of the Holocaust. The so-called ''Goldberg Report'' (for former Supreme Court Justice Arthur J. Goldberg) concluded that American Jewish organizations were unduly timid and slow to respond to the Nazi menace. Often, their attitude was one of business as usual. See *American Jewry During the Holocaust* (New York: Ralph Bunche Institute on the U.N., 1984). For a critical assessment of the report by an historian who resigned from the commission after reading its interim report, see Yehuda Bauer, ''The Goldberg Report,'' *Midstream* (February/1985): 25–28. Bauer calls the report a ''flop.''
32. Rolf Hochhuth, *The Deputy*, trans. by Richard and Clara Winston (New York: Grove Press, 1964).

2

The Jews and the Papacy

Hatred of Jews reached its zenith with the annihilation of approximately six million European Jews by the minions of Adolf Hitler. Of course, the Nazis did not invent the loathing of Jews. Such hatred had been nourished for centuries by organized Christianity. Century after century, countless Christian leaders taught the faithful that the Jews were an accursed people since, in their blindness, they had rejected Jesus, the Christ or messiah, God's only begotten son. Moreover, in their iniquity, Jews had murdered Christ. For their perfidy, Jews as a people deserved punishment, generation after generation, for all time. They were branded ''deicides''—Christ-killers—and treated as pariahs: shunned, persecuted, expelled, and often killed. Misery was to be their lot, one and all. Except for John, writers of the Gospels do not hold all Jews living in Palestine in Christ's time culpable in the matter of the crucifixion. The medieval tradition shaped by the Church, however, was less scrupulous in distinguishing between a handful of chief priests who conspired against Jesus and the great Jewish multitudes.

In the opinion of some scholars, excoriation of the Jews for their role in the crucifixion intensified in the second century, and was largely motivated by a desire to denigrate Judaism in the eyes of vacillating converts still attracted to the faith of their ancestors and unwilling to make any definitive break with the synagogue.[1] Roman guilt for Christ's death was downplayed while that of the Jews was stressed. Animosity towards Jews deepened further as the gulf between Christianity and Judaism widened. Israeli historian David Rokeah argues that when Christians realized the futility of their evangelizing efforts among Jews ''they saw no point in imposing self-restraint'' and a new ''abstract, one-dimensional, negative and Satanic figure'' of the Jew developed.[2]

Underscoring Paul's censure of the Jews, some early Church theologians, among them, John Chrysostom, fourth-century Bishop of Antioch, inveighed against Jews and their houses of worship as diabolical and sources of contamination. In future centuries, calls for the expulsion of Jews would be greeted with enthusiasm in a number of diverse lands.

Paul's words in his Epistle to the Romans also inspired a second school of Christian thought which held that the conversion of the Jews was a necessary prelude to the second coming of Christ. According to this interpretation, Christians were dependent upon Jews, who thus came to occupy a special place in Church thinking. Jews had been present at Christ's passion on the cross and his triumphant resurrection, but they had, nevertheless, obstinately rejected him as savior. In 1199, Pope Innocent III proclaimed that the infidelity of the Jews deserved condemnation, but that ''because through them the truth of our faith is proved, they are not to be severely oppressed by the faithful.''[3] Innocent's disclaimer did not prevent the Church from promoting ill will and disdain for the Jews.

The Church taught that Christians were the new Chosen People in contrast to the Jews who had killed the redeemer and were thus destined by God to do the devil's bidding.[4] Christian society was to grant some basic rights to Jews, but just the same, these Jews were to be consigned to a degraded, second-class status. Kenneth R. Stow emphasizes that prohibitions laid upon Jews were aimed at establishing the ''relative inferiority of the Jew to the Christian. Reality was thus to mirror the belief that Christianity had superseded Judaism, liberating the Christian through grace while the Jew remained enslaved under the 'Law.' ''[5]

At the behest of Innocent III, the Fourth Lateran Council convened in Rome in 1215, marking the apogee of medieval papal hegemony. The Council enacted several limitations on Jews; among them, that commercial interaction with Jews practicing usury (then defined as charging virtually any interest at all) was prohibited. Also, Jews over twelve years of age, along with Muslims, were to don distinctive garb to distinguish them from Christians. Likewise, Jews were to be quarantined during Holy Week lest they insult Christians, and special taxes were levied on them at Easter. An additional ruling made it impermissible for rulers to allow Jews to hold any public office in which they would wield power over Christians. That most glittering assemblage of prelates in medieval Church history also decreed that Jews who had been baptized into the Christian faith were proscribed from observing any Jewish customs.[6] All of the foregoing guidelines were officially announced in the name of the pontiff.

As Joshua Trachtenberg demonstrated in his classic, *The Devil and the Jews,* the literature spawned by the medieval period was completely dominated by one perspective on the Jew: that of an orthodox Christianity. Morality plays, poems, legends—not to mention folklore—all stereotyped Jews as the "fount of evil," bent on destroying Christendom and Christianity.[7] Reviled as sworn enemies of the Catholic Church, Jews were deemed to be demonic, that is, creatures of the devil: not human in the way Christians were. Furthermore, medieval popular belief in the existence of Satan was real, no less so than belief in Jesus as the Christ. Trachtenberg argued cogently that for medieval Europe "Satan was the archenemy of mankind, seeking to destroy it, as Jesus had come to save it."[8]

Artists during the Middle Ages commonly represented the devil as a grotesque being who travelled either on the back of the Hebrew or was borne by Synagoga, a mythical damsel who could not see Christianity's truth because her eyes were blindfolded. Such iconography can be traced to the apostle John who told how Jesus had informed those Jews rebuffing him that their father was the devil. To be bracketed with the devil was to insure disastrous consequences for the Jew in the Middle Ages, a fact not lost centuries later on the Nazi Jew-baiter, Julius Streicher, whose propaganda claiming a nexus between Jews and the devil led to even greater catastrophic consequences.[9]

If Jews were truly diabolical to medieval Christians, they were capable of any crime, no matter how unspeakable. Sons and daughters of the devil were open to all manner of credible accusations. Jewish physicians were thus charged with deliberately administering lethal substances to Christian patients. Jews were alleged to have poisoned wells, an allegation that provided a convenient scapegoat when the Black Plague ravaged Europe in the fourteenth century. Despite the fact that Pope Martin V in 1422 forbade Christians to spread word of Jewish responsibility for the Black Death, the canard retained currency.[10]

The previously mentioned Fourth Lateran Council defined the dogma of transubstantiation which stated that, through consecration, the host used during Mass was miraculously transformed by the priest into the body and blood of Christ. The consecrated host soon became the object of fervent popular veneration. This paved the way for tales about Jews who desecrated the host, sometimes in their houses of worship as part of their own ritual. To the easily manipulated masses, this profaning of the host was equal to the abuse, even mutilation, of the Christ present in the wafer. For such sinister actions, all Jews were held accountable.[11]

Another fallacious tale had it that Jews desecrated crucifixes. To the unschooled imagination, Jesus was as present on the crucifix as he was in the host. A companion falsehood which enjoyed some popularity thus claimed that during the process whereby one was converted to Judaism—a capital crime incidentally—a crucifix would be pierced.[12]

Ritual murder was still another grave charge periodically levelled against the Jews, often with tragic results. According to this amazingly durable blood libel hoax, Jews murdered Christians, usually Christian children, to obtain blood then used to make matzoh (unleavened bread) during Passover. Typical was the report about a very young boy named Simon who had been ritually put to death in 1475 in the northern Italian city of Trent. Relatively new to Trent, the German-speaking Jewish community was held responsible as an entity for the crime, and its members were taken into custody and tortured until confessions were extracted. Many were executed. Two Jews who had hoped to save their skins by converting were also put to death, although through the more benign method of strangulation rather than the stake. A papal tribunal later sanctioned these grotesque proceedings and the Pope himself, Sixtus IV (1471–1484), voiced his approval for subsequent persecutions that included more executions, additional conversions, the seizure of Jewish-owned property, and expulsions. A contemporary poem by one Matthaus Kunig saw an analogy between the ritual murder of little Simon and Christ's death on the cross since both victims were stretched "crosswise" and each "tilted his head to his right/and gave up his noble spirit."[13]

Miracles were attributed to Simon of Trent, and he was subsequently canonized. About half a millennium after the murder, however, serious doubts about the veracity of the story led to a Vatican prohibition against the veneration of Simon. It is not coincidental that the ecclesiastical decree suppressing the cult of "Blessed Little Simon of Trent" was issued on 28 October 1965, the same day the Second Vatican Council promulgated its "Declaration on the Relationship of the Church to Non-Christian Religions," that opened a new era in Jewish-Catholic relations.

The conversion of the Jews to Christianity was a *sine qua non* for the accomplishment of Christianity's ultimate end, a point dogmatically asserted at the sixteenth-century Council of Trent.[14] Every generation has produced Jews who were willing, even eager, to forsake Judaism. Immersed in a Christian society, surrounded by a Christian culture, Jews have often succumbed to Christian concepts and ways. Commercial dealings with Christians, for example, have often entailed an exchange of ideas about a broad spectrum of matters. Regular contacts with Christians led to intermarriage. Along with the adoption of non-Jewish dress and diet, intermarriage and conversions should be viewed as expressions of acculturation. In every epoch, conversion carried with it the possibility of an easier, more comfortable existence. Tightly-shut windows of opportunity would be opened for the convert and his or her offspring. Upward social and economic mobility would follow baptism, it was hoped. To borrow Sam Waagenaar's caustic observation about those Jews who capitulated to the blandishments of the Church, "there were some who felt it better to follow Christ on a full stomach than to hunger with Moses."[15]

While some individuals were surely motivated by a belief in Christ's divinity, other, perhaps more insecure individuals, just as surely acted out of psychological need, particularly the need to conform. By affirming belief in the majority faith, these individuals bolstered their own sense of security, the more so because religious non-conformists often provoked the wrath of the majority. Like the 19th-century German poet, Henrich Heine, many of these converts saw Judaism as a misfortune that could be eliminated by baptism.

Sprinkled with holy water, the convert was an outsider no longer.[16]

Jewish resentment towards proselytes has always been intense. Spitting in the direction of renegade Jews or on the ground was a common expression of such resentment. Not surprisingly, Rabbi Zolli and members of his immediate family were the objects of ridicule by Roman Jews who felt that he had scorned them.

Most converts were content to melt into the majority community: indeed, they craved an anonymity that would conceal their Jewish past. Others, however, for reasons better understood by psychiatrists than by theologians, were driven to become more Catholic than the Pope. For centuries, Jewish apostates were in the vanguard of the ubiquitous denunciations of Judaism, and they dominated sporadic theological disputations with the still benighted defenders of the faith which they had abandoned. Sadly, it was often erstwhile Jews who suggested the coercive means by which their former coreligionists could be persuaded to embrace Catholicism.

Preeminent among these Jewish converts, who became venomous in attacking Jews, was Johannes Pfefferkorn. Born in Moravia in 1469, Pfefferkorn engaged in criminal behavior before he, his wife and his children converted to Christianity. Cologne's Dominicans took him under their wing, and Pfefferkorn moved into the forefront of the order's anti-Jewish campaign. In the first decade of the sixteenth century, he wrote a number of treatises sharply critical of Jews. In those treatises, Pfefferkorn advocated, *inter alia,* that Jews be compelled to attend conversion sermons. Those Jews who balked at attending such sermons were to be forced out of the cities where they resided.

Pfefferkorn claimed that the Talmud was replete with sacrilegious passages regarding the Christian faith and he sought to have all copies impounded. The derisive propaganda disseminated by Pfefferkorn prompted a controversy involving John Reuchlin, an outstanding Christian scholar of Hebrew, who defended Jewish texts by exposing the superficial nature of Pfefferkorn's supposed erudition. In 1517, Desiderius Erasmus, the "scholar of Europe," railed against Pfefferkorn whom he dubbed "a criminal Jew who had become a most criminal Christian."[17] To Erasmus, Pfefferkorn was an unwelcome convert, "a poisonous fellow . . . fit only for the hangman."[18]

At the end of the Middle Ages, Spain's national identity was forged by means of a Catholic crusade against Jews and Muslims. Spain inevitably produced more than its share of zealous converts. One case in point is that of the fourteenth-century physician, Abner of Burgos, who apparently decided of his own free will to become a Christian. Despite the sincerity of his Christian belief, Abner of Burgos admitted that his conversion, like countless other conversions, had been influenced by circumstances of the times. His comments on the tax burden of the oppressed Jews provide the backdrop to an epiphany, an experience not unlike that which Rabbi Zolli would undergo six centuries later. Abner of Burgos reported that one day, while alone and despondent in the synagogue, he saw the "figure of a tall man" who first admonished him to slumber no longer, and then informed him that "the Jews have remained so long in captivity for their folly and wickedness and because they have no teacher of righteousness through whom they may recognize the truth."[19] A second, similar vision reportedly occurred three years later.

The reborn Burgos emerged from a prolonged period of contemplation to develop a rationalization for the persecution of Jews that was anything but righteous. Indeed, his plan was malevolent. Jewish autonomy was to be eradicated since, as Burgos argued, the messiah would not appear and the Jews would not be saved until they had been stripped of all vestiges of communal self-government. Abner insisted that Christian ethics were superior to Jewish ethics, and he proclaimed rabbis and other Jewish dignitaries to be simply "coarse creatures."[20] He even found too moderate those Popes who had placed their imprimatur on the Inquisition. To compensate for the papacy's insufficient fanaticism, Abner of Burgos advised that nothing less than massacre of the Jewish communities would be required for their salvation.[21]

Another inhabitant of Burgos in the closing years of the fourteenth century who "swapped saddles" and stirred up the Catholic populace against his former coreligionists was Pablo De Santa Maria, born Solomon Halevi. Already middle aged and a Jewish scholar of considerable note, he was baptized, became a priest, and with papal backing, was eventually consecrated a bishop.

By 1483, overall control of the Spanish Inquisition was in the sadistic hands of Tomas de Torquemada, the Dominican who nearly a decade earlier had served as confessor to their royal majesties, Ferdinand and Isabella. According to the *New Catholic Encyclopedia,* Torquemada was "of Jewish descent."[22] He nevertheless became the scourge of the Jews, including the Marranos who ostensibly had become Catholics, but who furtively lived as Jews. Torquemada monomaniacally directed the punishment and persecution of large numbers of Jews. It is estimated that perhaps two thousand were put to death as religious militants ran amok in a papally sanctioned enterprise in intolerance. In his comprehensive study of Jewry in Christian Spain, Yitzhak Baer wrote that it is likely that Torquemada was among those who favored the ousting of Jews from Andalusia.[23] In 1490 Torquemada disseminated a report on the ritual crucifixion of a Christian child in La Guardia, a report that fanned the flames of religious ardor and helped set the stage for the mass expulsion of Jews from Spain two years later.

Periodically, historical circumstances have begotten crypto-Judaism, a phenomenon whereby imperilled Jews went through the motions of converting to Christianity, sometimes en masse. An example can be found in the thirteenth-century Kingdom of Naples where multitudes of Jews outwardly embraced Catholicism, while for three hundred years afterwards the *neofiti* and their descendants maintained a surreptitious Jewish existence.[24] Whenever European Jews were in danger of being deported or even killed, they understood that baptism, however perfunctory, could often save their lives. Such was the case in fourteenth-century Spain. Largely in self-defense, most Jews in Toledo and Valencia converted. Barcelona Jewry followed suit. According to Cecil Roth's sardonic comment, "So many came forward for baptism, it was said, that the holy chrism in the churches was exhausted and it was regarded as miraculous that the supply held out."[25] Although Roth thought hyperbolic the estimation of those who set the number of converted at two hundred thousand, he did conclude that the Spanish episode was unique among the annals of Jewish history.

Because the Church regarded baptism as irreversible, those *conversos* who had traded the Torah for the Gospels but regretted their decision, had to flee to where they could live incognito. Most, however, took on the trappings of Catholicism while practicing Judaism clandestinely. The *conversos* would have their children dutifully baptized and their marriages solemnized by priests who would also hear their feigned confessions, but in their heart of hearts they remained Jewish. Wherever and whenever possible, these underground Jews abided by Jewish dietary laws and observed the Jewish sabbath. The boldest among them had their sons circumcized, and some even worshipped secretly at synagogues. Inwardly, the *conversos* were completely faithful to the creed of their forefathers. To quote Cecil Roth again, "They were Jews in all but name, and Christian in nothing but form."[26] Crypto-Judaism passed from generation to generation. Indeed, this charade engendered by religious bigotry has continued on the Iberian peninsula into the twentieth century. As recently as 1989, some thirty-two male inhabitants of Belmonte in northern Portugal, a region that is home to perhaps thousands of Marranos, underwent ritual circumcision to signify their return to Judaism.[27]

The desirability of converting the Jews was never an issue for the papacy, although what means could lawfully be employed to convince the stiff-necked Jews of their error remained a burning issue. Between 590 and 604, Gregory the Great succeeded in fortifying the papacy in Italy as he encouraged proselytizing campaigns. Nevertheless, he objected to the use of duress in bringing about conversion, since force led to ephemeral and insincere professions of Christian faith.

Enduring Vatican doubts about the effectiveness of forced conversions are graphically epitomized by a relief in the Cologne Cathedral which shows a female hog, the so-called Jewish sow. As translated from the German, the caption below the animal reads, "As truly as the cat eats the mouse, the Jew never becomes a true Christian."[28] Meanwhile, Innocent III, who had striven at the close of the twelfth century to make the papacy supreme in matters temporal as well as spiritual, granted explicit protection to the Jews against coercive baptism, but he forbade baptized Jews to return to Judaism. Such backsliding would represent in the words of one historian, "an insulting negation of the sacrament of baptism."[29] In regard to the baptism of Jewish children conducted without the consent of their parents, no consensus of Catholic thought was achieved for centuries.[30]

Notwithstanding its uncanonical character, forced baptism was traditionally one of the most blatant manifestations of papal contempt for Jewish rights. Houses of Catechumens (i.e., residences for Jews who, of their own volition, chose to become Catholics) came into being during the religiously turbulent sixteenth century. In 1543, the papacy granted to the Jesuits, a new order at the time established on the principle of unconditional obedience to the Pope, the right to operate two *case di catecumeni*. The establishment of these Houses insured that the criterion of volition would often be stripped of any real meaning in the future. In *The Pope's Jews,* Sam Waagenaar succinctly describes the operation of the *case di catecumeni* when he states that ". . . before long, Jews who had no intention whatever to exchange the Star of David for the Star of Bethlehem, were to be dragged through its doors."[31]

In the final quarter of the eighteenth century, Pope Pius VI's pontificate marked what is perhaps the nadir in the fortunes of Rome's ghettoized Jews, as indignity was piled upon indignity. Pretexts, some unbelievably flimsy, were at times invoked to justify wrenching a Jewish child from his or her family. Church authorities would honor the wishes for the minor's baptism voiced by already converted relatives holding the most tenuous claims over the child's spiritual life. Parentally unsanctioned baptisms, sometimes approved only by individuals completely unrelated to the Jewish children, would be deemed irreversible by papal authorities. It has been estimated that, in Rome alone, at least two thousand four hundred and thirty Jews travelled to the baptismal font between 1634 and 1790.[32] Exactly how many did so under pressure or through chicanery may never be known.

In 1787, intensified oppression led representatives of the Roman Jewish establishment to explore the possibility of having the whole community emigrate to what they surmised would be more hospitable surroundings in London. Their overtures to the English king, however, were rebuffed.[33]

One instrument for converting Jews to Christianity was the proselytzing sermon. Such sermons can be traced as far back as the ninth century. Still, it was not until the rise of the Dominican order in the thirteenth century that this practice became systematized and explicitly supported by ecclesiastical authorities. A decree of 1577 ruled that Jews residing in Rome and throughout the papal states had to provide a specified percentage of their number on certain days at designated churches.

Fifty females and one hundred male Jews were required to hear proselytizing preaching in Rome every week. Often the preacher himself was an apostate. To add injury to insult, honoraria for the sermons usually had to be paid by the Jews themselves. The French humanist, philosopher, and essayist, Michel de Montaigne (1533-1592), was impressed by the erudition of one renegade rabbi, Andrea del Monte, whom he heard deliver a conversionist sermon in Rome.[34]

The overpowered Jews resisted these forced sermons in a variety of ways. Despite the watchful eyes of papal proctors, some Jews took short naps. More courageous Jews discussed business matters in stentorian voices during the preachers' harangues.

In a fascinating watercolor done in 1829, Hieronymous Hess, a painter and graphic artist from Basel, delineated a groups of Jews seated in a Roman church and compelled to endure a conversion homily. It is clear to the observer that many in the captive audience would prefer to be elsewhere. Hess depicts such individuals as deliberately looking away from the cleric declaiming from the pulpit. Some in the painting are chatting; several are dozing; and one has his fingers plugging his ears to shut out the unwelcome message. Clerical monitors struggle in vain to curb this indecorous behavior.

Robert Browning conveyed the sentiments of Roman Jews forced to attend conversionist sermons in his poem, "Holy Cross Day." The title of the poem refers to a September festival commemorating what Christians believe was the moment when the Emperor Constantine witnessed the miraculous appearance of a cross in the midday sky. Browning, a philo-Semitic Christian and longtime resident of Italy who sometimes wintered in Rome, ridiculed the notion that, by compelling unwilling Hebrews to listen to religious teachings they detested, the Catholic Church was conferring blessings upon the Jews.

In "Holy Cross Day," Browning sympathetically viewed the proselytizing phenomenon from the Jewish perspective. Like "rats in a hamper, swine in a sty,"[35] the impoverished Jews of the ghetto would be trundled off to a church. The same hand which had gutted their purses would now throttle their creed. If a "doomed black dozen" accepted Christianity, Browning opined, the beggars among them would live more comfortably. The British poet well understood that it was often the promise of material betterment that actuated conversions.

As for the majority of Jews, they had withstood Christ eighteen centuries earlier. Now they would withstand Barabbas, the thief whom the mob wanted freed rather than Jesus.[36] For Browning, the Church was unquestionably the villain there, since what he mockingly called "the summons to Christian fellowship," was an integral element in the ongoing persecution of the Israelites.

Today, in an era of ecumenism, of religious goodwill, and more than a century after the Roman ghetto was liberated, there is a haunting reminder of the not so good old days of conversionist sermons. On the periphery of the ghetto—literally a stone's throw from the central synagogue—stands a small church whose facade bears a remarkable inscription in Latin and Hebrew taken from the Book of Isaiah. The inscription had originally appeared on the facade of the nearby Sant'Angelo in Pescheria where, in accordance with a 1584 papal bull, Jews were subjected against their will to Catholic sermons. The inscription reads: "I have spread forth my hands all the day to an unbelieving people who walk in a way that is not good after their own thought."[37] The words recall the Church's traditionally antagonistic attitude toward recalcitrant Jewry. The largely ineffectual mandatory sermons were discontinued in the nineteenth century during the pontificate of Pius IX, the longest in Church history.

Pio Nono was born Giovanni Maria Mastai Ferretti in Sinigaglia (Ancona) in 1792. Elected pope in 1846, his reign lasted thirty-two years during the turbulent Risorgimento period and its aftermath. It is commonplace for certain individuals to have their youthful liberalism eclipsed by the passage of time. Pius IX, an Italian nobleman, was a reformer, innovator, and a passionate advocate of things modern when he first ascended the throne of Peter. But in the years following the 1848 revolution that forced his temporary flight from Rome. Pio Nono grew increasingly conservative on political and theological matters.

Pius IX's position on the bloody American Civil War brings to mind the policies of Pius XII during World War II. Although he pronounced slavery incompatible with Christianity, Pio Nono pursued a neutral course between the Confederacy and the Union and expressed his wish for an end to hostilities. When the Northern victory appeared inevitable he asked for a peace that was not punitive.[38]

As far as theology is concerned, the pontificate of Pius IX is still associated with the 1854 declaration that the Virgin Mary, alone among human beings, had been born untainted by "original sin." It has been incumbent upon Catholics ever since to accept this doctrine of the "Immaculate Conception." Though Mary's corporeal assumption into heaven was first put forward sixteen years later, it was not solemnly defined as Church dogma until 1950 when Pius XII so defined it.

The polemical *Syllabus of Errors,* a document appended to Pius IX's encyclical, *Quanta Cura,* became Church teaching in 1864. Therein, liberal thought was savaged by the Pope. Specifically lambasted were secular education, civil marriage and divorce, freedom of the press in religious matters, liberty of conscience and worship, and the idea that Catholicism need not be the sole state religion. Condemned in no uncertain language was any notion that the pontiff ought to come to terms with progress or modern civilization.[39]

Pius IX convened the First Vatican Council in Rome in 1870. The council overwhelmingly supported a declaration that the Pope, whenever he speaks *ex cathedra* on matters of faith and morals, is incapable of error by virtue of his supreme apostolic authority. This decree made clear that there is no appeal from papal decisions. Should every other Catholic disagree on a particular matter, it would still be the Pope's view that was to prevail. At a critical historical moment when Italian nationalists were stripping the Pope of his temporal power and possessions, the Papacy was reasserting its absolute control over the spiritual realm.

How did Jews fare at the hands of this Pope whose pontificate was filled with turmoil? Acutely aware of the revolutionary spirit then rampant in Europe, Pius IX condescended in March, 1848 to permit a constitution of sorts for Rome. Some basic civil rights were vouchsafed to Catholics, but Jews—who numbered approximately twelve thousand—were specifically denied citizenship by the document.[40] Later in his pontificate, Pius IX wished to impede a rising tide of anticlericalism, and so he lashed out at Jewish journalists for the low moral tone of the press. Shortly thereafter, he charged Jews with being money-lusting enemies of Christ and Christianity.[41]

But, for Jews, it was the Pope's role in the scandalous Mortara case that guaranteed Pius IX a permanent place in their collective memory. Edgardo Mortara, the youngest child in a family of Bolognese Jews, became the focus of what developed into a firestorm of controversy in

Europe and the United States in the late 1850s. The simple facts of the case are as follows: when still an infant, Edgardo fell ill (the gravity of his illness is still a matter of debate). An adolescent Catholic maid in the employ of the Mortara family took advantage of the situation to secretly baptize the child, obviously without his parents' knowledge, much less their consent. One evening in June 1858, several years after little Edgardo's recovery, he was abducted from his home by officials of the Holy Office (Inquisition). At the time, Bologna was part of the Papal States, hence the Pope himself wielded far-reaching secular power.

Not yet seven years of age, Edgardo was dispatched to Rome where he became a ward of Pius IX. The Pope defended the abduction carried out by his gendarmes saying that it was his moral obligation to provide Edgardo with a Catholic education. Canon law then in effect held that the baptism, though unauthorized by the child's mother or father, was valid nonetheless. Precedent stretching as far back as the seventh century maintained that the offspring of Jews ought to be separated from their parents. Otherwise, the children would emulate their mothers and fathers in error.[42] Pio Nono was following the lead of Benedict XIV who, in the mid-eighteenth century, had ruled that the progeny of Jews (or pagans, for that matter) baptized without parental consent should be taken from their families to be raised in a properly pious fashion.[43]

Prevailing theological thought in the 1850s was clearly predicated on the belief that salvation outside the Catholic Church was impossible. Hence, little Edgardo's immortal soul was being safeguarded within the bosom of the Church. In this way, the Papacy was able to justify what much of the non-Catholic world adjudged to be a kidnapping that trampled upon the most fundamental rights of the Mortara family. In the eyes of the Pope and papal defenders, returning the child to his home would have consigned him to eternal damnation. As one apologist for the Papacy put it, Vatican state law "protected the baptized children of Jews from their parents."[44]

While custodians of a domicile for catechumens supervised the young Edgardo's education, his distressed parents pleaded in vain for their son's release. Moses Montefiore, the Italian-born and internationally renowned Jewish philanthropist, was asked to intercede with the Pope, but Pius IX refused him an audience.[45] Appeals and protests from Jews in many countries reached the Vatican. In addition, appeals from Emperor Franz Joseph of Austria, Napoleon III of France, and Count Camillo Cavour, a major figure in Italy's struggles for independence, fell on deaf ears. "Non possumus" (we can do nothing) was the Vatican's standard response.[46]

Despite the international outcry, Edgardo was never returned to his family. Under papal supervision, the Jewish youth was reared a Catholic. As a result, Edgardo refused to rejoin his parents unless and until they, too, converted. He took the name Pius Maria; it was common practice for Jews who became Catholic to adopt the name of Maria in honor of Christ's mother whose veneration was strongly encouraged by the Vatican. In 1945, Rabbi Zolli was to do the same. By choosing the name, Pius, Edgardo Mortara paid manifest tribute to his papal benefactor. In 1945, Rabbi Zolli was to honor Pius XII by adopting Pacelli's baptismal name.

At age fifteen Edgardo voluntarily opted to join the order of Canons Regular of the Lateran at the Canonica of St. Agnes. He was ordained a priest in 1873. Although it has often been charged that Mortara was utilized for proselytizing efforts among Jews, this apparently was not the case. With the passing years, the ordained Mortara earned a well-deserved reputation as an indefatigable educator who, in part due to his talents as a linguist, was sent on missions to many countries, including the United States.

When Mortara died at a ripe old age in Belgium in 1940, the furor that had surrounded him as a boy was largely forgotten. He died just before Hitler's juggernaut overran Belgium. Along with historian Bertram Korn, one wonders if Father Pius Maria Mortara would have shared the horrendous fate of six million Jews had he lived a little longer.[47] Other Jewish converts, including some who had become priests and nuns, perished in the gas chambers.[48] The Church championed Mortara as a bona fide Catholic. But to the Nazis, who used genetic rather than religious criteria in determining who was to live and who to die, Father Mortara would most likely have remained a Jew.

Almost three quarters of a century after the abduction of the Mortara child, one can still find a spirited defense of the Papacy's conduct. In 1929, Father A. F. Day asserted that Pius IX, whom he described as an "amiable and saintly" pontiff, had acted properly. Jewish carping, so went the argument, had shown a lack of understanding; Protestant agitation was based on anti-Catholic bigotry.

On the question of "valid" but unsanctioned baptism of Jewish infants, Day concurred with Benedict XIV, "perhaps the most learned" of Popes, "beloved and admired."[49] Day found no fault with a Church practice that justified the forced separation of baptized Hebrew children from their families so that they might be brought up as Christians. He wrote that parents could not be trusted in such weighty matters. Any injury done to the parents cannot equal "that which would be done to the dying child if the sacrament which opens heaven were withheld."[50] As late as 1935, when Cecil Roth published his *Short History of the Jewish People,* Day wrote to him, angrily objecting to Roth's statement that the Mortara youngster had been kidnapped. Father Day contended that Edgardo had been removed from the custody of his parents by a legal process.[51] The Church only abandoned this line of thinking in the wake of the Holocaust, by which time the relevant provisions had been deleted from canon law.

Edgardo Mortara's experience was by no means unique. There had been a number of similar previous cases.[52] And other such cases were to follow. It was only the eruption of world-wide indignation that set the Mortara case apart.

Despite the brouhaha over the Mortara abduction, the pattern was repeated in 1864 when an eleven-year-old Roman boy and apprentice cobbler, Giuseppe Coen, was taken to join the catechumens by a Sicilian priest noted for his proselytizing activities. The cleric in question had become the mentor and champion of many youthful neophytes. Vociferous objections by Giuseppe's parents, by some Catholics, and by the French ambassador as well, failed to have any effect. Giuseppe was pressured into an ecclesiastical career with the Carmelite Order. Allegations that the boy's ordeal caused the death of his older sister and the derangement of his mother, may be baseless.[53] Nevertheless, the boy's family did feel compelled to flee the Vatican's jurisdiction to safer territory in Livorno. When Rome fell to Italian nationalists in 1870, the papacy's temporal power was drastically reduced by the secular Italian government at home in its new capital of Rome. The Coens then pressured for the emancipation of their son through official and military channels. Ecclesiastical authorities meanwhile spirited the youngster to the island of Malta where he enrolled in the Carmelite novitiate. Coen later finished his studies at Castello, near Florence, and he was ordained a priest. A man of the cloth to the end, Coen died at the age of eighty-six on 13 September 1939.[54]

In the nineteenth century alone, there may have been as many as twenty verifiable cases of coercive baptism, most in Italy where the papacy wielded inordinate power throughout most of the century. Coercive baptisms of the past are almost completely forgotten nowadays. Selective historical amnesia dictates that there be little discussion of those appalling cases of pontifical abuse. Curricula in parochial schools, Catholic universities, and seminaries remain mute on what can only be described as Vatican-sponsored bigotry. No apology for these cases has ever been made by the Vatican. Furthermore, the cases described above make a mockery of Church claims to be pro-family, for in each instance, the prerogatives of Jewish families were subordinated to Catholic doctrinal biases.

Having been instrumental in the dehumanization of Jews for centuries, Church authorities have often been hoisted by their own theological petard. In its handling of the age-old myth of ritual murder, Rome's *Civiltà Cattolica,* the official Jesuit and semi-official papal magazine, is illustrative. From 1881, the year in which murderous pogroms became epidemic in Czarist Russia, to the outbreak of the First World War, *Civiltà Cattolica* repeatedly defamed Jews with blood libels that inevitably stirred up anti-Semitic feelings in the Christian world. An 1881 reference to ritual murder cited as its source a French rabbi, David Drach, who had embraced Catholicism, become an archivist in Rome in 1832, and who labored to bring Christian light to his former brethren. *Civiltà Cattolica* uncritically accepted Drach's false contention that Jews had been guilty of the infamous ritual murder of a Capuchin monk in Damascus in 1840.[55]

Dr. Charlotte Klein has noted that the virulent anti-Semite, Julius Streicher, resuscitated the ritual murder hoax on the pages of *Der Stürmer* in 1934.[56] In May of that year, an infamous special edition appeared which exposed the existence of the Jews' diabolical murder plan against "Gentile humanity." Ritual murder, as old as the Jews themselves, was the cornerstone of that plan. One prime example cited by Streicher was the savage killing of Simon of Trent in 1475. Supposedly, the source of his information about this gory affair was a book published in 1803 by a Jewish convert who had learned of it from his father, a rabbi. Whatever its provenance, the ritual murder myth remained for years a major weapon in *Der Stürmer's* anti-Semitic arsenal.[57] Still, *Civilità Cattolica,* which had not discussed the matter since 1914, did not disavow the views expressed in *Der Stürmer.* Rather, to its shame, the Jesuit periodical was silent on the issue during the Nazi era.[58] And this despite the fact that some popes through the ages had declared ritual murder to be a fiction. During the Holocaust, it was the silence of the then reigning Pope, Pius XII, that was to create a controversy. The echoes of that controversy can still be heard today.

Notes

1. David Rokeah, "The Church Fathers and the Jews in Writings Designed for Internal and External Use, "*Antisemitism Through the Ages,* Shmuel Almog (ed.), (Oxford: Pergamon Press, 1988), p. 64.
2. Ibid. The failure to convince Jews to adopt the new Christian faith led to Christian hatred of the Jews according to David Flusser who writes, "The Jewish origin of Christianity and the failure of Christianity to convert the Jewish people to the new message was precisely the reason for the strong anti-Jewish trend in Christianity." See David Flusser, *Judaism And The Origins of Christianity* (Jerusalem: The Magnes Press, The Hebrew University, 1988), p. 644.
3. Joshua Trachtenberg, *The Devil And The Jews: The Medieval Conception Of The Jew And Its Relation To Modern Antisemitism* (New Haven: Yale University Press, 1943), p. 165.
4. Robert Michael, "Christian Theology and the Holocaust," *Midstream,* 30, no. 4 (April 1984), p. 6.
5. Kenneth R. Stow, "Hatred of the Jews or Love of the Church: Papal Policy Toward the Jews in the Middle Ages," *Antisemitism Through the Ages,* Shmuel Almog (ed.), (Oxford: Pergamon Press, 1988), p. 81.
6. See Walter M. Abbott (ed.), *The Documents of Vatican II* (New York: Guild, America, Association Presses, 1966), p. 667.
7. Trachtenberg, *The Devil And The Jews,* pp. 12–13.
8. Ibid, p. 19.
9. Robert Bonfil, "The Devil and the Jews in the Christian Consciousness of the Middle Ages," *Antisemitism Through The Ages* ed. Shmuel Almog (Oxford: Pergamon Press, 1988), p. 91.
10. Trachtenberg, *The Devil And The Jews,* p. 107.
11. Ibid., pp. 109, 113.
12. Ibid., p. 118.
13. Quoted in R. Po-Chia Hsia, *The Myth of Ritual Murder: Jews and Magic in Reformation Germany* (New Haven: Yale University Press, 1988), pp. 44–45, Sixtus IV is not thought of very highly in Catholic circles. According to the *New Catholic Encyclopedia* (Volume XIII, p. 272–274), "The reign of Sixtus IV opened one of the saddest periods in papal history." Sixtus IV is accused of

nepotism and his contributions to the life of the Catholic Church are said to have been meager.
14. Stow, "Hatred of the Jews or Love of the Church," pp. 72–73.
15. Sam Waagenaar, *The Pope's Jews* (Open Court, La Salle, Illinois: A Library Press Book, 1974), p. 195.
16. See the chapter, "Shylock," in Hans Mayer, *Outsiders, A Study in Life and Letters,* trans. Denis M. Sweet (Cambridge: The M.I.T. Press, 1982) 269–395. Jewish folklore is rich in stories, jokes and proverbs about voluntary converts. Authentic Jews, according to one tale are incapable of experiencing a real change of heart and mind. Apostate Jews were never Torah-true Jews to begin with. It was often said that even the Almighty despised *meshummadim.* They truly belonged to the devil. Having forsaken the religion of their ancestors, they would be unwelcome to congregate with Jews in heaven. On the other hand, having been circumcized they could not congregate with Christians in heaven. Consequently, they are consigned to hell. See Haim Schwarzbaum, *Studies In Jewish And World Folklore* (Berlin: Walter De Fruyter & Co., 1968), pp. 341–342.
17. Quoted in *Encyclopedia Judaica* (Jerusalem: The Macmillan Company, 1971), vol. 13, pp. 355–356.
18. Shimon Marksih, *Erasmus and the Jews,* trans. Anthony Olcott, (Chicago: The University of Chicago Press, 1986), p. 70.
19. Yitzhak Baer, *A History of the Jews in Christian Spain* (Philadelphia: The Jewish Publication Society of America, 1961), vol. 1, p. 329.
20. Ibid., p. 350.
21. Ibid., p. 353.
22. *New Catholic Encyclopedia* (New York: McGraw Hill Book Company, 1967), XIV, 205.
23. Baer, *A History of the Jews In Christian Spain,* (1966), vol. 2, p. 331.
24. Cecil Roth, *A History Of The Marranos* (Philadelphia: The Jewish Publication Society of America, 1952), p. 5.
25. Ibid., p. 17.
26. Ibid., p. 20.
27. *Jerusalem Post International Edition,* Week ending 2 December 1989. Also see Michael Fink, "Marrano No More," *Jewish Monthly,* December 1989, pp. 16–21.
28. Joachim Prinz, *Popes From The Ghetto: A View of Medieval Christendom* (Dorset Press, 1966), p. 37.
29. Solomon Grayzel, *The Church and the Jews in the XIIIth Century,* Kenneth R. Stow, ed., (Detroit: Wayne State University Press, 1989), p. 166.
30. Stow, "Hatred of the Jews or Love of the Church," p. 83.
31. Waagenaar, *The Pope's Jews,* p. 164.
32. Cecil Roth, "The Forced Baptisms of 1783 At Rome And The Community of Rome," *The Jewish Quarterly Review,* 16 N.S., p. 108.
33. Ibid., pp. 111–112.
34. Waagenaar, *The Pope's Jews,* pp. 195–196.
35. Robert Browning, *The Complete Poetic and Dramatic Works of Robert Browning* (Boston: Houghton Mifflin Co., 1895), p. 281.
36. Ibid., p. 28.
37. Isaiah 65:2, *New Catholic Edition of the Holy Bible,* (New York: Catholic Book Publishing Co., 1957).

38. Benjamin J. Blied, *Catholics And The Civil War* (Milwaukee, 1945), pp. 68, 90.
39. J. H. Hexter, et al. (eds.), *The Tradition of the Modern World,* (Chicago: Rand McNally and Co., 1967), p. 727.
40. Harry Hearder, *Italy in the Age of the Risorgimento 1790-1870* (London: Longman, 1983), pp. 113–114.
41. Max Raisin, *A History of the Jews in Modern Times* (New York: Hebrew Publishing Co. 1949), p. 39. The Pope's verbal attack on the Jews is also referred to in Salo Baron, *A Social and Religious History of the Jews,* Vol. 2 (New York: Columbia University Press, 1937), p. 290.
42. *New Catholic Encyclopedia,* Vol. 9, p. 1153.
43. Eric John (ed.), *The Popes: A Concise Biographical History* (New York: Hawthorn Books, Inc. 1964), p. 397.
44. Quoted in Josef L. Altholz, "A Note On The English Reaction To The Mortara Case," *Jewish Social Studies*, 23 (April 1961): 115.
45. Montefiore became an unofficial roving ambassador for diasporan Jewry. Although raised in England, Montefiore had actually been born in Leghorn, the Italian port which, in the seventeenth and eighteenth centuries, had witnessed remarkable cultural and commercial development by a burgeoning Jewish population. See Sonia and V. D. Lipman, *The Century of Moses Montefiore* (Oxford University Press, 1985).
46. Edward H. Flannery, *The Anguish of the Jews: Twenty-Three Centuries of Anti-Semitism* (New York: The MacMillan Company, 1965), p. 169.
47. Bertram W. Korn, *The American Reaction to the Mortara Case: 1858-1889* (Cincinnati: 1957), p. 161.
48. Edith Stein, the Jewish-born philosopher and writer, who converted and became a nun is a case in point. Her beatification by Pope John Paul II in May 1987 exacerbated Jewish-Vatican relations. See the epilogue for a more detailed discussion.
49. A. F. Day, "The Mortara Case," *The Month,* 153 (1929): 506.
50. Ibid., p. 507.
51. See Cecil Roth, *Personalities and Events in Jewish History* (Philadelphia: The Jewish Publication Society of America, 1953), p. 273.
52. For example, in a case that foreshadowed the Mortara incident, a five or six year old Jewish child had been abducted in Ferrara in 1817. Supposedly, the child, Alessandra Ancona, had been secretly baptized as a sick infant by the family's maid. Roth wrote that the Jewish community in Ferrara lived in dread thereafter. Upon terminating the employment of Christian domestics, Jewish families would obtain affidavits in which the employees would declare that they had done nothing which could give the Vatican any claim on Jewish children in the household. Ibid., p. 270.
53. See Luciano Tas, *Storia degli ebrei italiani* (Rome: Newton Compton edition, 1987), p. 101 and Waagenaar, *The Pope's Jews,* pp. 272–273. The authors are grateful for additional information on the Coen case which was provided by Bruce Kupelnick.
54. More difficult to verify is the case of Graziosa Caviglia, age nine. According to reports, in 1863 or 1864 she was found crying close to the Roman ghetto by a very pious Catholic woman who escorted her directly to a house of catechumens. Over indignant remonstrations by the girl's family and the Jewish community at large, she was allegedly given the sacrament.

55. Charlotte Klein, "Damascus to Kiev: Civiltà Cattolica on Ritual Murder," *The Wiener Library Bulletin,* 27 No. 32 (1974), pp. 18–19. A German Jew by birth, the author converted to Catholicism and became a nun, Sister Louis-Gabriel. However, she chose to write this article under her original name.
56. Ibid., p. 25.
57. Randall L. Bytwerk, *Julius Streicher* (New York: Dorset Press, 1983), pp. 127, 129, 198–201.
58. Klein, "Damascus to Kiev. . .", p. 25. Jews were the butt of countless assaults in the pages of *Civiltà Cattolica* in the late nineteenth century. An anthology of the critical pieces was published in 1891 and was widely circulated. Jews, the "race which nauseates," were accused of triggering the French Revolution, of opposing the Catholic Church and of aiming at world domination. In the Hitler era, *Civiltà Cattolica* maintained its anti-Semitic stance, but was uneasy about Nazi antipathy towards Jews because it sprang from sources other than Christian principles. To make matters worse, the Nazis also exhibited ill will towards the Pope and the Church. See Daniel Carpi, "The Catholic Church and Italian Jewry under the Fascists (to the Death of Pius XI)," *Yad Vashem Studies* Vol. 4 (1960): pp. 44, 51.

POPE PIUS XII (Courtesy Catholic News Service).

3

The Controversy Over Pope Pius XII and the Holocaust Part I

Perhaps no other twentieth-century pope has left a more sizeable or indelible imprint on recent papal history than Eugenio Pacelli. Pius XII's protracted pontificate began as Europe was about to be plunged into the abyss of World War II. Among the *papabili* in early 1939, Pacelli, the Secretary of State since 1930, was the odds-on favorite to succeed Pius XI, and it was on his sixty-third birthday that the Roman-born Pacelli was given the keys to the kingdom. Legend has it that he refrained from voting for himself but humbly accepted his election as the will of God. The choice was extraordinary in several respects. Never before had a Camerlengo or papal chamberlain been elected Pope. Moreover, for more than two and a half centuries papal secretaries of state had been bypassed by the conclaves.

Of aristocratic lineage with close links to the papacy, Pius XII could boast of a grandfather, Marcantonio, who had served Pius IX as Under Secretary of the Interior for the Papal States from 1851 to 1870. Eugenio's father, Filippo Pacelli, had been a counsellor to the Papal Consistorial Court.

Pius XII has been called by one reporter "beyond doubt the best educated Pope of modern times."[1] Musical as a youngster, Eugenio also excelled academically. With a penchant for solitude, he became a voracious reader. After studying philosophy at the Gregorian University, Pacelli concentrated on theology at what is now the Lateran University.

Still in his early twenties in 1899, he was ordained a priest and then proceeded to develop expertise in canon law. His resumé would include no pastoral experience at all. It was diplomacy that was Pacelli's first love and his forté. He rose rapidly through the Vatican's diplomatic ranks, and from 1909 to 1914 served as a professor of ecclesiastical diplomacy.

In 1917, in the midst of the carnage of World War I, he was sent to Germany to explore the possibilities of peace and to represent the interests of the Vatican. By June 1920, Pacelli was the nuncio in Germany. A talented linguist, the future Pope easily mastered the German language which, by all accounts, he spoke with a quaint Italian accent. By the end of 1929 he had become one of the princes of the church and shortly thereafter Eugenio Cardinal Pacelli was appointed Secretary of State.

Seated on the throne of St. Peter at the time was Pius XI. Pacelli's record of restraint and reticence on the Jews has sometimes been compared unfavorably with that of his predecessor. For example, Rolf Hochhuth viewed Pius XI as a "very brave and very resolute man."[2] He had been born Ambrogio Damiano Achille Ratti on 31 May 1857 near Milan. A trained theologian, he was appointed nuncio in Poland in 1919 and, two years later, was made archbishop of Milan and given the cardinal's biretta. In February 1922, the year of Mussolini's momentous march on Rome, Ratti was elected Pope. It was during his seventeen-year pontificate that Fascism achieved power in Germany as well as Italy. Concordats were signed with the latter in 1929 and with the former in 1933. Pacelli was the driving force behind the treaty concluded by the Reich and the Holy See. From his perspective, the pact safeguarded vital Catholic interests in Germany. At stake was the spiritual well-being of twenty million German Catholic souls. The Vatican categorically rejected the notion that, in signing the accord, the Church was putting its imprimatur on the tenets of Nazism. From Hitler's perspective, the agreement not only conferred a degree of legitimacy on his shaky, somewhat disreputable regime then still in its infancy, but it called for the elimination of the Church from German politics.[3]

British Foreign Office documents reveal that Pacelli had no illusions about the Nazis in August 1933. In a discussion with Ivone

Kirkpatrick, the British Chargé d'Affaires in Rome, the Cardinal Secretary of State did not hide his disgust at Hitler's behavior. He lamented Germany's treatment of Austria, its persecution of the Jews, its actions against political opponents, indeed "the reign of terror to which the whole nation was subjected." The future pontiff was not at all sanguine that, with the passage of time, Hitler would moderate his conduct.[4]

Pius XI's dealings with Mussolini were somewhat circumspect, especially when Italian national sentiment backed Il Duce. No love was lost between the Papacy and the Italian dictator, but the former strove to avoid a collision with the Fascist regime over the Italian-Ethiopian War that began in 1935. The Holy See's timidity was obvious when it failed to respond to the claim of one fascist journal that the Italian cause was the cause of Roman Catholicism.[5] Nor did *L'Osservatore Romano* balk at accepting the Fascist version of the border incident that was used to justify Mussolini's military intervention in the Horn of Africa. Nor did the Pope see fit to find fault with the Italians' use of poison gas against the defenseless Abyssinians. Because the war of aggression enjoyed widespread support among the Italian citizenry, the Holy See straddled the moral fence. To have unsuccessfully challenged Mussolini might well have resulted in a considerable loss of prestige for the Vatican.[6] There appears to have been no difference of opinion between Pius XI and Pacelli on this matter.

Pius XI was much more willing than his successor to confront Hitler, the Concordat notwithstanding. A series of papal letters in the 1930s left no doubt about Ratti's antipathy toward Nazism. His 1937 encyclical, *Mit Brennender Sorge* (With Burning Anxiety), issued in German, pilloried those who would exalt and worship the nation or the race thereby perverting the divine will.[7] A livid Führer retaliated against the Catholic clergy in the Third Reich and in 1938, when Hitler journeyed to Rome on a state visit, he snubbed the Holy Father.[8] Some say it was the Pope who was unwilling to see the Chancellor.[9] In all likelihood, the hostility was mutual.

Luigi Cardinal Maglione, the Vatican Secretary of State, may have been exaggerating somewhat when, in 1940, he called United States Ambassador Myron Taylor's attention to the pro-Jewish labors of the late pontiff and stated flatly that, "His voice was the only important voice raised in Europe in their favor."[10] Nevertheless, Pius XI was somewhat more overtly sympathetic to the plight of Europe's Jews than his more discreet successor. "Anti-Semitism is inadmissible," he supposedly told pilgrims from Belgium in September 1938, and he identified himself with the Jews by adding, "spiritually we are all Semites."[11] Although Pius XI said nothing at all about the anti-Semitic Nuremberg Laws of 1935, in April 1938, the Sacred Congregation for Seminaries and Universities, at the urging of the Pope, requested that theology professors rebut the pseudoscientific racism by which the Nazis justified anti-Semitism. Regrettably, this comment was uttered in private and went unreported in *L'Osservatore Romano*.

As war clouds gathered over Europe, an encyclical containing an explicit stricture on racism and anti-Semitism awaited Pius XI's signature. The encyclical in question, "Humani Generis Unitas" (The Unity of the Human Race), had been drafted in secret at Pius XI's behest by Father John LaFarge, a highly respected American Jesuit. LaFarge came from a family of outstanding writers and artists, and was a distinguished journalist in his own right. He was also an authority on racial injustice.[12] On 22 July 1938 LaFarge was summoned to a private audience with the ailing pontiff who wished to issue a statement on the excesses of nationalism and racism. Aided by two other priests, one German, the other French, LaFarge toiled on the papal letter for three months in Paris.

In September 1938, the completed draft of the encyclical was delivered to Father Wlodzimierz Ledochowski, a Polish aristocrat, whose twenty-nine-year reign as Father General of the Society of Jesus (1915–44) was marked by personal absolutism and the establishment of closer bonds between the papacy and the Jesuits.[13] At Jesuit headquarters the encyclical was scrutinized and edited. Ledochowski may have delayed delivery of the document to the Pope. Some have speculated that he deliberately sabotaged the issuance of "Humani Generis."[14] Jesuit Father Walter Abbott was of the opinion that the Jesuit General was fearful of a direct confrontation with the great European powers.[15] Supposedly, Father LaFarge was chided for being too loyal to his superiors in giving the draft encyclical to Ledochowski.[16] On his deathbed, Pius XI requested that the document be sent to him without further delay, but it was too late. Before he could sign it, the pontiff succumbed to a coronary on 10 February 1939.[17] Thus "Humani Generis" was never published during Pius XI's pontificate. Moreover, the document was shelved by his successor. Along with other papers on the desk of Pius XI, the encyclical was deposited in the secret Vatican archives.

Nevertheless, unnamed Vatican sources had leaked word of the planned encyclical in late 1938. The existence of the document was reported in the *New York Times*[18] and the *New York World Telegram*.[19] With Pius XI's death, however, the encyclical remained largely forgotten. Not until 1972, when the *National Catholic Reporter* carried a front-page article on the unpublished encyclical, was the story of "Humani Generis" made public.[20]

One pivotal theme of the encyclical was that totalitarian governments which pursued racist, anti-Jewish, and chauvinist policies ignored the unity of all humankind and violated Catholic doctrine.[21] Racism and anti-Semitism were linked because "the struggle for racial purity ends by being uniquely the struggle against the Jews."[22] In no uncertain terms the encyclical lashed out against the persecution of the Jews:

> Denied legal protection against violence and robbery, exposed to every form of insult and public degradation, innocent persons are treated as criminals [though they] have scrupulously obeyed the law of their native land. Even those who in time of war fought bravely for their country are treated as traitors and the children of those who laid down their lives in their country's behalf are branded as outlaws by the very fact of their parentage.[23]

Obviously, it was with Nazi Germany in mind that the encyclical further asserted that the flagrant flouting of the human rights of Jews had transformed thousands into impoverished refugees wandering the globe.

The text was not wholly favorable to Jews. For example, it stated that contact with Jews could expose the faithful to spiritual contagion and other dangers. In addition, it expressed the opinion that "hatred of the Christian religion had driven misguided souls, whether of the Jewish people or other origins, to ally themselves with, or actively to promote revolutionary movements which aim to destroy society and to obliterate . . . the knowledge, reverence and love of God."[24] Such a reference would surely have strengthened the common equation of Communist and Jew.

Despite the foregoing, the encyclical spoke out very forcefully against anti-Semitism, calling it ineffective and self-defeating. Persecution of the Jews, it declared, was "totally at variance with the true spirit of the Catholic Church."[25]

Such sentiments would have been most welcome to the ears of world Jewry, but they were never proclaimed publicly. Gordon Zahn, for one, has written of the Vatican's missed chance. Publication of the encyclical "would have forced world attention upon issues and events that too many found convenient to overlook or ignore."[26] Instead, in the wake of *Kristallnacht,* the nationwide pogrom which the Nazis unleashed on the hapless Jews of Germany in November 1938, the papacy's silence was deafening.

Publication of "Humani Generis" might have radically changed the course of twentieth century Jewish history. Conor Cruise O'Brien believes that the Führer would have retreated in the face of "Humani Generis," that is to say, he would have soft-pedaled "the persecution of the Jews for the time being," and postponed the Final Solution until after the war. . . ." In his opinion, millions of Jewish lives could have been saved. For O'Brien, the Vatican's dereliction in not promulgating the encyclical was nothing less than "one of the most tragic missed opportunities in history."[27]

Airing "Humani Generis" during the pontificate of Pius XI might have drastically altered the course of papal history. Every bishop in Germany faithful to the Pope might have found himself in a concentration camp had the resounding denunciation of Nazi racism and anti-Semitism been printed, asserted Father Walter Abbott in a 1972 interview. It is "quite likely Cardinal Pacelli . . . might not have been elected to succeed Pius XI because of the resulting German crisis," Abbott added.[28]

Dealings between the Vatican under the mercurial Pius XI and Nazi Germany had deteriorated rapidly to the point where Ernst von Weizsäcker, later the German Ambassador to the Holy See, observed that had Pope Pius XI "lived a little longer relations between the Reich and the Church would probably have been broken off."[29] In Pacelli, the Nazis had a horse of a different color—someone much less temperamental, much less confrontational.

Convincing evidence exists to show that the new pontiff, Pius XII, not only knew of the draft of "Humani Generis" but drew upon it in his own maiden encyclical, *Summi Pontificatus* (Of the Supreme Pontificate), promulgated on 20 October 1939, seven weeks after the onset of World War II.[30] It too addressed the unity of human society. It too spoke of the evils of totalitarianism and racism. However, the grave and pressing matter of anti-Semitism was given a wide berth by the more circumspect and diplomatic Pacelli. In contrast with the lengthy (some seventeen pages), hard-hitting treatment of anti-Semitism contained in "Humani Generis," *Summi Pontificatus* did not mention the persecution of Jews at all. Poland, Pacelli averred, deserved the generous and fraternal concern of the entire world "for its fidelity to the Church, for its services in the defense of Christian civilization"[31] but nary a word was uttered about the Jews. That first pastoral letter set a precedent for the Vatican's future policy on the Jewish question. It was not the last time that Pius XII would, through his silence and inaction, acquiesce in the slaughter of the Jews.

At the beginning of his pontificate, Pius XII took a more forceful stand on another immoral, unchristian Nazi policy. Inspired by National Socialist racial ideology, a secret "euthanasia" program[32] was instituted in Germany in 1939 to rid the Third Reich of unproductive children and adults, that is, those who were physically or emotionally impaired. This category included the feebleminded, the insane, epileptics, and others. According to Nazi eugenicists, such people were "useless eaters," parasites on the body politic. Theirs was life unworthy of life.

In their use of medical personnel, gas chambers, and even crematoria, the notorious T4, and other "mercy killing" programs presaged the Holocaust to come. What is particularly noteworthy is that Nazi "euthanasia" elicited vociferous, though somewhat belated objections from the Vatican and from German Catholic prelates, especially the Bishop of Berlin, Konrad von Preysing, and the Bishop of Münster, Count Von Galen.[33] In a homily against Nazi "mercy killing," Bishop Preysing minced no words: "No justification and no excuse can be found for taking away the life of the weak or ill for any sort of economic or eugenic reason."[34]

In late 1940, on instructions from Pope Pius XII, the Congregation of the Holy Office castigated the murderous eugenics policies then well underway in Germany. In no uncertain terms it denounced homicide against defenseless, guiltless defectives.[35] But this pronouncement, because it was in Latin, the Church's official language, caused barely a ripple in Germany until Bishop Preysing made it known to his congregants.[36]

In an August 1941 sermon delivered under Gestapo surveillance, Bishop Galen inveighed against the morally disastrous policy of destroying innocent life. The "Lion of Münster" provided his stunned listeners with shocking details about the unconscionable murder of "incurables." He reminded his congregants that he was talking about "men and women, our compatriots, our brothers and sisters." They were "poor and unproductive," he conceded, "but does this mean they have lost the right to live?"[37]

Galen wanted the faithful to shun the Nazis and prophesied that divine justice would be meted out to the malefactors: ". . . a just God should and will pronounce upon all those who—like ungrateful Jerusalem—do not wish what God wishes."[38] Striking indeed in an otherwise brave and humanitarian homily was the bishop's clear linkage of the deity's supposed punishment of recalcitrant Jewry whose sole crime was their failure to embrace Jesus and the anticipated response of a God angered by the extermination of cripples and the mentally infirm. Is it really conceivable that Galen believed that the skepticism of disbelieving Jews was on a moral par with the mass murders committed by Nazi "eugenicists?"

From Rome, Pius XII lauded Galen for his "courageous intervention" and derived satisfaction and consolation from the bishop's bold initiatives. The pontiff wrote Galen personally to extoll him.[39] Pacelli's own statement on "euthanasia," more unequivocal than anything he ever issued on the "Jewish question," came in a pastoral letter issued in June 1943 to commemorate the twenty-fifth anniversary of his consecration as a bishop. Entitled *Mystici Corporis Christi* (The Mystical Body of Christ), the 14,500-word-long encyclical expressed Pacelli's profound grief over the Nazis "euthanasia" program.

> We see the bodily-deformed, the insane and those suffering from hereditary disease, at times deprived of their lives, as though they were a useless burden to society. And this procedure is hailed by some as a new discovery of human progress, and as something that is altogether justified by the common good. Yet what sane man does not recognize that this not only violates the natural and Divine

> law written in the heart of every man, but flies in the face of every sensibility of civilized humanity? The blood of these victims, all the dearer to Our Redeemer because deserving of greater pity, "cries to God from the earth."[40]

Germany was not specifically cited in the papal condemnation, but the Pope's target was unmistakable.

Catholic pressure unquestionably helped to bring about the termination of what Robert J. Lifton dubbed the "visible dimensions" of the medical killing project. Murder of defectives continued in a sub-rosa, less centralized fashion. Nothing comparable to the campaign against "euthanasia" was ever waged on behalf of beleagured Jewry, although history has recorded rare cases of extraordinary clerical courage such as that exhibited by Father Bernard Lichtenberg who was imprisoned for praying publicly for the Jews.[41]

Regarding the Nazi murder of defectives, Pius XII wrote, "We would not think we had done our duty if we had kept silent about such deeds."[42] But it is precisely Pacelli's public silence that is the gravamen of the charge against him on the Jewish question. The Church could reasonably anticipate that its outspokenness on "euthanasia" would strike a responsive chord in the German populace. But a defense of the Jews would be received quite differently. Consequently, the Church was essentially voiceless when the Nazis began their methodical, systematic assault on the Jews. Part of the explanation for these disparate approaches by the Church is certainly that the victims of the "mercy killings" were kith and kin, countrymen. They were, despite their handicaps, fellow Germans, whereas anti-Semitism victimized those whose loyalty to the fatherland was widely doubted. According to Nazi racial ideology, Jews, no matter how deep their roots in Germany, were aliens.

In addition, the Church had nurtured hatred of the Jews for almost two millennia. As a result, public opinion in Germany was favorably disposed to protect the disabled, but it was disinclined to go to the aid of Jews, perfidious in a theological as well as a political sense. Father Edward H. Flannery, author of *The Anguish of the Jews,* a frank treatment of Christianity's historic responsibility for anti-Semitism, has written that "Pius XII must have been aware that he could count on no firm constituency in Catholic—or Christian—Germany in the eventuality of a strong and specific denunciation of Hitler and Nazism or of those who supported and collaborated with him. . . . Perennial Christian antisemitism, now intertwined with a vicious racist Judaeophobia, had already taken its toll.''[43] In other words, Christianity had created what Rabbi Marc Tannenbaum has aptly called a ''climate of contempt'' for the Jews. Once released, the genie of Jew hatred could not be put back into the historical bottle.

Is it really possible that the Vatican did not know of the Judeocide being perpetrated by the Nazis? The answer is a resounding and unequivocal ''no.'' There is not a ''shadow of doubt with regard to its knowledge,'' Walter Laqueur has written in *The Terrible Secret.*[44] Indeed, Laqueur is of the opinion that the Vatican with its extensive web of clerics was ''either the first, or among the first, to learn about the fate of the deported Jews.''[45] ''No one was better informed than the Pope about the situation in Poland,'' Carlo Falconi has stated flatly. News arrived from diverse sources enabling the Vatican to ''know not only about the condition of the Church, but about that of every sector of the country's life—from the murder of the population (and especially the ruling class) to the depredation from the forced emigration of the people to the racial murder of the Jews, etc.''[46]

In early march of 1942, Msgr. Giuseppe Burzio, the nuncio in Slovakia, wired the Vatican that news had leaked out about the imminent mass deportation of Slovakian Jews. Deporting eighty thousand of them to Poland and to the mercy of the Germans was tantamount to condemning a great part of them to certain death, he said.[47]

In addition, Myron C. Taylor, President Franklin D. Roosevelt's personal emissary to the Vatican, told Cardinal Maglione by letter dated 26 September 1942 that the Warsaw Ghetto was being emptied and its inhabitants executed wholesale. Executions occurred in a camp established for that gruesome purpose, ''Belzek'' [sic].[48] Taylor, who indicated that his intelligence came from reliable ''Aryan'' eyewitnesses, added that there was ''not one Jew left in the entire district east of Poland, including occupied Russia.'' Jewish deportees from Slovakia, France, the Netherlands, Belgium, and Germany were earmarked for death. Did the Holy Father have any ideas about how the forces of ''civilized public opinion could be utilized in order to prevent'' further barbarities, Taylor asked.[49]

Kurt Gerstein, that most puzzling of Germans, also kept the Pope apprised of Nazi massacres. A devout Christian and an opponent of

Hitlerism, Gerstein paradoxically headed the technical disinfection services of the Waffen S. S. In that capacity he supplied the death factories in Poland with the deadly Zyklon B and had observed the methodical genocide.[50] He was a spectator when seven to eight hundred men, women, and children were crammed into a chamber to be gassed.

After he was rebuffed by the Legation of the Holy See in Berlin, he succeeded in providing ghastly details to Dr. Winter, the co-adjutor of Bishop Preysing and to Bishop Otto Dibelius who later quoted Gerstein's emotional plea: "The outside world must know! These things must become the talk of the world. There is no other means of putting an end to these atrocities."[51]

Gerstein's report, which historian Saul Friedlander, himself a Holocaust survivor, has publicized reveals Gerstein's profound disappointment over the Holy See's inaction. In that report, written shortly before Gerstein committed suicide in a French jail, he asked rhetorically

> What action against Nazism could one demand of an ordinary citizen when the representative of Jesus on earth himself refused even to hear me, although tens of thousands of human beings were being murdered every day; and although to wait only a few hours seemed to me criminal.[52]

One other invaluable conduit of information about developments in Poland was the embassy at the Vatican, maintained by the Polish government-in-exile in London. Its ambassador to the Holy See was the veteran diplomat, Kazimierz Papée. From 1940 to 1944 Papée exasperated the Pope with his periodic updates of appalling happenings in his native land coupled with entreaties of papal action. His tenure as ambassador from 1939 to 1958 coincided with the pontificate of Pius XII. Years after the pontiff's death, Papée was asked if it was possible that his missives about the desperate plight of the Poles, Jewish, and Catholic alike, had not been shown to the Pope. His reply was straightforward: "It is not possible. The Holy Father saw all such communications; it would not have been possible to withhold them from him."[53] Those communications did not skirt the ugly truths.

In October 1942, the Vatican Secretary of State was given particulars about the liquidation of ghettos in Warsaw and Vilna and the gassing en masse of Jews.[54] Two and a half months later, Papee estimated that in excess of a million Jews had already been slain by the Nazis.[55] In a note hand delivered by the Polish Ambassador to Monsignor Domenico Tardini, one of Maglione's main assistants, Papée minced no words about the extermination of Poland's Jews.

> The Germans are liquidating the entire Jewish population of Poland. The first to be taken are the old, the crippled, the women and children; which proves that these are not deportations to forced labor and confirms the information that these deported populations are taken to specially prepared installations, there to be put to death by various means [while] the young and able-bodied are killed through starvation and forced labor.[56]

This secret revelation was in the Vatican's hands four days before Pacelli broadcast his 1942 Christmas message.

For many months intense pressure had been exerted on the Vatican. Through Catholic channels, the executive of the World Jewish Congress repeatedly pleaded with the Vatican to have the pontiff openly proclaim his revulsion at Nazi crimes. More importantly, sundry governments pressed the Pope to speak out loudly, clearly, and precisely in condemnation of Nazi criminality.

In mid-1942, Hildebrando Pompeu Accioly, the Brazilian Ambassador to the Holy See, took the initiative to persuade the recalcitrant pontiff to do so. On several occasions, Harold H. Tittmann, Myron Taylor's assistant, reminded Vatican officials that the failure to "protest publicly against Nazi atrocities is endangering its moral prestige and is undermining faith both in the church and in the Holy Father himself."[57] Ambassadors from Britain, Uruguay and Belgium also approached the Vatican which remained adamant, arguing that Pius XII had denounced wartime immoral behavior. More specificity would only worsen matters. On 6 October 1942, Tittman wrote to the United States Secretary of State Cordell Hull that the "Holy See is still apparently convinced that a forthright denunciation by the Pope of Nazi atrocities, at least in so far as Poland is concerned, would only result in the violent deaths of many more people."[58]

However, after receiving a plethora of reports of Nazi butchery and numerous appeals from diplomats and others, the Pope finally relented. He agreed reluctantly to speak out in his 1942 Christmas talk. His remarks were bound to disappoint, for in the radio broadcast which emanated from his private study in the Vatican and which lasted three quarters of an hour, the pontiff saw fit only to make a brief, bland, and veiled reference to an unnamed group that might or might not be understood to be the Jews. He referred to humanity's obligation to the "hundreds of thousands of persons who without any fault on their part, sometimes only because of their nationality or race, have been consigned to death or to a slow decline."[59] These vague inscrutable words came after the Holy Father had spoken for more than half an hour. A front-page *New York Times* article which accompanied the complete text of the Christmas message was entitled "Pope Assails Peril of Godless State."[60] To the *Times,* the address was primarily a reaffirmation of the Vatican's "denunciation of Marxist socialism." Ostensibly the plight of the Jews was of peripheral concern. Jews were not identified as victims, nor were Nazis named as victimizers by the Pope. To future critics and a few contemporary ones, Pius had shown himself to be tone deaf to the screams of millions of Jews. A very recent Vatican document speaks approvingly about Pius' "vibrant appeal" in the Christmas message.[61] Critics would contend that "pontifical pussyfooting" would be a more felicitous description. Once again the supreme pontiff had declined to sound the tocsin.

Vincent McCormick, an American Jesuit resident in Rome, told one of Pius' closest advisers that the radio homily had been "much too heavy, ideas not clear-cut and obscurely expressed."[62] McCormick confided to his diary that the Pope was too dependent upon "German tutoring"[63] and that he should rely on Italians and Frenchmen to draft his statements. The New York-born McCormick concluded that the Vatican lacked the courage to confront the Germans, or, for that matter, the Italians.

When Harold Tittman had a forty-minute conversation with Pius XII at the traditional New Year's audience, the Christmas message was discussed. The American diplomat had the impression that the Pope was "sincere in believing that he had spoken therein clearly enough to satisfy all those who had been insisting in the past that he utter some word of condemnation of the Nazi atrocities."[64] Pius was taken aback when Tittman indicated that his meaning was unclear to some. Pacelli "thought that it was plain to everyone that he was referring to the Poles, Jews, and hostages."[65] Pius further told Tittman that he could not single out the Nazis for censure. The Communists would have to be mentioned also, and that would have been offensive to the Allies. In addition, he was persuaded, despite the mountain of evidence to the contrary, that the Western democracies had been guilty of exaggeration in describing German horrors. Pius, it must be remembered, had spent twelve of the happiest years of his life in Germany as a nuncio, admired Germany's rich culture and knew its history. He refused to believe the grim truth that the land of Beethoven, Bach, and Goethe had more recently produced mass murderers of unprecedented ferocity.

Tittman was of the opinion that the Pope's aversion to raise his voice against the Third Reich flowed from his fear that "the German people, in the bitterness of their defeat, will reproach him later for having contributed, if only indirectly to its defeat."[66] Given his long tenure in Germany, Pacelli knew that the Vatican had been sharply criticized because of Pope Benedict XV's perceived anti-German posture during the First World War.

Commenting on Hochhuth's *The Deputy* in 1963, Father Robert Leiber insisted that neither Pius XII nor the Allied governments truly understood the magnitude of the Nazis' criminality until Germany finally capitulated.[67] In 1966, Father Leiber, a member of Pacelli's inner circle and one of his staunchest defenders, still argued that Pius knew nothing of the "Final Solution." Prudence was required of the Pope in those troubled times. The Holy Father could not give credence to reports of savagery that might be false. Seventy-nine years old and retired, Father Leiber in a tape-recorded interview, asserted contradictorily that the "Pope protested against every wrong, wherever it was done. He did not go farther. He would have caused himself interminable embarrassment had he protested against every single occurrence. . . . The Pope was . . . quite aware that every one of his words would be exploited in a purely political way either by the Allies or by the Germans."[68] He had to avoid the appearance of taking sides, Leiber explained.

For the Vatican there was a moral symmetry to the Nazi and the Allied cases. Hilter's Germany was not seen as the aggressor, nor were her cruelties even against noncombatants viewed as greater than those of her foes. Without doubt, the fact that the Soviet Union, the fount of all evil in Vatican eyes, was aligned with the Western democracies, made it imperative for the Holy See to remain neutral.

Anti-communism had been a constant in the Catholic Church's policy ever since Pius IX issued his *Qui pluribus* encyclical in 1846. Even before Marx and Engels published their *Communist Manifesto,* Pio Nono spoke of that "infamous doctrine of so-called Communism which is absolutely contrary to natural law itself, and if once adopted would utterly destroy the rights, property and possessions of all men and even society itself."[69] Almost a century later when Nazi militarism began to flex its muscles, Pius XI saw entire peoples in danger of lapsing into barbarism. However reprehensible Nazism was, it did not pose the paramount immediate threat. As he made clear in his encyclical, *Divini Redemptoris,* the imminent danger was posed by "Bolshevistick and Atheistic Communism, which aims at upsetting the social order and at undermining the very foundations of Christian civilization."[70]

For the papacy after 1917, Catholicism's most formidable and tenacious enemies were to be found in Moscow. It was from there that the "false messianic idea" of Communism was disseminated. No doubt its atheism and its concomitant anti-clericalism were the elements in Communism that most strengthened Pius XI's resolve to save Christian civilization from what was seen as nothing less than a "satanic scourge."[71]

It is obvious that Pius XII shared this animosity toward the Soviet Union. As he navigated the perilous waters between the Scylla of Nazism and the Charybdis of Bolshevism, he perceived that while the former was no friend to Catholicism, it was less menacing than the thoroughgoing anti-religious ideology of the Kremlin. Indeed, whatever its defects, in his eyes, Nazism could serve as a bulwark against Marxism, perhaps as a destroyer of Marxism. Even more than the fact that Catholics were fighting on both sides during the Second World War, which militated against Vatican partisanship—he was loath to cause crises of conscience for Catholics fighting for the Third Reich[72]—dread of a Bolshevik victory contributed to the Pope's moral anesthesia in the face of Hitlerian-sponsored genocide.

In those troubled years Pius XII was inconsistent in responding to cases of aggression. If the malefactor was the Kremlin, the Pope was not tongue-tied. In late 1939 when Stalin invaded Finland, the Pope called the invasion the most cynical of the era. And when the League of Nations barred the Soviet Union, the Vatican could not contain its joy. John S. Conway has written that in this instance "there was no reluctance to take a firm stand, no talk of diplomatic neutrality or even the need to protect those Catholics who were now under Russian control."[73] In contrast, in the face of the Nazi conquest of Denmark and Norway, the Vatican remained mum and it failed to strongly take the Nazis to task for their brutal takeover of the Low Countries.[74] Not surprisingly, Operation Barbarossa, Hitler's long-planned assault on the Soviet Union, which took place on 22 June 1941, evoked no papal condemnation of Germany.

The Vatican and the Nazis were frequently at loggerheads because of the Führer's anticlerical actions in Germany. To Bernardo Attolico, the Italian ambassador to the Holy See, the pope complained that convents and other religious institutions had been padlocked, that Christ had been removed from the schools and that German youngsters were compelled to "recite that parody of the Our Father in which they thank Hitler for their daily bread."[75] Pacelli always feared that there would be no place for the Vatican in a new Nazi-ruled European order. After the Bolsheviks were vanquished, the Church might go from the frying pan into the fire.

Despite Hitler's hostile tendencies where Christianity was concerned, Germans were accorded preferential treatment in Rome. Attolico revealed that every day the pope receives "all the Germans who come to see him without even requiring them to kneel before him, as do all the others; at times he even interrupts the daily report of the Secretary of State, in order to receive them." The Italian envoy quoted Pacelli voicing the following lament in September 1941: "Oh, if my Germany had left me in peace . . . my attitude toward this war, especially at this time, would have been quite different. . . ."[76]

Despite Pacelli's misgivings about the Third Reich, there is little doubt that he preferred a German victory to one by Stalin. Captured Nazi documents strongly suggest such a preference. Fritz Menshausen, counselor at the German embassy to the Holy See, notified the Reich's Foreign Ministry in September 1941 that knowledgeable persons in authority had repeatedly assured him that the Holy Father, in his heart, stood on the side of the Axis powers.[77]

In the summer of 1943, the pontiff sent Count Enrico Galeazzi, a very influential Vatican banker, to New York City to confer with Francis Cardinal Spellman, an old friend and ideological bedfellow of

Pacelli's. Spellman enjoyed easy access to the White House. An ardent backer of Roosevelt, he served as Vicar of the United States Armed Forces and was sometimes used by FDR for diplomatic missions to Catholic countries. The Massachusetts-born prelate was urged by Galeazzi to speak to Roosevelt. Pius XII wanted Spellman to prepare the ground for what the pope termed a charitable peace with Germany. With such a negotiated peace as his objective, the pontiff through Spellman urged American ecclesiastics to promote tolerance and understanding toward Germany. Spellman visited FDR in early September 1943, but the American president had his own agenda. There would be no peace with charity with Germany. Rather Germany would be partitioned and the Soviet influence would be enhanced in postwar Europe. Spellman's report on the White House meeting must have caused great dismay in Rome.[78]

Despite the Nazis' unparalled barbarity, it was German soldiers who manned the ramparts against Marxism in the thinking of Cardinal Maglione and others in the Vatican in 1943. Without those ramparts European culture would be destroyed.

Pius XII still spoke of the Germans as a great nation battling against Bolshevism and shedding their blood "not only for their friends but also for the sake of their present enemies."[79] Left unsaid by the pontiff was the notion that the western democracies were fighting on the wrong side in World War II. It was a pity that the Allies were not aligned with the Third Reich against the Kremlin and the peril of Communism. Lost in the Holy Father's geopolitical calculations of the possible effects of the war on Christianity was the genocide of the Jews about which he was very knowledgeable in the summer of 1943.

* * *

What could Pius XII have done for the Jews? What should he have done? Excommunication of Hitler, Goebbels, and other Nazi luminaries who were at least nominally Catholic was one possible papal response to the tragedy that was unfolding in Europe.[80] As a penalty, excommunication had frequently been meted out for offenses far less serious than genocide. No one should be deluded into believing that fear of being ejected from the Church would have deterred the Nazi hierarchy from pursuing its murderous policies, but it would certainly have sent a clear message to millions of Catholics the world over:

Nazism was an unmitigated evil and all true followers of Christ had an obligation to oppose it.

Posterity can only speculate about what might have happened if the Pope had imposed an interdict, that is, an ecclesiastical censure denying Catholics in the Greater Reich access to most sacraments and to religious burial. We will never know for sure, for none was ever imposed. It is unlikely that Catholics would have turned against Nazism en masse. But again, where the Papacy stood regarding Hitler would have been made abundantly clear. The symbolic value of an edict of excommunication or interdict would have been inestimable.

As the catastrophe deepened, the Pope had many opportunities to take a stand. Hochhuth was not alone in believing that Pacelli was duty-bound to enjoin Catholics from playing any role in the policy of genocide, nor was he the only critic to speculate about ''how many people could have been saved just in Poland if the population had been summoned by the Church to offer Jews a hiding place.''[81]

In 1944, Jewish groups earnestly appealed to the Vatican through Myron Taylor to save Jews from total extinction. The appeal came at a time when Adolf Eichmann turned his attention to the substantial Jewish population in Hungary. It appeared that Eichmann's thirst for Jewish blood could not be slaked. After learning that some four hundred thousand Hungarian Jews had been transported to Poland and an additional hundred thousand had already been gassed, the World Jewish Congress entreated the Papacy to broadcast a public announcement which it felt was the only way to effectively mitigate the peril. Their appeal, could, the Congress hoped, lead to a Vatican denunciation of Nazi crimes and a clarion call to Hungarian Christians and others to protect Jews.[82] Month after month, the Pope temporized. No such broadcast was ever made. Joseph Lichten and others favorable to Pius XII have argued that the pontiff was restrained because he feared that stronger public criticism of the Nazis would worsen the plight of Europe's Jews. This appears to be a rationalization for papal inaction. Annihilation was the hellish policy of the Nazis and the Vatican knew that to be the case as early as 1942. By the millions, Jews were being slaughtered. What could possibly be worse than that?

With the notable exception of the French Thomistic philosopher, Jacques Maritain, most prominent Catholics did not question the Vatican's taciturnity. Rather, they satisfied themselves with the belief that the Pope knew best, that he was doing all that he could do behind the scenes. When the war ended, the full truth about the Pope's altruistic endeavors would be made known. Typical was Don Luigi Sturzo, an Italian cleric and an opponent of the Nazis, who wrote that he was sure that "Pius XII has made every effort, through diplomatic and personal channels, to influence Hitler and his staff."[83]

In the United States, Frances B. McMahon, president of the Catholic Association for International Peace, recognized that the Jewish predicament was the "most terrible single tragedy of the present war."[84] He expressed the opinion that passive acquiescence would mean complicity with the crimes of the Nazis, but was absolutely convinced that the Pope had attempted by various means to save Jews. When Germany was defeated, the record of those attempts would be disclosed.

Defenders of Pius XII contend that his representatives, especially the nuncios in several European countries, assisted the hapless Jews. Romania is often cited as a case in point.

At first in Romania, the Catholic Church acted exclusively on behalf of Jews who had converted to Catholicism. When, in 1940, the fascist, anti-Semitic Iron Guard pressed for the ouster of youngsters of Jewish lineage from Catholic schools, the papal nuncio, Andreia Cassulo, energetically remonstrated with the authorities. Again, in March 1941, he protested when Jews were prohibited from becoming Catholics, a practice which became widespread as vicious anti-Semitism was translated into terrifying disabilities for the Jews.[85]

Although the Vatican was principally concerned with guaranteeing that Catholics, including those of Jewish origin, enjoyed rights spelled out by the Concordat, the nuncio deserves the highest praise for his repeated interventions with General Ion Antonesco in 1942 and thereafter in support of non-converted Jews who were menaced by deportation. Father John Morley has written that the "nuncio in Bucharest was possibly the most active of the Vatican diplomats in matters concerning Jews."[86] On 6 September 1943 Cassulo prodded the Romanian Foreign Ministry to allow Jewish children to leave for Palestine.[87] His labors contributed to the survival of multitudes of Romanian Jews, including a substantial number of Jewish orphans. He served as a conduit for papal funds earmarked for the assistance of Transnistrian Jews.[88]

Alexandre Shafran, who served Romania's eight hundred thousand Jews as Chief Rabbi, had provided the nuncio with detailed graphic evidence of the pitiful conditions of Jews, evidence which the local Jews wanted placed before Pius XII.[89] Cassulo complied. There is no reason to doubt that the Pope was well aware of Cassulo's activities, but the initiative came from the nuncio rather than Rome.

Indeed, in his memoirs, Chief Rabbi Safran wrote that he "always had the feeling that all those humanitarian actions were more a reflection of Cassulo's own personality and derived directly from our relationship." Safran believed that "Cassulo used his official authority on our behalf more than was expected of him by the Vatican."[90]

Although Cassulo once complained to the Foreign Ministry that local officials were treating equally Catholics of the Jewish race and Jews of the Mosaic religion,[91] his altruism was undeniable. For the Jews of Romania, the nuncio's humanitarianism qualified him to be counted among the "righteous Gentiles."[92] Apparently, Cassulo's efforts and those of Angelo Roncalli, the future Pope John XXIII who served as apostolic delegate in Istanbul during the Second World War,[93] were the exceptions rather than the norm.

Father John Morley has scrutinized the Holy See's diplomacy in several countries during the Holocaust and has concluded that "Vatican diplomats only rarely acted on behalf of Jews as Jews, and this usually only for specific individuals. They sometimes had words of sympathy for the Jews, but little action followed from these words."[94]

Intercession for so-called Catholic Jews was much more common and more sustained. In accordance with their own racially-based definition of Jewishness, the Nazis were inclined to see baptism as meaningless. The baptized remained Jewish in Nazi eyes. But for the Vatican such converts were authentic sons and daughters of the Church who were entitled to its protection. Had the Church ignored the persecution of converts, it would have been cast in a decidedly negative light.

The Vatican was essentially undisturbed by the anti-Jewish legislation enacted by Mussolini and by Marshall Petain's puppet regime in France. It was only to the racial definition of Jewishness used by Il Duce and by Vichy which challenged the legitimacy of baptism into the Catholic faith and undermined the validity of some Catholic marriages that the Vatican took exception.[95]

Converted Jews could not be forsaken. Consequently, the Vatican felt obligated to work from March 1939 until 1945 trying to obtain visas for German Catholic Jews. But for the unconverted Jews of Germany and Europe as a whole, the Vatican did the minimum.

One atypical initiative by the Vatican occurred in November 1942 when the Nazis requisitioned between two and three thousand Jews, predominantly women, children, and the elderly, from the Italian-occupied zone of Croatia. Intervention by the Italians was asked by the Vatican Secretariat of State to prevent their deportation.[96]

In Slovakia, a puppet state created by the Nazis to fill the vacuum caused by the dismemberment of neighboring Czechoslovakia, the Papacy intervened more directly than elsewhere. The reason is obvious. Slovakia, which was granted de jure recognition by the Holy See on 25 March 1939, just eleven days after its birth, was a Catholic state, with "profound Catholic traditions" as Cardinal Maglione put it.[97] Both its president, Josef Tiso, and its prime minister, Vojtech Tuka, were Roman Catholic priests. The former possessed a doctorate in theology. Tiso, who was executed after the war, embarrassed the Vatican by declaring openly that Roman Catholic and National Socialist social doctrines were indistinguishable.[98] It was inevitable that what transpired in Slovakia reflected on the Roman Catholic Church. Indeed, Livia Rothkirchen has said that in a state run by clerics such as Tiso "every discriminatory law introduced during his presidency bore in a certain sense the imprimatur of the Church."[99]

At least initially, the Vatican's involvement in Slovakia was solely in its self-interest. Racial legislation adopted there appeared to nullify the validity of Jewish conversion to Catholicism. It treated so-called Catholic Jews as if they had not converted and banned marriages between such persons and bona fide Christians. That prohibition challenged the prerogatives of the Church in the sacramental matter of marriage. Fear that baptized Jews would be included among the deportees from Slovakia prompted several Vatican protests.[100]

Insofar as unbaptized Jews were concerned, what scandalized the Vatican most was the fact that Jewish girls were being forcibly transported from a Catholic state by a Catholic government to the eastern front, there to serve as prostitutes. Deportation of other unconverted Jews was also lamented as inhuman. In March 1943, in correspondence with Rome, Burzio stated unambiguously that deportation meant death.[101] Cardinal Maglione in reply expressed his wish that Burzio attempt to impede deportation projects.[102] The Secretary of State himself in May 1943 contacted the Slovakian legation at the Holy See to object to the transfer of the remaining Jews—men, women, and children, some of whom professed the Catholic religion. Maglione explained that his Church took to its bosom persons of all races. It regarded all of humanity with maternal solicitude.[103]

Unfortunately, the Holy See's exertions in Slovakia were essentially fruitless. It was a case of too little too late. Father John Morley ascribes the failure of papal diplomacy "as much to its own indifference to the deportation of the Jews as any other factor."[104] He faults the Vatican because it "issued not threats of excommunication or interdict against the president, the prime minister, or the people."[105] Morley believes that there was a chance for "a great moral and humanitarian gesture."[106] But it was lost.

Notes

1. John Gunther, *Inside Europe* (New York and London: Harper and Brothers, 1940), p. 265.
2. Patricia Marx, "An Interview With Rolf Hochhuth," *Partisan Review*, Vol. 31, no. 3 (Summer 1964), P. 367.
3. Public Record Office, British Foreign Office, 371/16727/5452, Ivone Kirkpatrick to John Simon, 19 August 1933; Guenter Lewy, *The Catholic Church And Nazi Germany* (New York: McGraw Hill Book Company, 1964), chapter 3. Also see Stewart A. Stehlin, *Weimar and the Vatican 1919-1933 German-Vatican Diplomatic Relations in the Interwar Years* (Princeton: Princeton University Press, 1983).
4. Kirkpatrick to Simon, 19 August 1933.
5. Anthony Rhodes, *The Vatican in the Age of the Dictators 1922–1945* (London: Hodder and Stoughton, 1973), p. 69.
6. Esmonde M. Robertson, *Mussolini as Empire-Builder: Europe and Africa 1932–1936* (New York: St. Martin's Press, 1977), p. 117. Rhodes, p. 69 and Dennis Mack Smith, *Mussolini's Roman Empire* (New York: The Viking Press, 1976), p. 74.
7. Michael Mashberg, "The Unpublished Encyclical of Pope Pius XI," *The National Jewish Monthly* (April, 1978), p. 41. Although the document alluded to the sacred nature of the Hebrew scriptures it characterized Jews as the people who had crucified Jesus.
8. J. S. Conway, *The Nazi Persecution of the Churches 1933–45* (London: Weidenfeld and Nicolson, 1968), p. 166.
9. Hans Kuhner, *Encyclopedia of the Papacy* (New York: Philosophical Library, 1958), p. 239.

10. Notes of Msgr. J. G. Patrick Hurley, 8 March 1940 re: Summary of Conversation between Cardinal Maglione and Ambassador Myron Taylor in *Records And Documents Of The Holy See Relating To The Second World War: The Holy See And The War In Europe March 1939-August 1940.* Volume 1. Edited by Pierre Blet, Angelo Martini, Burkhart Schneider and Gerard Noel (Washington: Corpus Books, 1965), p. 353.
11. Mashberg, "The Unpublished Encyclical," p. 41. Carlo Falconi, *The Silence Of Pius XII.* Trans. by Bernard Wall (Boston: Little, Brown and Company, 1965), p. 94.
12. Jim Castelli, "Unpublished encyclical attacked anti-Semitism," *National Catholic Reporter,* 15 December 1972, p. 1.
13. Malachi Martin, *The Jesuits: The Society of Jesus and the Betrayal of the Roman Catholic Church* (New York: Simon and Schuster, 1987), p. 221.
14. Castelli, "Unpublished encyclical . . ." Franz Greiner thought it improbable that Ledochowski had subverted the encyclical. See Franz Greiner, "The Unpublished Encyclical," *International Catholic Review Communio"* (March/April 1973):120.
15. Unpublished press release of National Catholic News Service based on an interview with Father Walter Abbott, 12 December 1972.
16. Ibid.
17. Ibid. and Mashberg, p. 40.
18. *New York Times,* 29 November 1938.
19. *New York World Telegram,* 28 November 1938.
20. Castelli, "Unpublished encyclical, p. 1 ff."
21. Ibid., p. 1.
22. "Humani Generis Unitas," p. 88. Copies of the draft of the encyclical are difficult to find. The best source is the Father Edward Stanton papers at Boston College (Burns Library).
23. Ibid., p. 88
24. Ibid., p. 95.
25. Ibid., p. 97.
26. Gordon Zahn, "The unpublished encyclical—an opportunity missed," *National Catholic Reporter,* 15 December 1972, p. 9.
27. Conor Cruise O'Brien, "A Lost Chance To Save the Jews?" *The New York Review of Books,* 27 April 1989, p. 35. O'Brien's speculation has been challenged by Jacques Kornberg of the University of Toronto. O'Brien's "might have been," writes Kornberg, "disregards the papacy's practical concern with maintaining religious institutions, based on its view of the church as the necessary channel for grace and salvation. Clearly this took priority over promoting Christian love, self-sacrifice and martyrdom." See *The New York Review,* 26 October 1989, p. 69.
28. Press release of the N.C.N.S., 12 December 1972.
29. Ernst Von Weizsäcker, *Memoirs of Ernst Von Weizsäcker,* trans. by John Andrews (London: Victor Gollancz, 1951), p. 282.
30. In its 1988 statement on "The Church and Racism," the Vatican acknowledged that Pacelli had borrowed elements from "Humani Generis" for his own *Summi Pontificatus.* No mention was made of the fact that Pius XII had expurgated his predecessor's trenchant criticism of anti-Semitism. See Pontifical Commission

"Iustitia et Pax," "The Church and Racism—Towards A More Fraternal Society" (Vatican City, 1988).

31. Pope Pius XII, "The Unity of Human Society" (Summi Pontificatus), *The Catholic Mind* 37, no. 885 (8 November 1939): p. 915.
32. The term "euthanasia" is clearly a misnomer when applied to Nazi policies. Derived from the Greek roots "eu" meaning good and "thanatos" meaning death, euthanasia truly refers to killing or making possible the death of terminally ill individuals for merciful reasons with their consent or that of their families.
33. While most Catholic spokesmen found "mercy killing" and Catholic teaching irreconcilable, one Catholic theologian, Prof. Joseph Mayer of the Paderborn Academy, justified "euthanasia for the mentally ill." See Robert A. Graham, "The 'Right to Kill' In the Third Reich-Prelude To Genocide," *The Catholic Historical Review,* Vol. 62 (1976), p. 59.
34. Quoted in J. S. Conway, *The Nazi Persecution of the Churches 1933–45* (London: Weidenfeld and Nicolson, 1968), p. 270.
35. Graham, "The 'Right To Kill,' " pp. 64–65.
36. Gitta Sereny, *Into That Darkness: An Examination of Conscience* (New York: Vintage Books, 1983), p. 74.
37. Philippe Aziz, *Doctors of Death,* vol. 4 (Geneva: Ferni Publishers, 1976), p. 96.
38. Ibid., p. 97 and Robert J. Lifton, *The Nazi Doctors-Medical Killing and the Psychology of Genocide* (New York: Basic Books, Inc. Publishers, 1986), p. 94.
39. Graham, "The 'Right To Kill,' " pp. 64–65 and Letter from Pope Pius XII to the Bishop of Munster, 24 February 1943 in *Actes Et Documents Du Saint Siège Relatifs À La Seconde Guerre Mondiale: Lettres De Pie XII Aux Eveques Allemands 1939-1944,* vol. 2, edited by Pierre Blet, Angelo Martini, and Burkhart Schneider (Vatican City: Libreria Editrice Vaticana, 1966), pp. 306–310.
40. Pope Pius XII, *Mystici Corporis Christi,* in *The Catholic Mind* 41 No. 971 (November 1943), p. 37.
41. Raul Hilberg, *The Destruction Of The European Jews* (New York: Harper and Row, 1979), pp. 299–300.
42. Graham, "The 'Right To Kill,' " p. 65. Letter from Pope Pius XII to Bishop von Preysing, 15 December 1940 in *Actes Et Documents,* vol. 2, pp. 180–183.
43. Flannery, *The Anguish of the Jews,* p. 226.
44. Walter Laqueur, *The Terrible Secret: Suppression of the Truth about Hitler's "Final Solution"* (New York: Penguin Books, 1982), p. 55.
45. Ibid, p. 56.
46. Carlo Falconi, *The Silence Of Pius XII,* trans. by Bernard Wall (Boston: Little, Brown and Co., 1970), p. 198.
47. Burzio to Maglione, 9 March 1942, *Actes et Documents,* vol. 8, p. 153. Laquer, *The Terrible Secret,* p. 56 and Livia Rothkirchen, "Vatican Policy and the 'Jewish Problem' in 'Independent' Slovakia 1939-1945, *Yad Vashem Studies,* 6 (1967):36.
48. *Foreign Relations of the United States: Diplomatic Papers* 1942, Vol III Europe, (Washington: United States Government Printing Office, 1961): 775–776.
49. Ibid.
50. Saul Friedlander, *Kurt Gerstein: The Ambiguity of Good,* trans. by Charles Fullman (New York: Alfred A. Knopf, 1969), p x.
51. Ibid., pp. 160–161.

52. Ibid., p. 2.
53. Quoted in Gitta Sereny, *Into that Darkness: An Examination of Conscience* (New York: Vintage Books, 1983), p. 333.
54. "Notes From The Polish Ambassador," 3 October 1942, in *Actes et Documents* vol. 8, p. 670.
55. John F. Morley, *Vatican Diplomacy and the Jews during the Holocaust 1939–1943* (New York: Ktav Publishing House, 1980), p. 138.
56. Polish Ambassador to Secretary of State, 19 December 1942, *Actes et Documents* vol. 8, p. 755. We have used the translation from the French by Sereny, pp. 330–31. Tardini was chief of the Section for Extraordinary Ecclesiastical Affairs.
57. Minister Harrison in Switzerland to U.S. Secretary of State, 3 August 1942, *Foreign Relations* vol. 3, p. 772.
58. Ibid., pp. 776–777. Sister Pascalina Lehnert who was very close to the Pope claimed that the pontiff was on the verge of publicly condemning the persecution of the Jews in August, 1942. However, when the Nazis retaliated against the Catholic Church following the open protest of the Dutch bishops, he changed his mind. In her autobiography, Sister Pascalina recalled the Pope saying that a papal protest could cost two hundred thousand lives. He then allegedly burned his statement which was to have been published in *L'Osservatore Romano*. Sister Pascalina wanted to keep a copy of his protest as it could be useful some day, but he was fearful that Nazis could penetrate the Vatican and discover the papers. See Pascalina Lehnert, *Pio XII il privilegio di servirlo* trans. Marola Guarducci (Milano: Rusconi, 1984), pp. 148–149.
59. *New York Times*, 25 December 1942, p. 16.
60. Ibid., p. 1.
61. "The Church And Racism: Towards A More Fraternal Society" (Vatican, 1988), p. 15.
62. James Hennessey, "American Jesuit In Wartime Rome: The Diary of Vincent A. McCormick S. J. 1942-1945," *Mid-America; an historical review*, 56 No. 1 (1974):36.
63. Ibid., p. 49.
64. Harrison to Secretary of State, 5 January 1943 *Foreign Relations*, vol.2 Europe (1943) (Washington United States Printing Office, 1964), P. 912.
65. Ibid., At the beginning of 1943, Wladyslaw Raczkiewicz, the President of Poland, wrote to the Pope about the supernatural courage of Warsaw's Catholics in protesting the maltreatment and killing of Jews. The Pope's reply made no mention of Jews. The letters are reproduced in Kazimerz Papée, *Pius XII A Polska 1939-1949* (Roma: Editrice Studium, 1954), pp. 62–65. Piux XII has also been pilloried for his diffidence in responding to Hitler's persecution of the Roman Catholic Church in Poland. Lukas has written that the pontiff ". . . at no time made a clear, unequivocal statement in defense of the Polish church against the barbarities inflicted upon it by the Germans." See Richard C. Lukas, *The Forgotten Holocaust—The Poles Under German Occupation 1939-1944* (Lexington: The University Press of Kentucky, 1986), p. 16.
66. Tittman to Secretary of State, 6 October 1942, *Foreign Relations*, Vol III (Europe), p. 777.
67. Falconi, *The Silence of Pius XII*, p. 46. Leiber made his comment to the *Frankfurter Allgemeine Zeitung*.

68. "Pius XII And The Third Reich," *Look,* 17 May 1966, p. 45.
69. *Seven Great Encyclicals* (Glen Rock, New Jersey: Paulist Press, 1963), p. 178.
70. Ibid., p. 177.
71. Ibid., p. 179.
72. Guenter Lewy, *The Catholic Church and Nazi Germany* (New York: McGraw-Hill, 1964), pp. 303–304. Lewy quotes Pius' remarks on the subject made to the Berlin correspondent for *L'Osservatore Romano.*
73. John S. Conway, "The Silence of Pope Pius XII," *The Review of Politics,* 27, No. 1 (January 1965), pp. 116.
74. Ibid.
75. The Royal Italian Embassy to the Holy See, 16 September 1941 in *Documents on German Foreign Policy 1918-1945* (Washington D.C.: United States Government Printing Office, 1964) Series D., Volume 13, p. 526.
76. Ibid., p. 527. In December, 1941 two months after he was informed by Msgr. Burzio in Slovokia that the Einsatzgruppen were annihilating Russian Jewry, the pontiff extended an invitation to the Berlin Opera to perform at the Vatican.
77. Fritz Menshausen to State Secretary Weizsacker, 12 September 1941 in *Documents on German Foreign Policy,* Series D, Volume 13, p. 489.
78. John Cooney, *The American Pope: The Life And Times Of Francis Cardinal Spellman* (New York: Times Books, 1984), pp. 134–135. Cooney drew his information from Cardinal Spellman's memorandum to the Vatican summarizing his meeting with Roosevelt. Also see "Pius XII Papst der Deutschen," *Der Spiegel,* 18 November 1964, p. 124 and *Journal de Genève,* 27 July 1964.
79. Saul Friedlander, *Pius XII and the Third Reich: A Documentation,* trans. by Charles Fullman (New York: Alfred A. Knopf, 1966), pp. 190, 192. Friedlander drew his information from telegrams sent to Berlin by Weizsäcker in September, 1943.
80. Lewy, *The Catholic Church and Nazi Germany,* p. 303.
81. Patricia Marx, "An Interview With Rolf Hochhuth," *Partisan Review,"* 31, no. 3 (Summer 1964):373.
82. The text of the telegram from Alex Easterman of the W. J. C. to Myron Taylor was quoted in a letter from Taylor to Maglione, 6 July 1944. Taylor File, National Archives, RG 59, Box 4.
83. Letter from Sturzo to A. Leon Kubowitzski, 30 May 1943. Reprinted in Aryeh L. Kubovy, "The Silence of Pope Pius XII and the Beginnings of the 'Jewish Document' ", *Yad Vashem Studies,* VI (1967), p. 12.
84. *New York Times,* 26 July 1943, p. 19.
85. Theodore Lavi, "The Vatican's Endeavors on Behalf of Romania Jewry During the Second World War," *Yad Vashem Studies,* Vol. 5 (1963), pp. 405–406.
86. Morley, *Vatican Diplomacy,* p. 45.
87. Cassulo to Foreign Minister Antonesco, 6 September 1943 in *Actes Et Documents,* vol. 9, p. 474.
88. Ibid.
89. Nora Levin, *The Holocaust: The Destruction of European Jewry 1933–1945* (New York: Schocken Books, 1978), p. 586.
90. Alexandre Safran. *Resisting the Storm Romania, 1940-1947: Memoirs.* (Jerusalem: Yad Vashem, 1987), p. 106.
91. Cassulo to Foreign Minister Antonescu, 6 September, 1943 in *Actes Et Documents* IX, p. 475. This demarché on behalf of converted Jews was contained in a

separate letter, not the one of the same date in which he pleaded for Jewish children.

92. Lavi, "The Vatican's Endeavors," p. 417.
93. His serious reservations about Zionist solutions notwithstanding, Roncalli worked to aid persecuted Jews in several countries including Romania, Slovakia, Croatia, and Germany. Did Roncalli act on his own initiative or on instructions from the Vatican? Pinchas Lapide claims that in 1957 when he had an interview with the future John XXIII—he was still the Patriarch of Venice at the time—Cardinal Roncalli credited Pius XII not himself with saving thousands of Jews in Turkey and the Balkans. On those agonizing matters, Roncalli said "I referred to the Holy See and afterwards I simply carried out the Pope's orders: first and foremost to save human lives." Lapide, *The Last Three Popes And The Jews,* p. 181. Also see Leiber, "Pio XII e Gli Ebrei . . ." p. 455. Cynics wonder if Roncalli in 1957 was simply acting in a characteristically modest fashion. Published Vatican documents do not contain any such written instructions from Pacelli, but they might have been conveyed orally.
94. Morley, *Vatican Diplomacy,* p. 196.
95. Ibid., pp. 18–22. and Michael R. Marrus, "French Churches and the Persecution of Jews in France, 1940-1944" in *Judaism And Christianity Under The Impact of National Socialism* (Jerusalem: The Historical Society of Israel and the Zaliman Shazar Center for Jewish History, 1987) pp. 311–314.
96. Daniel Carpi, "The Rescue Of Jews In The Italian Zone Of Occupied Croatia," *Rescue Attempts During The Holocaust—Proceedings Of the Second Yad Vashem International Historical Conference—Jerusalem April 8-11, 1974* (Jerusalem: Yad Vashem, 1977), pp. 490–491, 521.
97. Secretary of State to the Slovakian Legation, 5 May 1943 in *Actes Et Documents . . .,* IX, p. 275.
98. Morley, *Vatican Diplomacy,* p. 77.
99. Rothkirchen, "Vatican Policy and the 'Jewish Problem' in 'Independent' Slovakia," p. 5.
100. Ibid., p. 44.
101. Burzio to Maglione, 7 March 1943 in *Actes Et Documents . . .,* IX, pp. 175–176.
102. Ibid., Maglione to Burzio, 9 March 1943, pp. 179–180.
103. Ibid., Secretary of State to the Slovakian Legation, 5 May 1943, p. 275.
104. Morley, *Vatican Diplomacy,* p. 101. Deportations were suspended in 1943 but not until the vast majority of Slovakian Jews had been deported. Some historians cite ecclesiastical intervention as the reason for the suspension. Others do not. When the Nazis took over Slovakia directly in 1944 almost all of the remaining Jews were sent to Auschwitz. See Morley, *Vatican Diplomacy . . .,* p. 96 and Yeshayahu Jelinek, "The Vatican, the Catholic Church, the Catholics, and the Persecution of the Jews during World War II: The Case of Slovakia," Bela Vago and George L. Mosse (eds.) *Jews and Non-Jews in Eastern Europe,* 1918–1945 (New York: John Wiley, 1974), p. 222.
105. Morley, *Vatican Diplomacy,* p. 101.
106. Ibid.

4

The Controversy Over Pope Pius XII and the Holocaust Part II

In his penetrating study of Jewish Rome under Nazi occupation, Michael Tagliacozzo states: "It has been said, rightly so, that few days among the bimillennial history of the Jews in Rome will ring as doleful as the 16th of October, 1943."[1] At approximately four o'clock on that October morning, troops under the command of *SS-Obersturmbannführer* Herbert Kappler, chief of the Gestapo in Rome, together with SS militia belonging to the *Ordnungspolizei* (uniformed police) and the *Sicherheitspolizei* (security police), surrounded Rome's ancient ghetto, blocking any possible exit from that area's maze of sinuous streets and alleys. Then, at 5:30, and with teutonic precision, these SS troops commenced their carefully planned[2] *Judenaktion*, a raid on the Jewish inhabitants that was to spare no one, not infants, the infirm, nor the aged.[13] Armed with lists containing the names and addresses of the ghetto's population, SS officers ordered their troops to gather at gunpoint all those caught at home.[4]

Scenes of unspeakable grief were enacted as hapless victims, many still in their nightclothes, were forced through the ghetto's main street to a gathering point in the open space at the base of the Theater of Marcellus. The raid continued until about one o'clock when convoy trucks were sent to transport the Jews to the first stop on their long voyage into exile. Giacomo Debenedetti, a Jewish writer in hiding in Rome and eyewitness to these events, has captured all the terror and pathos of 16 October 1943 in his homonymous novella. His description of the raid's denouement dramatizes the tragic premonition experienced by these victims of Nazi barbarism:

> All morning long the weather had remained dreary and wet. Around eleven there was a brief break when a bit of sun broke out on the steps of the *Portico d'Ottavia*. It was toward these steps that those poor feet had been dragging for hours: poor, flat feet already tired and aching before their journey had even begun. On Sabbaths—by now so long ago—that ray of sunshine used to pierce the Synagogue's stained glass and emblazon the organ's pipes that glittered in a luster of gold. That same ray of sunshine would then reflect off the faithful gathered in a harmony of jubilation, in a dazzle of sainted cheerfulness. The children would sing: "Holy, Holy, Holy, Lord God of Hosts, the Earth is full of Your Glory." Now, from the depths of the ditches where they were awaiting deportation, those same children emitted only sobs, sobs that know no chorus and rise not to heaven like the smoke of sacrifice. Having once again turned gloomy, the heavens out here seem to reject those cries . . . . How much time will yet have to pass before that weeping is transformed into the canticle of children in the gas ovens?[5]

SS convoys brought those Jews seized in the raid to the Italian Military College in Via della Lungara, down the Tiber a short distance and a stone's throw from the Vatican. Those slated for deportation[6] spent two brutal nights under guard in the Military College. On Monday, October 18, the prisoners were transported by convoy to the Roma-Tiburtino train depot and loaded onto eighteen livestock cars. Pressed into the cars like worthless cargo, Rome's captured Jews were forced to wait for six hours on dead track in the most inhuman conditions while the *Sicherheitspolizei* kept at bay any friend or relative who so much as dared approach the convoy. At five past two that afternoon, the convoy set off from Rome. On board were 1,007[7] prisoners, for the most part, women and children. On October 22, the convoy reached its final destination: Auschwitz. Of the 1,007 transported to Auschwitz, fifteen returned at war's end, fourteen men and one woman.

No sooner had the raid begun on October 16 than all Rome was abuzz with talk of the German atrocity. What surprised most Romans, apart from the display of barbarity, was the Germans' audacity in conducting such a *Judenaktion* in the papal city, under the very balcony of Pius XII. Jews, too, were stunned despite their awareness that "Pope Pius XII was hardly their staunch defender."[8] Indeed, many historians and witnesses attribute the complete lack of preparations by Rome's Jews to their belief that they enjoyed immunity because of the Pope's presence. Preparations might have saved no small number of them. Too many of Rome's Jews, both the poor residents of the ghetto and those more prosperous and assimilated living in other parts of the city, trusted in the Pope's presence and expected that some form of Vatican intervention would discourage any desire on the Germans' part to carry out in Rome what they had for some time been carrying out in other areas of occupied Europe. These Jews, rich and poor, were immobilized by their illusions.

Anxious for news, relatives and friends of those arrested on October 16 deluged the Vatican with entreaties. Requests for public intervention on behalf of the forlorn Jews were given short shrift, though Vatican authorities did make some discreet inquiries about the fate of Roman and other Jews who had been taken into custody by the Nazis. As was the case elsewhere in Nazi-occupied Europe, the Vatican expressed its greatest concern for baptized Jews who had been arrested despite their change of faith.[9]

It is still unclear just how effective Vatican efforts on behalf of unbaptized Jews really were. A secret communiqúe sent by the British Ambassador, Sir Francis d'Arcy Osborne, to the Foreign Office in late October 1943 reported that Ernst Weizsäcker, the German Ambassador, had secured the release of large numbers of Jews at the urging of the Cardinal Secretary of State. However, the vague wording of Osborne's message suggests that Italian Jews were not actually among those freed. He did state that those who had one Aryan parent were released.[10]

Rabbi Panzieri, an assistant to Zolli, wrote to the Pope on October 27 in the name of the Israelite community in Rome. While the language of the epistle was flowery, the tone was emotional, even desperate. Panzieri entreated the pontiff to intervene on behalf of the Roman Jews who had been rounded up eleven days earlier and then deported. Specifically, he wanted warm clothing for those transported from Rome: infants, children, pregnant women, the elderly. The deported had been pulled from their beds with scent clothing, and winter was fast approaching.[11] Unlike those at the Vatican, Panzieri did not realize the much graver danger posed by deportation to Auschwitz.

Other representatives of Rome's Jewish community had likewise planned to petition Pius XII directly. Edited by Dante Almansi and

Settimio Sorani, head of *Delasem*, a Jewish organization helping refugees, an appeal requesting information on the deported and pleading for the liberation of at least the women, children, elderly, and infirm had been drafted by community leaders. The appeal was supposed to be delivered by hand to the Pope's entourage within the Vatican by Sorani and Dr. Cyril Kotnik, a member of the Yugoslavian legation to the Holy See. Sorani was arrested by agents of the Gestapo, however, the moment he stepped into the apartment of the Yugoslav diplomat. Just hours before, those agents had carted off Kotnik's entire family. The appeal never arrived at its destination.[12]

Jesuit Father Pietro Tacchi Venturi, who frequently acted as a middleman between the Holy See and the Italian government on Jewish issues, also beseeched the Pope for help. Roman Jews and Catholics had been barbarously shipped like "butcher's beasts,"[13] and Venturi wanted the Holy Father to find out what had happened to them. He saw the Pope as the vindicator of those whose rights had been trampled.

Apparently, the deported Jews themselves also thought that the Pope was their best hope. According to the Bishop of Padova, Carlo Agostini, when the deportees passed through his city, they pleaded that Pius XII be informed of their dolorous condition in order that he could come to their aid. So tenacious was this belief in the possibility of papal intervention that Roman Jews, say witnesses, clung fast to their hopes right up to the moment of their extermination at Auschwitz.[14]

The Pope's presence alone did not suffice to halt the Nazi juggernaut, nor did any meaningful intervention on the part of Pius XII and the Vatican hierarchy come to the aid of Rome's Jews before, during, or after the raid. From the very beginning of the Nazi occupation of Rome, Pius XII had settled on a general policy of silence. True, that silence was punctuated, but only intermittently and with certain pronouncements of vague disapproval whose cryptic "Vaticanese" ensured an ambiguity that posed no threat to Nazi programs or policies. Apologists for this line of inaction defend the Pope's behavior, claiming that any forceful move on the Vatican's part would have caused a rupture with the Reich that could only have made matters worse for the Roman population in general, and for Rome's Jewry in particular. Indeed, so goes the argument, such a rupture might have endangered the Church and the Pope's very person—abduction of Pius XII was one danger—thus eliminating a potential source for the subtle persuasion the papacy might have managed to exert on the most ardent advocates of Nazi racial policies.

Such is the thrust of the apologia offered by the Jesuit Father R. Leiber, confidant to Pius XII, in his 1961 article in *La Civiltà Cattolica.*[15] Father Leiber went on to tell *Look* magazine in 1966 that, at the time of the Nazi raid in Rome, Pacelli had done everything he could; indeed, the Pope had even exhausted his personal fortune on behalf of the Jews, he claimed. In the same article, Leiber states that Dr. Raffaele Cantoni, a Jewish leader, supposedly once informed the Jesuit that Roman Jews wanted not papal pronouncements but practical assistance. Leiber quotes Cantoni as having said: "This he [Pius XII] gave us as much as he was able to."[16] The Jews were allegedly happy that the pontiff did not make a public statement on their situation since Nazi reaction would have been unpredictable.

But an opposing line of argument can likewise be made, for papal interdiction of Nazi genocide might have caused some form of dissension within German, and especially Roman Catholic German, ranks (a dissension already present, albeit slight, submerged, and unorganized). Furthermore, Vatican condemnation of Nazi genocidal policies might have intensified the already deep-seated hostility of the occupied peoples, the Italians in particular, and could have served to increase the ranks of those who had passed from passive resistance to open rebellion.[17] At the very least, papal interventions might have abated the full brunt of Nazi butchery, saving some lives in the process. Admittedly, conjecture of this kind always remains tenuous, but such conjecture is necessary when responding to a justification that many would consider without foundation. The defense of Pius XII on the grounds that his quiet response to the deportation of Rome's Jews was the consequence of Vatican *Realpolitik* still leaves too many moral concerns as regards an institution that claims divine inspiration and whose leader is considered a moral as well as a political guide. Holding Pius and the Vatican hierarchy accountable for their professed moral guardianship, one can only judge their combined silence before, during, and after the Nazi raid and deportations in Rome as basically accommodating, even immoral. It must be kept in mind that Pius XII had not spared words, nor had he couched his denunciations in ambiguous phraseology, when attacking what he considered evils perpetrated by the Soviets or the Spanish Republicans. Are we to consider the extermination of innocent Jews residing within earshot of the papal apartments a less heinous crime than others, and by what moral measure? As to the argument that a forthright stand by the Pope in Italy or elsewhere would have placed his Church and his flock in greater jeopardy, Irving Greenberg has asked, "If true faith means taking up the cross for God, then when will there ever be a truer time to be crucified, if necessary? Even if the attempt to help is doomed to failure, when will it ever be more appropriate to risk one's life or the church's life than to stop the crucifixion of children?"[18]

Less risky to the Vatican than a public criticism of Nazi policy would have been a discreet warning whispered to key members of the Jewish community. Susan Zuccotti believes that such a tip could have saved the lives of hundreds.[19]

The Vatican was well aware of plans for the raid in advance of October 16th through the German Ambassador to the Holy See. Weizsäcker[20] had learned of the raid through the actions of the German Consul, Eitel Friedrich Mollhausen,[21] who had inadvertently got his hands on secret messages from the *Reichsführer*, Heinrich Himmler, to Kappler in Rome. Those messages made reference to previous secret communications from Himmler that called for the application of the "Final Solution" through the mass deportation of Italy's Jews. Responding to these top-secret dispatches sent to Kappler from Himmler's headquarters in Rastenburg, Mollhausen, because of personal disagreement with Nazi genocidal policies he considered not only inhuman but politically inappropriate,[22] rushed a telegram on October 6 to the *Wilhelmstrasse* offering an alternative to the deportation scheme.[23] About twenty hours later, Mollhausen sent a second urgent dispatch to Berlin that read:

> Field Marshal Kesselring has asked Obersturmbannfuhrer Kappler to postpone planned *Judenaktion* for the present time. If however it is necessary that something be done, he would prefer to utilize the able-bodied Roman Jews in fortification work near here.[24]

Mollhausen was unsuccessful in thwarting the Nazi Command's plans for a raid and deportations. By his actions, however, he brought to the attention of German diplomatic and military circles in Rome the designs of the High Command, designs which then became known with the upper echelons of the Vatican. Katz has written that

> The Vatican too was informed by Weizsäcker of Mollhausen's intervention; it was good news of course, but from that moment on the highest authorities of the Church, including Pope Pius XII, knew beyond any doubt that the Germans were planning to deport the Jews of Rome.[25]

For years there have been persistent allegations that the Holy Father told the German ambassador that if the Roman Jews had to be transported, the deed should be done without delay. The source of these rumors was an unidentified German officer who had gone to the Via Flaminia on October 16 to arrest a family of Jews residing there. Although the veracity of the officer was challenged, the Vatican was concerned because apparently there were witnesses to the incident.[26]

Only when the October 16th raid and deportations already constituted a fait accompli did the Vatican break its long silence through an editorial that appeared in the *Osservatore Romano* in its Monday-Tuesday edition of October 25–26, 1943. In that editorial, the Vatican expressed its discomfort with the German actions, though no direct reference was made either to the raid or to the deportations. In language both veiled and, to the uninitiated, hopelessly abstract, the Holy Father was hailed for his indefatigable efforts in alleviating the pains of an afflicted world.

> Persistent and pitiful echoes of calamities, which as a result of the present conflict do not cease to accumulate, continue more than ever to reach the Holy Father.
>
> The August Pontiff, as is well known, after having tried in vain to prevent the outbreak of the war by striving to dissuade the Rulers of the nations from taking recourse in force of arms, which today are so fearsome, has not desisted for one moment in employing all the means in his power to alleviate the suffering, which, whatever form it may take, is the consequence of this cruel conflagration.
>
> With the augment of so much evil, the universal and paternal charity of the Pontiff has become, it could be said, ever more active; it knows neither boundaries nor nationality, neither religion nor race.
>
> This manifold and ceaseless activity on the part of Pius XII has intensified even more in recent time in regard for the increased suffering of so many unfortunate people.
>
> Such blessed activity, above all with the prayers of the faithful of the whole world, who unanimously and with ardent fervor never cease to look to Heaven, can

> achieve even greater results in the future and hasten the day on which the shining glow of peace will return to the earth; and men, laying down their arms, will put aside all their differences and bitterness, and becoming brothers once more, will finally labor, in all good faith, for the common weal.[27]

Unfortunately for those who already lay dead at Auschwitz, this news of papal solicitude fell on deaf ears.

These, the only words to issue from the Vatican in the wake of the deportations, did succeed in ultimately bringing solace to at least one segment of the paper's readership: the German Command. Weizsäcker immediately translated the *Osservatore Romano* piece and sent it off to Berlin. Katz informs us that certain inaccuracies in the Weizsäcker translation were most likely due to the haste with which it was prepared. Nevertheless, the substance of the Vatican's pronouncement was clearly understood by officials in Berlin. In a letter that accompanied the translation, Weizäcker wrote:

> The Pope, although under pressure from all sides, has not permitted himself to be pushed into a demonstrative censure of the deportation of the Jews of Rome. Although he must know that such an attitude will be used against him by our adversaries and will be exploited by Protestant circles in the Anglo-Saxon countries for the purpose of anti-Catholic propaganda, he has nonetheless done everything possible even in this delicate matter in order not to strain relations with the German government and the German authorities in Rome. As there apparently will be no further German action taken on the Jewish question here, it may be said that this matter, so unpleasant as it regards German-Vatican relations, has been liquidated.
>
> In any event, there is one definite sign of this from the Vatican. *L'Osservatore Romano*, of October 25–26, gives prominence to a semi-official communique on the loving-kindness of the Pope, which is written in the typical roundabout and muddled style of this Vatican newspaper, declaring that the Pope bestows his fatherly care on all people without regard to nationality, religion and race. The manifold and growing activities of Pius XII have in recent times further increased because of the greater sufferings of so many unfortunate people.
>
> No objections need be raised against this statement, insofar as its text, a translation of which is enclosed, will be understood by only a very few as alluding in any particular way to the Jewish question.[28]

Revealing is the fact that, after the translation's arrival in Berlin, someone took care to underline the following key words and phrases: <u>Pope . . . not . . . pushed into demonstrative censure of the deportation of the Jews of Rome . . . done everything possible even in this delicate matter . . . it may be said that this matter, so unpleasant as it</u>

regards German-Vatican relations, has been liquidated. Coupled with the silence on the part of Pius XII after the *Osservatore Romano*'s abstruse public pronouncement, the underlining that took place in Berlin speaks volumes to the effect that Vatican reticence had in regard to what had already occurred in Rome and elsewhere, as well to what was yet to occur in occupied territories until the end of the war. If Pius XII had refused to speak directly and with the full force of his persuasive powers in an attempt to save the Jews of Rome, what hope for eventual papal intervention had the Jews of lands far removed from St. Peter's Square? Father Morley has written of the Vatican's efforts to aid Rome's thousand-plus deported Jews of whom only about fifteen survived the war, ''the steps taken were so slight as to be out of all proportion to the crime committed.'' Morley's assessment of the Vatican record on this deportation is that it was ''so minimal as to be disappointing and, possibly shameful.''[29]

Those who believe that Pius XII had been unjustly treated argue that his deeds on behalf of Jews in need of asylum far outweigh his words in importance. They frequently cite the fact that thousands of Jewish lives were spared because refugees were given sanctuary by church officials.

Joseph L. Lichten, who led the Anti-Defamation League office in Rome from 1971 to 1986, is one such Jew who came to the defense of Pius XII. Writing on the period of the Nazi occupation shortly after the Pope's death in 1958, Lichten said:

> Thousands of Jewish refugees poured into Vatican City; thousands of others sought shelter in the basilicas and other buildings of the Holy See outside the Vatican wall. No less than 15,000 were sheltered at Castel Gandolfo. The Pope sent by hand a letter to the bishops instructing them to lift the enclosure from convents and monasteries so that they could become refuges for the Jews. More than 180 places of refuge were made available in Rome and secret asylum given to more than 7000 fugitive Jews.[30]

Several books report this number of fifteen thousand allegedly harbored at Castel Gandolfo, the Pope's summer residence fifteen miles southeast of Rome.[31] The claim has never been substantiated.

In a confidential conversation with a member of Myron Taylor's staff, in early 1945, Monsignor Tardini estimated that during the months when the swastika flew over the ''Eternal City'', six thousand

Jews were given protective hospitality by Catholic clergy. They were given sanctuary in religious institutions including the Gregorian and Lateran Universities.[32]

Italian historian Renzo DeFelice has published a detailed list of the religious houses in Rome which afforded the Jews security. Fifty-five were male houses and one hundred female. Using data supplied by the houses involved and compiled by Father Robert Leiber, DeFelice concluded that 4447 persons were hidden, but he pointed out that some names appear more than once because certain individuals in their frantic quest for greater safety relocated from one building to another.[33]

Father Leiber wrote in 1961 that the Pope had made known his feeling that the religious houses could and should give refuge to the Jews.[34] Meir Michaelis agrees. He has written that, "Pius XII personally ordered the clergy to open these sanctuaries to all non-Aryans in need of refuge." Pinchas Lapide, a Jewish writer on papal matters who has extolled Pius XII for his altruism during the Holocaust, has stated that the Pope clandestinely instructed clerics "to save human lives by all means."[35] How these instructions were transmitted remains nebulous.

It is true, of course, that many Jews were able to find sanctuary in religious houses both within Vatican City and in greater Rome where some Vatican-owned structures could not be touched because of their extraterritorial status. It is also true that rules were suspended that would ordinarily have kept the doors of convents and monasteries closed to lay people and to those of the wrong gender. There is no hard evidence that this was done at the behest of Pius XII, but he must have been well aware of the situation.

Clerical rescuers were by no means unusual in Italy where there had historically been no deep-seated, institutionalized anti-Semitism and where Jews were a tiny, highly assimilated minority. One heroic Italian priest saved several members of a Jewish family by hiding them in his own house. He even calculated the time of the Passover festival and made it possible for his guests to celebrate the traditional seder.[36] There is no reason to believe that the priest acted at the direct or indirect urging of the pontiff. It is more likely that he and other caring padres acted as Italian patriots and as humanitarians.

In Assisi, the home of the venerable St. Francis, several priests, including Salvatore Rufino Niccacci, risked their lives to provide safe hiding places in religious edifices for at least three hundred Jews. Still more remarkable is the fact that the beneficiaries were not neighbors but strangers, for there was no prewar Jewish population in Assisi. Fraudulent documents were put at the disposal of refugees, some of whom were successfully smuggled to Allied-controlled territory by a dedicated band of nuns and priests.

Although Bishop Giuseppe Placido Nicolini, a Benedictine monk, richly deserves the credit he has received for his role in Assisi's life-saving network of guardian angels, the Pope himself was found wanting by Father Niccacci. He could not understand why Christ's vicar on earth remained silent when the Nazis transformed the cross into a swastika. "Isn't his role as the spiritual leader of the Church more important than his role of politician or head of state?" asked the peasant turned priest. Father Niccacci was clearly chagrined because the pontiff had left it to his subordinates to succor the persecuted. He could have done more. Father Niccacci inquired rhetorically of the Almighty why he had not furnished his followers in the hour of their greatest need with a "leader who would have stood up to the devil who twisted your Cross."[37]

Sharply conflicting testimony was offered by another priest, Don Aldo Brunacci, who worked with Bishop Nicolini in Assisi. In the 1980s Father Brunacci wrote that in September 1943 the bishop had shown him a letter from the Vatican Secretary of State and had declared that it was the pope's wish that they organize aid to the persecuted, especially to the Jews. Prudence and secrecy were urged. Not even priests were to be informed. Father Brunacci did not make clear if he had read the letter himself. His use of the ambiguous phrase "mostrandomi una lettera" can be interpreted to mean that the bishop had summarized the contents for him.[38] Although he quotes some of the bishop's words verbatim, Father Brunacci admits that he is drawing on memory in the absence of notes. No such letter from Rome was ever found in the bishop's correspondence, Father Brunacci reported in 1975 to another forum.[39]

Of all clergy who earned places for themselves among the so-called "righteous Gentiles" when the Nazis were making Europe into an abbatoir, none is more highly esteemed than Father Maria Benedetto (Father Marie-Benoit). Father Benedetto, a French Capuchin, had scholarly credentials as a specialist in Judaica and had taught Hebrew at a Marseilles seminary prior to the war. During the war, under the collaborationist Vichy regime, he labored without respite to provide sanctuary in his monastery for Jews and others who were hunted like animals by the predatory Nazis.[40]

When the Nazis took over Rome in September 1943, Father Benedetto and his deputies buoyed the flagging spirits of Jews, found lodgings for them, obtained false papers and provided food as well as financial support. His operation, one fraught with peril for all involved, was exceedingly expensive. According to historian Susan Zuccotti, none of the desperately needed funds came from the Pope's coffers.[41] Nor is there any documentation to show that Benedetto's philanthropic endeavors in Rome were initiated or even encouraged by the Vatican.

Caution was Pius' watchword even when the victims of Nazi persecution were non-Jews. Ample evidence of this was provided by the Via Rasella-Fosse Ardeatine episode. Via Rasella is a short, narrow, cobblestoned street which slopes downhill from the Barberini Palace on Rome's Quattro Fontane. It was there on the afternoon of 23 March 1944 that an S.S. column was ambushed by Italian partisans who then eluded capture. Thirty-three S.S. lost their lives in the surprise attack.

The Nazi hierarchy responded with furious alacrity. On orders from Hitler himself, Herbert Kappler saw to it that several hundred hostages were rounded up and transported to the Ardeatine caves located on the fringes of the city near the Appian Way's Christian catacombs. Three hundred and thirty-five Italians, ten for every S.S. fatality, were methodically, cold-bloodedly executed. The victims, all of whom were dispatched with a bullet to the neck, came from sundry walks of life. They ranged in age from fifteen to sixty-nine. The vast majority were Catholics, at least nominally. In fact, less than a quarter were Jews. Many of the Catholic martyrs of the bloody Nazi reprisal had been active in the Resistance. Most of the Jews were killed simply because they were Jews and a quota had to be filled. Regardless of religion, none had been implicated in the Via Rasella incident.

In the hope of preserving the secret of their crime, the S.S. sealed the cave opening. But literally within days, the Nazis'.dirty work was discovered. After the German interlude ended in June, 1944, some of those responsible for the massacre, including Kappler, were tried and convicted. Today an awe-inspiring monument to the Fosse Ardeatine martyrs stands at the site of the killings.

Where was the pope when this catastrophe was unfolding? Pro and anti-papal writers have noted that the pontiff had been outraged by the Via Rasella bloodshed. He considered the perpetrators Communists and fanatics whose irresponsible violence had jeapardized the negotiations to make Rome an open city.[42] As far back as October 1943 the pontiff had told Harold Tittman of his anxiety over the possibility that Communist bands active in Rome's environs would take violent action before the Nazi evacuation.[43]

What of the Nazi retribution? The most comprehensive treatment of the Ardeatine carnage is Robert Katz's masterful *Death in Rome*, first published in 1967. Without any doubt, the most explosive of Katz's allegations was that the pope had advance knowledge of the Nazis' intention to exact revenge by murdering innocent Italians and he opted not to act. "A miracle was not necessary to save the 335 men doomed to die in the Ardeatine caves," Katz wrote. "There was one man who could have, should have and must be held to account for not having acted to at least delay the German slaughter. He is Pope Pius XII."[44]

Perhaps inadvertently, in 1980 the Vatican published a document that showed that the papacy had prior knowledge of the Ardeatine massacre. The document which consisted of notes of the Secretary of State briefly summarized the surprise attack on Via Rasella. Based on information provided by the government of Rome, the notes foresaw that the Nazis would execute ten Italians for every German who had been killed. The document was dated 24 March 1944, the day after the ambush. It is significant that the document was also stamped with the time it was received—10:15 a.m., some hours before the reprisals commenced and many hours before they were finished.[45]

Father Robert Graham has conceded that there is no documentary evidence that shows that the Pope intervened to avert the impending massacre of March 24. Nevertheless, he surmises that Pius did send Papal emissaries, but, of course, to no avail.[46]

Katz, an American writer-historian and a longtime resident of Rome, was hauled into criminal court on a charge filed by Contessa Elena Rossignani, Pius XII's niece. Katz, along with Carlo Ponti, the well-known film producer and George Pan Cosmatos, a film director, were accused of criminal libel, this, years after Pacelli had gone to his reward. All had collaborated on the movie "Massacre in Rome" featuring Richard Burton which was adapted from Katz's book. In the fall of 1975 the three defendants were found guilty of defaming the late pontiff. Although Ponti and Cosmatos were sentenced to six months imprisonment and Katz was given fourteen months, the sentences were suspended.[47]

Not content to debate the historical role of Pius XII in the court of public opinion, some papal protectors had resorted to the Italian criminal justice system. For such people who view the occupant of the Chair of St. Peter as Christ's vicar on earth, there is a virtual taboo about chiding Pius XII for what he did or did not do during World War II. His manner and mien are not fit subjects for debate.

The mystique which envelopes the papacy confers security on those who believe that popes, without exception, speak with moral certainty. If Pius was culpable as Katz and others charge, that security is undermined and along with it the conviction that the supreme pontiff is a virtually infallible rudder on moral matters. To err as grievously as Pius XII did is not divine, but human. In shielding the reputation of Pius XII, his defenders are shielding the "godly" institution which he led. Well understood is the danger that Pius XII's record of moral lapses is more likely to tarnish than burnish the papacy's image. As Father Robert Graham once succinctly put it, " . . . while his detractors can no longer injure him, their slanders and insinuations continue to plague the Church, for when a pope is defamed, the Church suffers."[48]

By May 1945, hostilities in Europe had ceased. Germany had surrendered unconditionally. Adolph Hitler, "a maniac of ferocious genius, the repository and expression of the most virulent hatreds that have ever corroded the human race," to use Churchill's apt description, was dead by his own hand. The crematoria went cold and the stench of slaughter evaporated, but not before roughly six million Jews, including well over a million children, had perished.

One more chapter in the complex saga of the Vatican and the Holocaust was still to be written. Nazi criminals desperately sought to evade Allied justice by fleeing Europe. Many followed the so-called "monastery escape route" to safety. Exactly what part the Vatican played in establishing and maintaining, in financing, or at least in condoning that conduit to freedom for Nazis has yet to be resolved to everyone's satisfaction.

According to a top secret 1947 United States State Department memo, fugitive Nazis were assisted in Italy by the Vatican which exerted pressure on various Latin American countries where Catholic influence was substantial to admit immigrants.[49] Argentina, Mexico and Cuba were three such countries. As a result of Vatican urging, those countries gave preferential treatment in their admissions policies to anti-Communists, even if they had Fascist or Nazi backgrounds. With succor provided by sympathetic German agents in Barcelona, Nazis, including hunted war criminals, made their way to havens in Latin America.

In the opinion of American foreign service officer, Vincent La Vista, who wrote the memo, the Vatican's objective in this immoral traffic was to propagate the faith. To that end, a helping hand was extended to any Catholic refugee, regardless of nationality, regardless of previous conduct. Supposedly, the Vatican was eager to funnel into both Latin American and some European nations, persons who were known to be supportive of the Church and opposed to Communism.[50] La Vista referred to the existence of a German group at the Vatican that facilitated the emigration of their countrymen to Latin America with valid passports obtained from the International Red Cross.

In 1984, shortly after the LaVista memo was made public, it was described as artificial, false, and inaccurate by Father Robert Graham and Father Pierre Blet, two Jesuit historians who were among the editors of the multivolume collection of Holy See documents relating to the Second World War. Father Graham, an American priest, denounced the charges of Vatican complicity contained in the memo as "propagandistic maneuvers" by individuals who "never lose the occasion to crucify" the Catholic Church.[51] A third cleric, the German-born Reverend Antonio Weber of the St. Rafael Society in Rome which furnished aid to refugees, denied that the Vatican ever hid or helped Nazis following the war, although a small number of German diplomats were temporarily sheltered before returning to their native land.[52]

To Monsignor John M. Oesterreicher, the founder of the Institute of Judeo-Christian Studies at Seton Hall University in New Jersey, and a victim of Nazi persecution himself, the accusations levelled against the Vatican by La Vista and others were "not true nor made in good faith."[53] He characterized the evidence cited as "hearsay" which would be inadmissible in an American court. Oesterreicher further suggested that the Vatican and the Pope had replaced the Jews as whipping boys. If Catholic clerics aided fugitive Nazi war criminals, Oesterreicher wrote, it was because they were "truly convinced, or deceived into believing, that the wrongdoer had turned from his godless way."[54] It strains credulity to believe that Nazi mass murderers had become remorseful overnight. Moreover, even if absolution had been granted by clergy, justice would still require that malefactors be held legally accountable for their horrendous crimes. Clerics assisting cold-blooded war criminals to escape were not performing acts of compassion. They were accessories after the fact.

Of course, La Vista was not alone in indicting the Holy See for assisting runaway Nazis. In his biographical portrait of Pius XII, Constantine Prince of Bavaria explained that he was informed that the hiding places in monasteries, emptied of Jews and anti-Fascists, were quickly filled with new occupants.

> The fugitives had been released, but it was their former pursuers who now sought safety in ecclesiastical territory. In the Seminario Lombardo, for instance, the Communist Giovanni Roveda was succeeded by a Gauleiter and a Government Administrative official. In San Paolo there are still Fascists of high rank awaiting an amnesty . . . one *may* hazard a guess that the mysterious corpse recently interred in another Monastery was the Gauleiter of Tyrol who had been sought in vain.[55]

Several historians have joined in the chorus of condemnation. Christopher Simpson, in his recently published penetrating study of America's recruitment of Nazis in the postwar period, has written that the most important network spiriting Nazis to the West "operated in and through the Vatican in Rome."[56] In its zeal to protect Catholic anti-Marxists, the Papacy, which had battled godless Communists for decades, conveniently overlooked the sordid pasts of those who were guilty of heinous murders of innocent men, women, and children.

Simpson held Pius XII personally accountable for making Church channels available to an entire Ukrainian Waffen SS division of eleven thousand men. Bent on exploiting Ukrainian manpower and Ukrainian anti-Communist sentiment, the Nazis in 1943 organized the "SS Volunteer Division Galicia." Most of its members were not war criminals, but this unit supposedly included some individuals who had worked in Nazi death factories such as Treblinka and Sobibor and had participated in anti-Jewish and anti-communist excesses. They surrendered to the British in 1945 and were interned in Italy. Through the intervention of the Ukrainian Catholic Archbishop Ivan Buchko, a Ukrainian specialist in the Roman hierarchy, Pacelli arranged for their safe passage out of reach of the Soviets. As told by Pavlo Shandruk, a Lieutenant General in the Ukrainian National Army, it was only because of the Holy Father's involvement that his men were not extradited to Stalinist Russia.[57] Instead, they were settled in Britain and various other places in the non-Communist world. In 1950 perhaps two thousand settled in Canada, especially in Toronto.

More than three decades later charges of war crimes were still being levelled against some of the Ukrainians by Canadian Jews. At long last in 1985 a commission headed by Jules Deschenes, a former chief justice in Quebec, held hearings on the criminality of members of the Galicia division. To the joy of the Ukrainian community and the consternation of at least some Jews, the commission's final report exonerated the Ukrainian veterans.[58]

In other instances the criminality of Nazi fugitives and the complicity of certain Vatican elements are beyond dispute. Among individual Nazi escapees abetted in their flight from justice was Franz Stangl whose claim to infamy was that he had been camp commandant first at Sobibor and later at the Nazi killing center at Treblinka where almost a million Jews from ten different countries were put to death for the crime of being Jewish. Having escaped from Linz prison in the spring of 1948, the Austrian-born Stangl made his way to Rome. He had heard about a German bishop there who aided "Catholic SS officers." The bishop in question was Alois Hudal, a fellow Austrian who served as father confessor to Germans living in the Italian capital. The prelate knew Stangl's name and stated that he was awaiting his arrival.[59] Interviewed in a Düsseldorf prison in 1971 after he had been extradited from Brazil, convicted by a West German court and sentenced to life imprisonment, Stangl informed historian Gitta Sereny that Hudal had provided funds, a Red Cross passport, passage on a ship and a Syrian entry visa.[60] He had also arranged employment in Damascus. A few years later Stangl and his family left the Middle East for Brazil where he was eventually discovered.

His patron, Bishop Hudal, an ardent pan-Germanist, an admirer of the Führer and an obsessive anti-Communist, was the central personality in the postwar Nazi escape route. It is for good reason that he has been dubbed the "Nazi Scarlet Pimpernel" after the fictional English nobleman who rescued French aristocrats during the French Revolution's Reign of Terror.

Hudal held doctorates in philosophy and theology, fields in which he published widely. His 1937 volume on the foundation of National Socialism was purportedly a dispassionate account of the Nazi movement. While Hudal eschewed crude anti-Semitism, the book is at best an uncritical investigation and at worst a thinly veiled rationalization of Nazism and racism. The author's convoluted prose is imbued with and appeals to a whole conceptual system revolving around the *Volk* and the German national soul.[61]

Hudal had been a friend of Pacelli's since the latter's days as nuncio in Germany. It was Pius XII who pressed his candidacy for the rectorate of Santa Maria dell' Anima in Rome and who consecrated him a bishop.[62]

Funds for the escape of war criminals may not have always come from the Vatican's coffers. American Catholics may have unwittingly financed the ocean passage and visa fees for Nazis on the run. Such was the claim made in an article that appeared in the German press in 1984. The key player was allegedly the War Relief Services, a creature of the National Catholic Welfare Conference. From October 1944 on, its Rome office was headed by an American priest, Andrew P. Landi, who distributed funds to refugee committees representing various nationalities. Money may have gone to Bishop Hudal.[63]

Looking back to those turbulent times, Monsignor Landi denies consciously assisting war criminals. He presumed that all of those individuals who sought help from his agency were bona fide refugees. He did not try to screen emigrants but left that task to the refugee nationality committees each of which was led by a priest. Landi has no recollection of working with or knowing Hudal.[64]

A major conductor in the Vatican underground railroad was Father Krunoslav Dragonovic, a Croatian priest who belonged to the Franciscan order. Dragonovic, a longtime Fascist, had strongly supported the pro-Nazi self-proclaimed "pure Catholic" puppet state of Croatia headed by Ante Pavelic which was responsible for the bestial murder of countless Orthodox Serbs and several thousand Gypsies and Jews. After the Third Reich collapsed, Dragonovic directed a seminary in Rome. He was also the chief representative of the Croats on the council of Intermarium, a lay Catholic group which played a crucial role in the "monastery escape route." Father Dragonovic used his connections with Latin American diplomats, the Red Cross, the National Catholic Welfare Organization and the C.I.C. (the United States Army Counterintelligence Corps) to evacuate many Nazi war criminals. Among them was the notorious Klaus Barbie, the "butcher of Lyon," who, in 1951, was dispatched via Genoa to asylum in Bolivia under the pseudonym, Altmann.[65] Barbie's visa issued at the Bolivian consulate in Geneva bears the signature of Father Dragonovic who vouched for him.[66]

Another Nazi beneficiary of the Vatican's policy of "hear no evil, see no evil, speak no evil," but rather harbor evil, was Walter Rauff. It was Rauff, an S. S. Colonel, who developed the mobile gas vans as an early instrument of genocide. Rauff worked closely with the Catholic hierarchy in northern Italy during World War II. He dealt with Cardinal Ildefonso Schuster, for example. Schuster, Roman-born but of Swiss descent, had been the archbishop of Milan since 1929 and was known to be an anti-Bolshevik zealot. Rauff was also in cordial contact with Monsignor Don Giuseppe Bicchierai, Cardinal Schuster's secretary, as well as with Bishop Hudal.

After the defeat of the Nazis, Rauff fled to Naples from a detention camp in Rimini. A Catholic priest in Naples enabled Rauff to make his way to Rome. La Vista said that the Rimini escapees were assisted in Rome by a Padre Bayer who concerned himself with the "German refugee action of the Vatican." According to a sworn statement made by Rauff to the Chilean Supreme Court in 1962, he was sheltered in Rome for about eighteen months "always in convents of the Holy See." Reunited with his family thanks to the largesse of the Church, Rauff went to Syria and ultimately to South America.[67]

In defense of the Papacy, Father Blet has pointed out that in the aftermath of the collapse of the Third Reich "there were people of every type harbored in convents, under false identities." He has implied that the Church authorities could not distinguish and had no obligation to distinguish between, on the one hand, bona fide refugees, that is, innocent victims who were dislocated by the war and, on the other hand, wanted Nazi war criminals. As to the Walter Rauff case, Jesuit Father Blet observed that there were no convents in Vatican City, a point which critics would find jesuitical. On this, Benno Weiser Varon has written that Rauff did not say that "he hid for 18 months in convents and monasteries in Vatican City." In all probability he said ". . . in convents and monasteries of the Vatican."[68] Varon was correct. In his 1962 statement made in Santiago, Chile, Rauff spoke of staying for more or less a year and a half "siempre in Conventos *de* las Santa Sede. [emphasis ours]."[69] Rauff mistakenly believed that his ecclesiastical places of protection were in Vatican City proper. It is likely that Rauff associated all convents in and around Rome with the Catholic Church and used the term "of the Holy See" to describe such entities.

Serge Klarsfeld, an internationally acclaimed Nazi-hunter whose father was gassed at Auschwitz, believes that Rauff meant to say that he was harbored in the facilities of the Vatican, but doubts that Pius XII was aware of the sanctuary granted Rauff. However, Klarsfeld also doubts that the pontiff strongly opposed such a practice.[70]

Just how much did the Pope know? The Vatican's argument that the Holy Father was oblivious to the so-called "ratline" smuggling Nazi killers to safety in the Middle East and Latin America, that it was the work of a few misguided rogue clergymen, has a hollow ring. If it is contended that the courageous rescue efforts of clergy who sheltered Jews from Nazi persecution in churches, priories, and other Church edifices, could not possibly have been carried out without the pontiff's knowledge and encouragement, tacit or explicit, then the same may be said about rescue activities that benefitted Nazis guilty of unspeakable crimes. The Vatican cannot have it both ways.

* * *

Pope Pius XII breathed his last on 11 October 1958. An era had ended. For many of the faithful, the papacy without Pacelli was almost unimaginable. Just three years after his death, his canonization was confidently predicted in a book on the Vatican written by a Protestant.[71] Countless Catholics who saw him as a person of heroic virtue shared that expectation. Unless a nominee for canonization was martyred, he or she must have lived a life of heroic virtue. According to those who have promoted the cause of Pius XII "hundreds of thousands" of believers have petitioned the Holy See to begin the process that could lead to sainthood for Pacelli. When Pope Paul VI told the Second Vatican Council that the cause of beatification and canonization would be initiated, the announcement drew sustained applause. Separate processes have already been held in a variety of places including Warsaw, Munich, Lisbon, Montevideo and, of course, his birthplace, Rome. Witnesses have been heard and relevant evidence amassed. In due course, a *Positio* or printed volume containing pertinent supporting material will be examined by theologians and, after that, by bishops and cardinals.[71]

Of course, canonization is often lengthy, complex, and tortuous. One miracle attributable to the intercession of the candidate for a halo is ordinarily a prerequisite for canonization in the era of John Paul II. It is considered proof that the Almighty approves of the individual and the life lived by the future saint. For Pacelli this should be no impediment. Miracles ascribable to him have previously been documented to the satisfaction of many in the Church.

Before a servant of God is deemed worthy of being inscribed in the book of saints, it must also be shown that he lived an exemplary life as a Christian. Despite his piety, his devotion to the Madonna and his missionary zeal, Christopher Columbus has never been canonized because he fathered a son out of wedlock and had an illicit affair after his wife's death. His genius, notwithstanding, Dante Alighieri has never made the grade either, perhaps because he consigned some popes to hell in his masterpiece, *The Divine Comedy*, perhaps because of his self-confessed sexual appetite.[73] In sharp contrast, the ascetic Pacelli's private morality appears to have been above reproach and it is inconceivable that further investigation will reveal any sexual peccadilloes on his part. But, in light of the obloquy heaped on Pius XII because of his conduct during the Holocaust, his case will surely be exceptionally intricate and delicate.[74] Officials whose task it is to investigate the candidate's qualifications may well ask if from 1939 to 1945 Pius XII was heroic or virtuous. At the very least, would-be saints can be expected to have been guided by principles rather than pragmatism. On that score Pius XII failed to pass muster. It may be some time before the Catholic church, which he ruled so autocratically, declares that he is indeed seated next to God. On the basis of the historical record it appears that Pius XII hardly merited the honor ex-rabbi Zolli paid him when he adopted the name Eugenio.

Notes

1. Michael Tagliacozzo, ''La Comunità' di Roma sotto l'incubo della svastica, La grande razzia del 16 ottobre 1943,'' in *Gli ebrei italiani durante il fascismo: Quadereni del Centro di Documentazione Ebraica Contemporanea*. 3, Milano, novembre 1963, p. 21.
2. That the plan to deport Rome's Jews had been in the making since the early days of the Nazis' occupation of the city is substantiated in a series of top-secret communiqués directed to Kappler in Rome by officials at Himmler's headquarters at Rastenburg. It is clear that these directives were part of the general plan for a ''Final Solution of the Jewish problem'' promulgated at the Wansee Conference of 20 January 1942. See: Tagliacozzo, *La Comunita' di Roma*, pp. 8–13.
3. The majority of the Jews captured by the Nazis were residents of the city's small and ancient ghetto. Nonetheless, Nazis invaded the homes and carried away a number of Roman Jews residing in Trastevere and elsewhere. See: Robert Katz, *Black Sabbath: a Journey Through a Crime Against Humanity* (Toronto, Macmillan, 1969), *passim* and Susan Zuccotti, ''Rome, 1943: The October Roundup,'' in *The Italians and the Holocaust: Persecution, Rescue and Survival* (New York: Basic Books Inc. Publishers, 1987), pp. 101–138.
4. ''By a fortuitous circumstance, a relatively high number of younger men succeeded in avoiding capture. The local Command had in those very days issued a mobilization order for obligatory work service with threats of severe sanctions for all those who did not comply.'' Tagliacozzo, *La Comunita' di Roma,* p. 22.
   '' . . . this one time the weekly distribution of cigarettes proved to be a visit of providence since many men were saved because they happened to be in line at the tobacconists' . . . . '' Giacomo Debenedetti, *16 ottobre 1943-Otto ebrei*. (Rome: Editori Riuniti, 1978), p. 56.
   Nevertheless, and as once again Tagliacozzo points out, this apparent stroke of luck had other, darker consequences: ''On the other hand, however, this fact proved fatal for many, especially women, the elderly and children, who believed the roundup was being directed exclusively against able-bodied men slated for the work force or for military service.'' Tagliacozzo, *La Comunita' di Roma*, p. 22. The implication here is that many of these same women, elderly and children made no attempt to flee while watching their fathers and brothers escape ''on the roofs, in cellars or to the homes of non-Jewish neighbors.'' Ibid.
5. Debenedetti, *16 Ottobre 1943*, pp. 58–59.
6. On the morning after the raid, those captured and held overnight in hellish conditions at the Military College underwent a rigorous selection process: ''Towards dawn on Sunday, after a meticulous examination of identity cards and other documents, the spouses and children of mixed marriages, boarders and domestic help considered 'Aryans,' and finally, Jewish foreigners, including, according to . . . Kappler's report, one citizen of the Vatican, were released. Following the selection process, 252 persons were released.'' Tagliacozzo, *La Comunità di Roma,* p. 27.

7. There is some discrepancy in reporting the total number of those deported after the raid. Tagliacozzo sets the number of deported at 1,007; Katz says 1,041 were deported (Katz, *Black Sabbath* p. 331); Zuccotti likewise sets the number at 1,007 (Zuccotti, *The Italians and the Holocaust,* p. 131). Readers should consult note 1 to "Appendix 1" in Katz for possible clarification: Katz, *Black Sabbath,* p. 380.
8. Susan Zuccotti, *The Italians and the Holocaust*, p. 105. Zuccotti adds: "He had not opposed the Italian racial laws [in 1938]. He had not condemned occasional Catholic press articles and bishops' speeches approving religious, if not racial, discrimination. He had not tried to protect Jews in other European countries." Zuccotti, ibid. Readers should also see the previous chapter in the present work.
9. Notes of the Secretary of State, n.d. October 1943, *Actes et Documents*, Vol 9, p. 307; Father Tacchi Venturi to Cardinal Maglione, 26 October 1943, ibid., pp. 525–526.
10. Public Record Office (London), Foreign Office 371/37255, Sir Francis d'Arcy Osborne to the Foreign Office, 31 October 1943.
11. Rabbi Panzieri to Pope Pius XII, 27 October 1943, *Actes et Documents,* vol. 9, p. 529.
12. See, Tagliacozzo, *La Comunità' di Roma*, pp. 34–35.
13. Father Pietro Tacchi Venturi to Cardinal Maglione, 25 October 1943, *Actes et Documents,* vol. 9, pp. 525–526.
14. See note 34 in Tagliacozzo, ibid. p. 29 and Bishop Carlo Agostini to Cardinal Maglione, 25 October 1943, *Actes et Documents,* vol. 9.
15. See especially, R. Leiber, S. J., "Pio XII e gli Ebrei del 16 ottobre a Roma," in *La Civiltà Cattolica*, n. 1657, 4 March 1961, pp. 454–458.
16. "Pius XII And The Third Reich," *Look,* 17 May 1966, p. 40.
17. Tagliacozzo underscores this claim through citation of a leaflet distributed by the underground Resistance in Rome. The excerpt cited reads:
    Germans have gone around Rome all night and for a whole day pulling people from their homes. The Germans would like to convince us that those taken are aliens, that they are of another race; but we recognize them as our flesh and blood: they have always lived, struggled and suffered with us. Not only able-bodied men, but the elderly, children, women, infants, all have been crammed into sealed wagons and sent to their fate. There is no heart that doesn't tremble at the thought of that fate. But the soldiers who have carried out so inhuman a task with unflinching frigidity, without a glimpse, without a trace of mercy in their eyes, they, too, have their families far away: mothers, wives, children, sisters; and they, too, must be overcome at times with nostalgia at hearing again the songs of their childhood. A party or State discipline that shrivels and ossifies the heart to that point, that stills every voice of humanity and reduces man to a robot is a poison that must be counteracted by fire and steel. Ours is no longer hatred, it's horror. Until Europe is liberated from this nightmare, there will remain no hope of peace. No one considers tomorrow's retailiation to be in letting loose a hunt after German women and children, but these Nazi soldiers and their servants, spies. Fascist hired assassins must be silenced, forever, buried forever in this every earth which they dare to besmirch with so much shame." Tagliacozzo, *La Comunita' di Roma*. p. 33. According to Tagliacozzo, words such as the above expressed the true "state of mind of the Roman population," a state of mind that papal condemnation of Nazi atrocities might have helped to encourage. Tagliacozzo, *ibid*. Any objection to the idea of papal support for military violence should be balanced against longstanding Church teaching on the 'just war,' as well as the

recent behavior of the Vatican hierarchy in relation to Mussolini's Ethiopian campaign and the Spanish Civil War.

18. Irving Greenberg, "Cloud of Smoke, Pillar of Fire," *Holocaust-Religious and Philosophical Implications,* ed. by John K. Roth and Michael Berenbaum (New York: Paragon House, 1989), p. 330.
19. Susan Zuccotti, "Pope Pius XII and the Holocaust: The Case in Italy," *The Italian Refuge-Rescue of Jews During the Holocaust* ed. by Ivo Herzer, Klaus Voigt, and James Burgwyn (Washington D.C.; The Catholic University of America Press, 1989), p. 261.
20. Weizsäcker, whom the British Jewish historian, Sir Lewis Namier, saw as cautious, crafty, untrustworthy and a "past master in camouflage," came from a distinguished family that boasted of its academics and civil servants. In 1943 he replaced the longtime ambassador to the Holy See, Diego von Bergen, who was popular at the Vatican because of the central role he had played in negotiating the 1933 Concordat. Leonidas E. Hill credits Weizsäcker with warning the leaders of the Roman Jewish community of the impending roundup. "As a consequence many Jews fled to the Vatican properties protected by the notices of Weiszäcker's embassy." Lewis Namier, *In The Nazi Era* (London: Macmillan and Co. Ltd., 1952), p. 68 and Leonidas G. Hill, "The Vatican Embassy of Ernst Von Weizsäcker, 1943–1945," *The Journal of Modern History*, 39 No. 2 (June 1967), p. 147.
21. "By a curious twist of fate, the consul, Eitel Friedrich Mollhausen, had literally overnight become one of the most important men in occupied Rome. Late in the previous day [September 24, 1943] the Nazi ambassador to the new Mussolini government, Rudolf Rahn, had been seriously injured in an automobile accident in northern Italy. It had now become clear that Rahn would be incapacitated for at least several weeks, and in any event most of his future activities would take place in the north, seat of the neo-Fascist regime. The consul in Rome, who was only thirty years old, was thus placed in charge of the embassy with the full powers of a chief of a diplomatic mission." Katz, *Black Sabbath,* p. 55.
22. In regard to the Nazi High Command's insistence that the "Final Solution" be applied to occupied Italian territory, "Consul Mollhausen was . . . contrary to this line of action for reasons of temperment and perhaps because he considered it useless as well as inhuman." Tagliacozzo, *La Comunitá di Roma,* p. 10.
23. The telegram read: "Rome, 6 October 1943. Received: 6 October 1943, 1330 hours. No. 192 from 10/6. *Very very urgent!* For Herrn Reichsminister personally. Obersturmbannführer Kappler has received orders from Berlin to seize the eight thousand Jews resident in Rome and transport them to Northern Italy, where they are to be liquidated [wo sie liquidiert werden sollen]. Commandant of Rome General Stahel informs me he will permit this action only on approval of the Herrn Reichsminister for Foreign Affairs. In my personal opinion it would be better business to employ the Jews for fortification work as was done in Tunis, and, together with Kappler, I will propose this to Field Marshal Kesselring. Please advise. Mollhausen." Reported in Katz, *Black Sabbath,* p. 136.
24. Robert Katz, *Black Sabbath,* pp. 136–137.
25. Ibid., p. 136.
26. Notes of the Secretary of State, 23 October 1943, *Actes et Documents,* vol. 9, p. 519.

27. Katz, *Black Sabbath*, pp. 286–287; Zuccotti, *The Italians and the Holocaust*, p. 130 and *Tagliacozzo, La Comunita' di Roma*, p. 31. From 1939 to 1945 *L'Osservatore Romano* did not distinguish itself by championing the Jewish cause. *Civiltà Cattolica* which unofficially reflected Vatican views was also predictably diffident about Jewish persecution. The one article on Jews that the Jesuit periodical published focused on Jewish responsibility for the crucifixion of Christ and declared that "the crime of the sons of the Synagogue has been repeated in every generation." As late as 1952, the genocide of the Jews still evoked no comment in the pages of *Civilità Cattolica* which lamented the fact that the post-war Bonn government in Germany was paying compensation to Jews whose property had been seized by the Nazis. See Charlotte Klein, "In the Mirror of *Civilità Cattolica*: Vatican View of Jewry, 1939–1962," *Christian Attitudes on Jews and Judaism*, 43 (August 1975): pp. 12–13.
28. Katz, *Black Sabbath*, p. 287.
29. Morley, *Vatican Diplomacy*, p. 186.
30. Joseph L., Lichten, "Pius XII and the Jews," The *Catholic Mind*, 57 No. 1142 (March-April 1959), p. 161. Dr. Lichten who died in 1987 at the age of eighty-one, pioneered in organizing Catholic-Jewish dialogues. Shortly before his death, Lichten was designated a Knight Commander of the Pontifical Equestrian Order of St. Gregory the Great by Pope John Paul II.
31. Alden Hatch and Seamus Walshe, *Crown of Glory: The Life of Pope Pius XII* (New York: Hawthorn Books, Inc. Publishers, 1958), p. 168 and Paul I. Murphy with R. Rene Arlington, *La Popessa* (New York: Warner Books, 1983), p. 205. Another writer puts the number of Jews hidden at one time in Castel Gondolfo at three thousand. See Fernande Leboucher, *Incredible Mission*. trans. J. F. Bernard (Garden City, New York: Doubleday & Company, Inc., 1969), p. 118.
32. National Archives, Microfilm 1284-56 Myron Taylor to the Secretary of State, 26 March 1945.
33. Renzo DeFelice, *Storia degli ebrei italiani sotto il fascismo* (Rome: Einuadi, 1961), II, pp. 568, 746–751. Michael Tagliocazzo believes that 4,238 Jews found asylum in the religious edifices of the Italian capital and an additional 477 were protected in the Vatican proper and its enclaves. See Michaelis, *Mussolini And The Jews*, p. 365.
34. Robert Leiber, "Pio XII e gli ebrei di Roma 1943–1944," *La Civilità Cattolica*, I, 4 March 1961, p. 451.
35. Michaelis, *Mussolini and The Jews*, p. 364 and Lapide, *The Last Three Popes and The Jews*, p. 134. Sam Waagenaar, a critic of the papacy, believes that virtually no Jews were sheltered within Vatican walls. See Waagenaar, *The Pope's Jews*, pp. 426–427.
36. Emanuele Pacifici, Personal interview, Rome, 21 May 1987.
37. Alexander Ramati (As told by Padre Rufino Niccacci). *The Assisi Underground: The Priests Who Rescued Jews*. (New York: Harcourt, Brace and Jovanovich, 1978), p. 175. Similar rescue operations existed in Genoa, Turin, and Perugia, all with the support of archbishops in those cities. See Susan Zuccotti, "Pope Pius XII and the Holocaust: The Case in Italy," *The Italian Refuge: Rescue of Jews During the Holocaust*, eds. Ivo Herzer, Klaus Voigt, and James Burgwyn (Washington, D.C.: The Catholic University of America Press, 1989), p. 268.
38. D. Aldo Brunacci, *Ebrei In Assisi durante la guerra: Ricordi di un protagonista*

(Assisi: Libreria Fonteviva, 1985), p. 9. From the text it is not clear whether it is the papacy or the bishop who is urging patience and secrecy.

39. D. Aldo Brunacci, *L'opera di assistenza, del clero e del Vescovo di Assisi dopo l'8 settembre 1943*. Talk originally delivered 28 June 1975. Reprint of proceedings of a conference on "Cattolici e fascisti in Umbria (1922–1945)" (Bologna: Società Editrice Il Mulino, 1978), p. 22.
40. Zuccotti, *The Italians and The Holocaust,* pp. 209–210. Sam Waagenaar has stated bluntly that "the Vatican kept its purse strings securely closed, and gave nothing". Waagenaar, *The Pope's Jews,* p. 402.
41. Zuccotti, *The Italians and The Holocaust,* p. 210.
42. Constantine, Prince of Bavaria, *The Pope: A Portrait From Life*. trans. Diana Pyke (New York: Roy Publishers, n.d.), p. 227.
43. Harold H. Tittman to U.S. Secretary of State, 19 October 1943, *Foreign Relations of the United States: 1943,* II (Washington: United States Government Printing Office, 1964), p. 950.
44. Robert Katz, *Death in Rome* (New York: The Macmillan Company, 1967), pp. 249–250. Also see Michael Tagliacozzo, "Le responsabilita'di Kappler nella strage degli ebrei di roma," *La Rassegna Mensile Di Israel -Volume Speciale in Memoria D'Attilo Milano*. Vol. XXXVI (July-September 1970); 389–414. According to Eugenio (Eugen) Dollmann, an S.S. officer whose excellent command of Italian qualified him to interpret for the Führer on his 1938 trip to Italy and who served under several German ambassadors in the Italian capital, it was Heinrich Himmler, the S.S. leader, who was mainly responsible for the massacre.
45. Notes of the Secretary of State, 24 March 1944, *Acts et Documents,* Vol. X (Vatican City: Libreria Editrice Vaticana, 1980), p. 189. When Katz wrote his *Death in Rome,* he did not know that the Vatican actually anticipated the ten to one ratio of victims. Letter from Robert Katz to the authors, 11 November 1990.
46. Robert A. Graham, *Pius XII's Defense of Jews and Others: 1944–45* (Milwaukee: Catholic League for Religious and Civil Rights, n.d.), p. 15.
47. Robert Katz, personal interview, 21 June 1985. *New York Times,* 28 November 1975 and 24 January 1976 and *The London Times, 28 November 1975*.
48. Graham, *Pius XII's Defense*, p. 1.
49. Memo from Vincent La Vista to Herbert J. Cummings on "Illegal Emigration Movements In And Through Italy," 15 May 1947, p. 10.
50. *Ibid.*, p. 2.
51. *New York Times,* 30 January 1984.
52. Ibid.
53. John M. Oesterreicher, "Accusations not true nor made in good faith," *National Catholic Reporter,* 2 March 1984.
54. Ibid.
55. Constantine, *The Pope,* p. 230.
56. Christopher Simpson, *Blowback: America's Recruitment of Nazis and Its Effects on the Cold War* (New York: Weidenfeld and Nicolson, 1988), p. 176.
57. Ibid., p. 180; Pavlo Shandruk, *Arms of Valor* trans. Roman Olesnicki (New York: Robert Speller and Sons Publishers, Inc. 1959), pp. 291–292.
58. Harold Troper and Morton Weinfeld, *Old Wounds-Jews, Ukrainians and the Hunt for Nazi War Criminals in Canada* (Chapel Hill: University of North Carolina Press, 1989), p. 315. Sol Littman of the Canadian Friends of the Simon Wies-

enthal Center calls the Deschenes Commission "inept" and its conclusions "biased." He claims that he offered to provide that Commission with damaging evidence about the Ukrainian unit. His offer was not accepted, he recently informed a researcher. Sol Littman, telephone interview, 24 April 1990. Alti Rodal, a Jewish scholar who wrote a supplementary report for the Commission, found no evidence of criminality sufficient to warrant legal action against the Galicia Division personnel, but neither was she prepared to exonerate them. Alti Rodal, telephone interview, 24 April 1990. In her report, Ms. Rodal concluded that, "it is likely that at least some persons who had served with Nazi-sponsored Ukrainian police/militia units used in killing actions in 1941–1942 found their way into the ranks of the Division either before or after the Battle of Brody." Alti Rodal, Unpublished report on "Nazi War Criminals In Canada: The Historical And Policy Setting From The 1940's To The Present" prepared in 1985 as an annex to the Deschenes Commission Report, p. 408. In her report Rodal also pointed out that Canadian authorities initially balked when Karol Sidor, the founder and first commander of the pro-Nazi, para-military Hlinka Guard in Slovakia, sought asylum. For a while Sidor, who had once been premier and minister of the interior before his appointment as Slovakian ambassador to the Holy See, was persona non grata. Only in 1950 after Pius XII interceded with the Canadian prime minister through the apostolic delegate was Sidor admitted to Canada where he died three years later. Ibid., pp. 413–415.

59. Gitta Sereny, *Into that Darkness: An Examination of Conscience* (New York: Vintage Books, 1983), p. 275.
60. Ibid., p. 289.
61. Alois Hudal, *Die Grundlagen des Nationalsozialismus: Eine ideengeschichtliche Untersuchung* (Leipzig: Johannes Gunther Verlag, 1937).
62. Benno Weiser Varon, "The Nazis' Friends in Rome," *Midstream,* vol. 30, no. 4 (April, 1984), p. 11.
63. Hansjakob Stehle, "Passe vom Papst?," *Die Zeit,* 4 May 1984, p. 10.
64. Andrew P. Landi, Telephone Interview, 2 May 1990. The treatment of German ex-diplomats in Vatican City was another troublesome issue. Montini pleaded with the British and the Americans to help the Vatican save face by making concessions. The Germans, Montini hoped, would not have their liberty restricted and they would be permitted to proceed directly to Germany. The Allies were unsympathetic and Harold Tittman's impression conveyed in a secret telegram was that the Vatican was more concerned with "appearance and possible adverse publicity than with anything else." Harold Tittman to Secretary of State, 13 July 1945 in National Archives, General Records of the Department of State, Box 3725 B.
65. Erhard Dabringhaus, *Klaus Barbie* (Washington, D.C.: Acropolis Books, 1984), pp. 176–179. Also active in the Lyon area during the German occupation was the collaborator Paul Touvier. He joined the pro-Nazi militia, the Milice and, after the war, was convicted in absentia of war crimes. With clerical help Touvier managed to escape. He eluded the French authorities by hiding in a series of religious houses until he was arrested in a monastery on 22 May 1989. His protectors over the years had been clerics who were motivated in the main by right-wing ideology. See Ted Morgan, "L'Affaire Touvier: Opening Old Wounds," *The New York Times Magazine*, 1 October 1989, pp. 32 ff.

66. The visa was reproduced in *Die Zeit,* 4 May 1984, p. 9.
67. English translation of Walter Rauff statement, 5 December 1962, Santiago, Chile. This document is Exhibit H of the "Summary of Facts and Documents—Simon Wiesenthal Center Investigations on Rauff and the Church."
68. Varon, "The Nazis' Friends," p. 10.
69. Spanish original of Walter Rauff statement, 5 December 1962, Santiago, Chile.
70. *New York Times,* 26 January 1984.
71. Corrado Pallenberg, *The Vatican From Within* (London: George G. Harrap & Co., Ltd., 1961), p. 46.
72. Letter from P. Peter Gumpel to the authors, 28 February 1988. Father Gumpel represented the Postulazione Generale della Compagnia di Gesù. Also see the *New York Times,* 19 and 20 November 1965.
73. Pallenberg, *The Vatican From Within,* pp. 209–210.
74. See Kenneth L. Woodward, *Making Saints: How the Catholic Church Determines Who Becomes a Saint, Who Doesn't and Why* (New York: Simon and Schuster, 1990.) Ideological rivalry between conservatives who wish to see Pius XII canonized and liberals who support the canonization of John Paul XXIII may also prove to be an impediment.

5

Chief Rabbi Zolli in Trieste

Few would quarrel with the assertion that, except for the years 1938–1944, twentieth-century Italy has provided its Jewish population with one of the most congenial milieus in the Christian world. Throughout the middle of the nineteenth century, the liberal, anti-clerical spirit permeating much of Italy's struggle for national independence—the *Risorgimento*—mustered enthusiastic Jewish support and militated against any emergence of popular anti-Semitism.[1]

The Jewish community's two millennia-old history—there were Jews on the peninsula before Christ's birth in Palestine—afforded Italians of the Mosaic faith a special niche in Italian history.[2] Unlike the majority of their traditional co-religionists in Poland who were readily identifiable by their language (most Jews were Yiddish speakers and spoke Polish badly or not at all) and by their dress (men often sported caftans and head coverings while a married woman wore a *sheitl* or wig), at the time of the *Risorgimento,* Jews of Italy, with few exceptions, had become highly acculturated. Despite local variations and certain idiomatic idiosyncrasies, their language was Italian, and their garb much the same as that of their Catholic neighbors. It would have been preposterous—at least prior to 1938—to consider Italian Jews as foreigners in their homeland.[3] In fact, Mussolini's Race Laws in 1938 did not mirror the thinking of most Italians about Jews.[4]

Compare this with Poland whose government informed the impotent League of Nations in 1938 that its predominately urban Jewish minority, about 10 percent of the overall Polish population, constituted an intolerable "foreign element." Even though they had been in the country for about a thousand years, Jews were seen by most Polish Catholics as strangers.

Since the total Jewish population was extremely small in relation to the social whole (Jews comprised just one-tenth of one percent of the Italian population), Italian Jews were perceived neither as a formidable commercial force nor as a political threat to be feared. Moreover, the lack of a centralizing political structure prior to the decade, 1860–70, had allowed for a wide variety of regional traditions to develop. For the most part, Jews of Northern Italy, especially those concentrated in the regions of Piedmont and Tuscany, as well as in the cities of Livorno, Milano, and Trieste, had already experienced a degree of emancipation by 1860 unheard of in Rome, the Papal States, and the south in general.[5]

With the seizure of the Papal States by Italian patriots and the final establishment of united Italy's capital in Rome in 1870, Jewish emancipation extended throughout the new kingdom. The absence of legislative and political restraints, the complete lack of any governmentally sponsored anti-Semitism, allowed for a sudden and dramatic assimilation of Italian Jews in a manner unparalleled elsewhere in Europe. By the end of the nineteenth century, and in the early years of the new century prior to World War I, Jews in Italy gained entrance into all spheres of Italian society. In 1902, for example, a Jewish army general, Giuseppe Ottolenghi, was appointed Minister of War, while in 1910, another Jew, Luigi Luzzati, became Prime Minister. In Italy it was not extraordinary for Jews to reach the highest echelons of the army, the navy, or the judiciary. In Rome, a city infamous for previous dark periods of papally-sponsored anti-Semitism, Ernesto Nathan served honorably and efficiently as mayor between 1907 and 1913 as head of a lay-Masonic coalition. During these same early years, two other Italian Jews, Claudio Treves and Giuseppe Emanuele Modigliani, distinguished themselves as leading figures in the Italian Socialist Party. Italian Jews were likewise prominent in the arts and sciences: the novelist, Italo Svevo, the artist, Amedeo Modigliani, and the philologist, Graziadio Isaia Ascoli, are but three of many who can be called to mind.[6]

Such total Jewish integration into Italian society, then, the result, states Mario Toscano, of the fact that: "In Italy, unlike other European countries, the formation of a national consciousness by Jews paralleled the formation of a national consciousness by the rest of the population,'"[7] further explains the very low degree of Italian anti-Semitism, even on a popular level. This happy confluence of historical and social factors sets Italy of the early twentieth century apart among other Christian nations, and thus renders even more disturbing and dramatic the later shift in Italian-Jewish fortunes that history had in store.

* * *

Although Israele Zolli was to spend virtually his entire professional life in Trieste and afterwards in Rome, his tortuous trail began not in Italy at all, but in Brody, in a prostrate, dismembered, Poland. Brody, a predominantly Jewish city, was located in the Austrian-controlled section of Poland after that unhappy land was partitioned in 1795. It was the proud birthplace of a surprisingly large number of outstanding rabbis in the eighteenth and nineteenth centuries and, in 1881, it also produced Israele Zoller who was the youngest of five children. His mother could boast of many learned rabbis in her genealogy. His father, a man known for his integrity, operated a silk factory in the textile city of Lodz, then under Russian dominion. When the Czarist authorities padlocked the factory, hard times befell the family. It is understandable that young Israele was encouraged by his mother to study for the rabbinate rather than consider the risky business world.[8]

Zolli's rabbinical career may be said to have been launched at the age of twenty-three or twenty-four, shortly after the death of his beloved mother. Following a semester at the University of Vienna, Zolli—his name then was still Zoller, of course—went to Florence where he studied simultaneously at the university eventually earning an advanced degree in psychology and at the nearby Italian Rabbinical College. Rabbi Samuel Hirsch Margulies, a distinguished scholar who like Zolli had been born in Galicia—in Brody to be precise—was then the director of the Rabbinical College. Margulies also served as the Chief Rabbi of Florence and was an enormous influence on the young Zolli, his protégé. He often journeyed to Poland and it was, in fact, Margulies desirous of replenishing the chronically short supply of rabbis in Italy, who brought Zolli to Florence. In straitened circumstances, Zolli also received some material help from Margulies. There is some evidence that Margulies considered Zolli his most brilliant student.[9]

In 1911, Zolli took up his position as Vice-Rabbi in Trieste, a picturesque city strategically situated on the Adriatic where Italy and the Balkans meet. Indeed, it had long been a cockpit for the competing territorial aspirations of the Italians and the multiethnic Austro-Hungarian Empire. As the major seaport of the ruling Hapsburgs, Trieste boasted a wealthy and sizable Jewish community—perhaps six thousand souls at the turn of the century. In 1912, the year in which the new Byzantine-style synagogue in Trieste was completed, Hirsch Perez Chajes, five years Zolli's senior and a noted Zionist leader, scholar and rabbi, was appointed Chief Rabbi there. Zolli had studied under Chajes in Florence, but relations between the two ambitious rabbis were strained. Zolli descried their relationship as "cool, often tense and never friendly."[10] He somewhat simplistically ascribed their inability to get along to the fact that his own sympathies were with the Italians who saw Trieste a unredeemed Italian soil whereas Chajes was pro-Austrian and really coveted the Chief Rabbi's post in Vienna, which he assumed in 1918. Despite some opposition, Zolli was promoted to Chief Rabbi in Trieste in February 1920 after the city was incorporated into the Kingdom of Italy. Finally, he was out of the long shadow cast by Chajes who was both idolized as a human being and honored as a scholar. Or so he thought. In fact, for decades to come Zolli would be unfavorably compared with the legendary Chajes.

Zolli's personal life had also been less than joyous in the second decade of the new century. Right after his arrival in Trieste he married an Austrian woman, Adele Litwak, and the short-lived union produced a daughter, Dora. However, Zolli suffered a severe trauma when Adele died tragically a few years later.

Matrimonial records in Trieste's synagogue show that in August 1920 Zolli remarried. His bride, Emma Angiolina Majonica, had been born in Gorizia, Italy in May 1883.[11] The wedding ceremony was performed by Rabbi Ermanno Friedenthal, a former classmate of Zolli's in Florence. When asked by Rabbi Friedenthal which of two *haftorhas** should be read at the service, Zolli characteristically replied, the shorter one.[12] Where observance of Jewish law was concerned, Zolli would usually prove to be more like the willow than the

*A *haftorah* is a portion of the Books of Prophets of the Hebrew Bible read after the reading of the Torah on festivals, fast days, and Sabbath.

oak. By all accounts, Emma, who was to bear Zolli a second daughter, Miriam, was quiet, unobtrusive, simple, and somewhat unsophisticated. Matrimonial bliss may have eluded Zolli but the marriage would last almost thirty-six years until his death.

Zolli's rabbinical career was clearly less tranquil and gratifying than either his personal life or his scholarly life. Indeed, his tenure as Chief Rabbi in Trieste was almost never free of tension. The same pattern of behavior that was later to put Zolli at loggerheads with Roman Jewry caused discord in Trieste. Everybody admired his erudition and he was deferentially addressed in writing as "Rabbino Maggiore Prof. dott.," but he was unable to endear himself to his congregants. Actually, he never tried. Ministering to his flock was never high on his list of priorities. He was openly contemptuous of those with less learning than he. As a result he was always more reviled than revered.

It is not hyperbole to say that Zolli had a talent for alienating his congregants. Some, such as Nives Castelbolognese, did not want to be married by the Chief Rabbi. Her sister had a sickly child who died after a few months. Notwithstanding the fact that his own adherence to *Halachah* or Jewish law was often very flexible, Zolli refused to allow the baby to be buried in the family crypt because it had never been circumcised.[13] One community leader stated passionately that he did not even want Zolli present at his funeral.[14] Silvia Suadi Volpi remembers when she lost her post as a teacher in 1938 because of the newly promulgated racial laws, her mother sought out Zolli hoping that her daughter could find employment in the Jewish schools. Half a century later, Suadi Volpi recalled with bitterness that Zolli did not wish to deal with the problem. He did not offer consolation. It was not just what he said, but the unsympathetic way he said it.[15]

Interviews conducted in 1988 with octogenarian and nonagenarian Trieste Jews yield a picture of Zolli as cold, distant, unfriendly, unapproachable, overly concerned with money and insensitive to people. Many, including his longtime secretary, Clementina Ianni, remember Zolli as not being truly devout.[16] Owing to the fact that he came from a long line of rabbis, he had Judaism in his blood, Ianni said, but not in his spirit. He liked being the professor, not the rabbi.[17] For the rabbinical profession he had little respect and actively discouraged one young Triestino from becoming a rabbi.[18] He had no Jewish protégés in Trieste and left no disciples. Mario Stock, an historian of the Jews of Trieste and President of the Jewish community there, has stated unequivocally that Zolli contributed absolutely nothing to Trieste's Jews. Baptism was the logical end of Zolli's career of nothingness, Stock said in a recent interview.[19] Stock does not mention Zolli's name even once in his history of Jewish Trieste although Zolli was there for almost three decades.[20]

Skeptics might conclude that the uncomplimentary Jewish assessments of Zolli made with hindsight reflect vindictiveness over his 1945 defection. However, dusty files perused in the attic of Trieste's synagogue shed light on Zolli's prickly personality and confirm his perennially troubled relations with the lay leaders and the community at large.

Events that unfolded at the end of 1928 bespeak the poor rapport that existed. Ostensibly in that year there was a dispute over the desire of the presidency to have Zolli teach Biblical history and reading to a group of young boys, a task which the Chief Rabbi believed was beneath his dignity. At one point Zolli stormed out of the room where this matter was under consideration. In a letter replete with hostility and sarcasm, Zolli expressed his view that any schoolteacher was adequate to do the kind of instruction he had been asked to do. He declared that the lay leadership did not know how to request anything higher of him than to give "private lessons in alpha-bet." Nevertheless, he condescended to provide the lessons for the "ragazetti" (little kids).[21]

To the lay leaders this affray was but a symptom and an index of the sorry state of affairs in Trieste's Jewish community. In a lengthy epistle, J. Capi, the chancellor of the community, wrote that he had great admiration for Zolli's intellectual assets, but he would have been pleased to be able to praise him as a rabbi. He referred to the unceasing complaints of the administrators that they had to make peace between Zolli and the community. It was the rabbi who ought to have been the peacemaker but the roles were reversed. It was expected of the rabbi that he set a good example, but Capi lamented the fact that Zolli attended temple functions infrequently and failed to carry out the most important acts of his ministry. Zolli was accused of lacking interest in various charitable works. Institutions that were languishing because of a deficiency of support could be helped by vigorous aid from the rabbi. Zolli was reminded that he had been entreated to join in a fund-raising effort, but had replied that he had a "higher charge." As to Zolli's annoyance at not being invited to meetings of the presidency, Capi said that he was loath to involve the rabbi in purely administrative matters. Capi concluded by reiterating his appreciation of Zolli's uncommon intellect and added that if the esteem the Chief Rabbi enjoyed in literary and academic circles pleased him, then it would be a still greater pleasure to win not only the esteem, but the love and veneration of his brethren.[22]

Apparently, Zolli was unconvinced. He wrote a terse one sentence reply to a four-page typewritten letter and stated bluntly that is was easier to clarify such issues in a conversation than through correspondence.[23]

Over the years conflicts continued to erupt periodically. An incident in September 1931 involved Zolli and Alberto Levi, an Orthodox Jew in the Trieste community who sometimes served as *chazan* or cantor. On one occasion he shocked the assembled worshipers by shouting irreverent remarks at the Chief Rabbi during religious services. Precisely what caused the dispute is not clear, but Levi wrote to Zolli, vowing that except on the anniversaries of his parents' deaths, he would never again don the vestments of a cantor to officiate in Trieste.[24]

In June 1934, a battle was fought over the matter of Zolli's rent. The Italian government had authorized the lowering of rents and Zolli wanted his reduced accordingly. However, the community agency which provided the rabbi's housing argued that Zolli had long received preferential treatment, that he resided in their best apartment at a ridiculously low rent which had not been raised in many years. Lowering his rent further would have brought about an abnormal and unacceptable situation. Gratuitously added was the accusation that Zolli was wrongly receiving remuneration for presiding at funerals.[25]

At about the same time the housing conflict was raging and surely as a result of it, Zolli asked that the names of his daughter, Dora, and his wife Emma be removed form the list of contributors to the community's nursery school and that his own name be deleted from the board of directors.[26] Carlo Morpurgo, the president of the nursery school, wrote to Zolli that it was an old tradition for the Chief Rabbi to be represented on the nursery school board. This was intended to confer an honor, not to impose a burden. Excessive demands would not be made of the rabbi,[27] he was assured. Zolli answered that he was always willing to put his modest work at the disposal of the school. However, true to form, he was adamant about expunging his name from the board of directors.[28]

Given the uneasy, sometimes tempestuous association between the Chief Rabbi and the community, why was it not dissolved until 1939 when Zolli went to Rome? Perhaps the explanation may be found in the chronic paucity of qualified Italian rabbis. Language was one significant impediment to the recruitment of first-rate spiritual leaders. Few foreigners could speak fluent Italian. Zolli was a notable exception. He mastered Italian quickly. Furthermore, many Italian Jews were backsliders in their religious practices. Rabbis had to gingerly walk a tightrope to satisfy both those, a minority, who were truly Orthodox, and those whose outlook was really that of Reform Judaism. Zolli, whose own religiosity was in general elastic, was probably successful most of the time in this respect. His many difficulties had much more to do with an abrasive nature than with a particular religious philosophy.

In the wake of Zolli's conversion, a few of his detractors—and they were legion—accused him of having had Fascist proclivities.[29] It was suggested that Zolli's selection as Chief Rabbi of Rome was influenced by his willingness to make "himself solid with the Fascist authorities and their Jewish agents."[30] On this point, the documentation remains unconvincing. Zolli was specifically alleged to have held a unique Torah service in the Trieste synagogue sometime during the Mussolini era. Supposedly, the "scrolls of the Law were taken from the Holy Ark, carried in procession through the aisles of the Temple, which was [sic] lined by Fascist, Jewish soldiers in uniform giving the Fascist salute."[31] Corroborating evidence for this anecdote cannot be found and nobody in Trieste can recall such a service.

In October 1935, Mussolini's regime, using a border incident as a pretext, invaded Ethiopia which had vanquished and humiliated the Italian military in the battle of Adowa forty years earlier. Italian Jews, in general, ardently backed this imperialistic reprise, this naked aggression against a peaceful nation located in the horn of Africa. Jewish Trieste was no exception. On the evening of Yom Kippur, 1935, a crowd packed the Tempio Maggiore for a patriotic "manifestation." After invoking divine blessings on King Victor Emmanuel and on the national government, Chief Rabbi Zolli delivered a speech in which he referred to the ancient concept of God as a God of armies. He then invited the assembled throng to direct their thoughts towards the valorous soldiers of Italy who, in distant eastern Africa, were fighting for the greater power and glory of the fatherland.[32]

According to the account in the local Trieste daily, Zolli's words struck a responsive chord. The crowd rose to its feet, begging the Lord for a military victory. At the conclusion of the service, the president, speaking on behalf of the entire congregation, expressed his belief that Zolli's sentiments were those that animated the whole Jewish community.[33] If such was the case, it was one of those very rare instances where Zolli and the community spoke with a single voice.

To galvanize morale and help finance the unprovoked invasion of Ethiopia which was aimed at re-capturing the glory of ancient Rome, the Duce entreated Italian women to magnanimously donate their wedding rings to the state. In December 1935, Zolli wrote to the Fascist leadership in Trieste that the Jews there would be happy to surrender their rings. Perhaps rings other than wedding bands could be donated as the latter had religious as well as material value for Jews, he believed. Zolli obsequiously said he would be pleased to have a donation ceremony at the temple with Fascist officials in attendance. The ceremony would be announced ahead of time in the press and would be held in front of the plaque commemorating Jewish dead from World War I.[34]

By the time the ceremony took place, the Union of Italian Jewish Communities had notified the Trieste Jewish elders that the Italian rabbinate had concluded that wedding rings did not have any sacred character according to the Hebrew rite. Therefore they could be donated after all. For its part, the Union asserted that Jewish women would not be second to other Italian women in their sacrifices to the fatherland.[35]

Before the actual offering of the wedding rings by Trieste's Jewish women, there was a brief religious service accompanied by choral singing. Fascist representatives were present at the gathering and witnessed the large crowd congregate before the World War I dedication plaque to contribute their rings to the war effort and to the state. The process of giving lasted several hours.[36]

The foregoing indicates that many, probably most, in Trieste's Jewish community were willing, even eager to align themselves openly with Il Duce. Jewish support for him was considerable throughout the country. Jews were probably proportionately represented in the ranks of Italian Fascism which, until 1938, unlike its German counterpart, had no anti-Semitic ideological component. When a petition was circulated in Trieste in 1936 paying homage to the fatherland and the regime, seven hundred signatures of Jewish heads of families were collected in just three days.[37] In addition, to demonstrate their unswerving loyalty, the community allowed the Jewish schools in Trieste to be thoroughly indoctrinated so that they might provide an undiluted Fascist education to youngsters.[38]

Zolli surely did not challenge these conformist actions, but neither is there reason to believe that he initiated them. Synagogue records reveal that he had little to do with the day to day functioning of the community, and decision-making on major issues was the prerogative of the lay leadership. Although he spoke in support of the Ethiopian venture and was involved in the ring donations campaign, although he frequently signed his letters to government officials with the words "Saluti fascisti,"[39] although he was willing to sign the loyalty oath to safeguard his professorship at the University of Padova when a few other braver faculty members preferred to forfeit their posts rather than identify themselves with the Fascist government,[40] Zolli was probably not a Fascist sympathizer. Nor was he an opponent of Fascism.[41] Italian politics did not engage him any more than the mundane affairs of the Jewish community. He was a pragmatist who opted to navigate in safe political waters which, in the intensely nationalist Italy of the 1930s, meant external compliance with Fascism. Like most mortals, Zolli lacked the high principles, the idealism, and the courage of which heroes are made.

Aimed at the creation of a Jewish national home in Palestine, Zionism was an ideology which made less than impressive inroads among the highly assimilated Italian Jewish population in the 1920s and 1930s. It was an ideology on which Zolli expressed himself, albeit somewhat inconsistently. Zolli doubtlessly considered himself a Zionist, but of the cultural rather than the political variety. It is true that in 1922 he deified Theodor Herzl, the Budapest-born journalist who founded modern political Zionism, calling him a man of political intuition close to prophecy. He also praised Chaim Weizmann, a tireless fighter for the establishment of a Jewish state who later became the first president of Israel,[42] but it was Ahad Ha-Am who was Zolli's model.

Dubbed the "agnostic rabbi," Ahad Ha-Am—his real name was Asher Zvi Ginsberg—emphasized a cultural and spiritual renewal rather than a mass influx of diasporan Jews into Palestine. Writing in 1927, Zolli echoed the ideas of Ahad Ha-Am who had died that same year. Zionism was not simply a response to anti-Semitism. It would resolve the problem of Judaism not that of the Jewish people. Returning a majority of Jewish people to Eretz Israel was not the highest priority. What was needed was the rise of a Jewish spiritual center in Palestine, a center in which the loftiest ideals of all humanity and a superior morality would be realized. This goal would be brought about, said Zolli, neither by the rigid Orthodox nor by assimilated intellectuals forgetful of their origins. In the new elevated spiritual hub, Hebrew, the ancient national tongue of Israel, would be given vigor and splendor. For the Yiddish language, the Jewish vernacular in most of Eastern Europe including his native Galicia, Zolli could muster only disdain.[43]

Over the years, Zolli evinced some interest in developments in Palestine, then a British mandate in which Arab nationalists and Zionists vied with one another. In 1930, he sojourned there with the help of the Italian government, visiting Egypt en route. He spent much time in Jerusalem with the Ashkenazi Chief Rabbi, Abraham Isaac Kook, the founder of the chief rabbinate there, and with various academics. Upon his return to Trieste, Zolli gave several lectures to both Jewish and Christian audiences on his impressions of the Holy Land.

Four years later in Trieste, he eulogized the preeminent Hebrew poet of his time, Chaim Nachman Bialik, who had died in Vienna following surgery. The Chief Rabbi and other Jewish dignitaries in Trieste saw Bialik's body off for burial in Palestine. On that solemn occasion Zolli gave a talk in Italian and modern Hebrew on the work of the Russian-born poet in the life, thought, and art of Israel.[44]

During the biennium beginning in the summer of 1934, Mussolini tried to curry favor with political Zionism despite the fact that he long harbored suspicions of the movement because of its close associations with Britain and its international character. There were pro-Zionist utterances and parleys with influential Zionists.[45] Late in 1935, Mussolini dispatched Corrado Tedeschi, a loyal follower and a Jew, to Palestine to win Zionists over to the Fascist cause.[46] Consistent with his own authoritarianism, the strutting Duce preferred the revisionist Zionism of Vladimir Jabotinsky to the dominant Labor Zionism with its socialist ideology. Mussolini's transitory flirtation with Zionism was evident in 1934 when Jabotinsky's Betar youth organization was allowed to establish a Jewish Maritime School at Civitavecchia as an autonomous entity within the seaman's school operated by the Italian government.[47]

After the Ethiopian war, as Hitler and Mussolini cemented their Fascist alliance, anti-Zionism became a staple of Italian Fascist rhetoric. Aspersions were cast upon Zionists for their foreign loyalties, while their allegiance to Rome was called into question. In that daunting atmosphere Zolli remained silent on the Zionist question.

But after he left the Jewish fold in 1945, an emboldened Zolli voiced his disillusionment over the progress of Zionism. In fact, less than a month after his baptism, he set down his thoughts. He had been a lover of Zionism, he protested. He had wanted to see persecuted Jews safely ingathered, working productively in Uganda[48] or elsewhere with a nucleus of spiritual and intellectual life in Jerusalem. But, after endless suffering, the end result appeared to be a strip of earth, nothing more than earth. Heaven was denied for a piece of earth. For Zolli there were already too many nationalisms.[49]

Examining the available evidence, one gets the distinct impression that Zolli had few if any strong political convictions. He lacked a real commitment to Zionism, Fascism, or any political philosophy, for that matter. He was similar to the chameleon which, to reduce its vulnerability to predators and thereby enhance its chances of survival, changes its pigment and merges with its surroundings. He was similar to Proteus, the sea god in Greek mythology who could change his shape at will. Zolli altered his opinions, switched allegiances and, as we shall see later, adopted new names. Where prudence required him to vacillate or temporize, Zolli did so. His political and maybe his theological views were clearly peripheral to his academic undertakings.

Study and research, especially Biblical research, were Zolli's great passion, his grand obsession. He was most contented when he was cloistered with his manuscripts and his books. Comforting the afflicted or counselling the troubled, i.e., playing the pastoral role, were not at all to his liking and were probably seen as unwelcome demands on Zolli's time better spent on scholarship.

Even before his arrival in Trieste, Zolli had written a number of journal articles in German and Italian. His scholarly production during the Trieste period was sizable. In 1922 he published an anthology entitled *Letture ebraiche*, which contained essays on a variety of topics ranging from Dostoyevsky and the Jews, to Chaim Weizmann and history, to Biblical poems in the *Risorgimento* poetry of Pascoli. 1924 was a particularly fruitful year for Zolli. Volume I of his *Tre milleni di storia*[50] appeared in print, as did his historical demographic study of the Jewish community of Trieste.[51] That year also marked the appearance of Zolli's manual on the introduction of the Hebrew language and literature which thousands of persons, adults and children, used to learn Hebrew with ease and pleasure. In 1932, *La vita religiosa ebraica*[52] was published, followed in three years by *Israele-Studi storico-religiosi*.[53] About *Il Nazareno*,[54] his less than dispassionate study of Jesus, published in the turbulent year of 1938, much more later in this volume.

For many years Zolli taught Hebrew and Semitic languages at the University of Padova where he enjoyed an enthusiastic following and lectured widely to non-Jewish audiences. By all accounts, he was much more involved with his students than with his coreligionists. Some of his students, including a number who were ordained as priests, remained friendly with Zolli until his death. In his 1954 memoirs, Zolli asserted that some of his former pupils subsequently confided to him that even "at that time they were remembering me in their holy Masses, asking God . . . for my conversion."[55]

There is little doubt that Zolli was more highly regarded by Catholics than by his fellow Jews in Trieste. He was personally close to Luigi Fogar, the Bishop of Trieste and Capodistria who would later confirm him in Rome.

In the late 1920s and 1930s, as an economically depressed and jingoist Europe moved inexorably toward the abyss of World War II, Zolli, a non-Italian living among Italians, a Jew largely isolated from his own people, in his insecurity may have undergone an identity crisis. In 1933, he legally changed his surname from Zoller to Zolli to reaffirm his identification with his adopted homeland.

It has also been stated that from time to time Zolli employed various first names as alternatives to Israele. For example, at least once he authored an article in an Italian scholarly journal on religion as "Italo Zoller." Adoption of Italo as a Christian name was often an expression of chauvinism in the Mussolini era. When he forwarded an offprint of the article to the library of what is today the Hebrew Union College-Jewish Institute of Religion, Zolli crossed out Italo and substituted Israele in its place.[56] Was this another example of his "chameleonism" at work?

Ignazio, which was the baptismal name of Loyola, the Basque founder of the Jesuit order of which Zolli was enamored, is another given name that the Chief Rabbi is reported to have used,[57] but the proof here is very flimsy. In a long article on Italy which appeared in the 1941 edition of the *Universal Jewish Encyclopedia*, there is a reference to "Prof. Ignazio Zolli, former chief rabbi of Trieste."[58] However, the *Universal Jewish Encyclopedia* entry on Zolli himself gives his first name as Israele.[59]

One critic of Zolli's has written that "in 1932 he took the name of Antonio in honor of St. Antonio, the patron saint of Padua, on the occasion of his 7th centenary."[60] Here too the evidence is very skimpy. Inexplicably, two *New York Times* articles published in the summer of 1944 identified the Chief Rabbi as "Anton."[61] A 1945 biographical sketch accompanying an article of his in a Catholic publication describes him as "Israele Anton Zolli, former chief Rabbi of Rome." Yet the author of the piece is listed on the title page as Eugenio Zolli.[62]

It is curious that not one of the surviving Trieste Jews, some of whom knew him quite well, can recall Zolli ever using Antonio, Anton, or for that matter, Italo or Ignazio. Is it possible that the Chief Rabbi and the professor, in a sense lived emotionally separate lives, one in the Jewish sphere, the other in a Catholic milieu?

His commitment to Judaism which, for decades was probably less than steadfast, may well have become even more tenuous in the late 1930s when Mussolini's racial laws rendered Jewish existence increasingly precarious. In early 1938, in an atmosphere of burgeoning racism following the Ethiopian war, the Italian dictator resigned himself to Italy's subservience to Nazi Germany and its deification of race. Press and radio criticism of the Jews were escalated and the July 14 Manifesto of the Racial Scientists laid the groundwork for the anti-Semitic legislation soon to be enacted. That "scientific" document declared that the Jews were not part of the pure Italian race which, it claimed, was Aryan in nature.[63]

Speaking in Trieste in September 1938, the sometime philo-Semitic Duce offered a defense of his new strident anti-Semitism. Race was the burning question of the moment, he asserted in language that might have originated in Berlin. Clear-cut racial consciousness was required in Italy. Moreover, international Jewry had, for sixteen years, proven to be an irreconcilable foe of Fascism.[64]

In the fall, the first race laws segregated Jewish children in public primary schools or banished them altogether from public secondary schools. November saw the adoption of new statutes, modeled on Hitler's Nuremberg Laws, which forbade Italian Jews to marry Christians or to employ Gentile domestics. Jews were ousted from the Fascist party. They were no longer welcome in the Italian military which theretofore boasted Jewish generals and admirals. Jewish ownership of land was restricted and Jews lost their jobs in government agencies and in the insurance and banking fields.[65]

While some previously acculturated Jews made a new psychological identification with Jewishness, others sought a respite from discrimination in flight or conversion. As many as six thousand opted to flee from the peninsula, and an equal number were baptized by the summer of 1943.[66] Formal conversion did not guarantee exemption from the draconian racial laws, but one could always hope for special treatment.

Conditions were certainly propitious for the repudiation of Judaism. Jews were not simply outsiders, aliens in their own land. They were now an endangered species.

Among the converts was the mother of Dan Vittorio Segre, author of the riveting *Memoirs Of A Fortunate Jew*. Segre's mother had been drawn to Catholicism for at least two decades, but her son's emigration to Palestine and the tensions generated by the anti-Jewish laws precipitated a crisis: ". . . the world crumbled around my parents, my mother found herself once again isolated and unprepared to face events greater than herself."[67]

Another convert was Roberto Melli, the painter of "Il Pastore" and other oils. A few years after publication of the race laws he, too, abjured his faith.

Zolli followed neither the path of emigration nor of conversion although he was in a particularly vulnerable position. Foreign-born Jews who had become citizens after 1919 had had their citizenship revoked by the 1938 anti-Semitic Laws. In Zolli's case, the Prefect of Trieste had stripped him of his Italian citizenship by decree in May 1939, and the state had rejected him as Chief Rabbi because he was technically a Polish national.

According to his secretary, in his Trieste phase, suffering at the hands of an unappreciative Jewish community, Zolli made some personal identification with the Christ-figure. He kept a photograph of himself in his office. When his wife commented that he looked Christ-like in the photograph, he did not disagree.[68] Persecution under the racial laws may have deepened his identification with Christ. It is known that in parts of his 1938 study of Jesus, Zolli came across more as a worshiper than as a neutral, detached scholar. Furthermore, his overly long but learned sermons delivered just before his departure for Rome reportedly included the kind of language more readily associated with Christianity than with Judaism.[69] Under the pressure of deteriorating circumstances, Zolli may have been emotionally scuttled. At the same time, he may have been theologically adrift. If he was not a crypto-Catholic, Zolli was certainly moving in that direction, but even he may not have been able to envision the extraordinary trajectory his future life would follow.

In any case, he opted to remain a rabbi and to exchange the chief rabbinate in Trieste for the more prestigious post as spiritual leader of Rome's Jews. Perhaps it was fitting that his last correspondence with the elders in Trieste dealt with financial matters inasmuch as it had been money that often put them at sword's point.

On 10 December 1939, the president of the Trieste community wrote somewhat accusingly to Zolli that it seemed that the outgoing Chief Rabbi had been unable to distribute some five hundred lire which had been placed in his hands by one Eduardo Breitner for the benefit of poor families. Zolli was requested to either return that sum or to account for its disbursement.[70] Later in the month, Zolli formally tendered his resignation and requested severance pay. One day later, the Jewish council met and approved the final financial arrangements. The president officially accepted his resignation and so notified Zolli.[71] Unverified rumor has it that Zolli, in his farewell homily in Trieste, tactlessly but typically told his congregants, "Finally I leave you."[72]

Whether the anecdote is true or not, Zolli was certainly pleased to end what had been a misalliance, a mutually unsatisfying relationship with the Jews of Trieste. At best, it had been a marriage of convenience. His new relationship with the Jews of Rome would prove even more loveless, and the 1945 divorce would be of seismic proportions.

Notes

1. See, Mario Toscano, "The Jews in Italy from the Risorgimento to the Republic," in *Gardens and Ghettos: The Art of Jewish Life in Italy.* Catalogue of an Exhibition held at the Jewish Museum of New York 1989–1990, edited by Vivian B. Mann (Berkeley: University of California Press, 1989), especially pp. 25–32.
2. For general histories on the Jews of Italy, see: Cecil Roth, *The History of the Jews in Italy* (Philadelphia: The Jewish Publication Society of America, 1946); Attilio Momigliano, *Storia degli ebrei in Italia* (Torino: Einaudi, 1963); Luciano Tas, *Storia degli ebrei italiani* (Roma: Newton Compton editori, 1987); Gina Formiggini, *Stella d'Italia Stella di David: Gli ebrei dal Risorgimento alla Resistenza* (Milano: Mursia, 1970); David Ruderman, "At the Intersection of Cultures: The Historical Legacy of Italian Jewry," in *Gardens and Ghettos,* pp. 1–23.
3. There were approximately 45,000 Italian Jews at the end of the 1930s. Demography was surely one factor in minimizing anti-Jewish sentiment in Italy as it was elsewhere, in Denmark for example. Historians do not agree about the role of Jews in Italy's economy and its relation to the fact that Judeophobia was of secondary or even tertiary importance. Andrew Canepa points out that Jews were visible in journalism, insurance, and textiles, but there was no Italian Rothschild symbolizing Jewish financial hegemony. Canepa argues that Italy's tardy involvement in the Industrial Revolution was of utmost importance in explaining the low level of Jew-hatred: " . . . the damage to the material position and social status of the lower middle classes, occasioned elsewhere by monopolistic concentration in the closing decades of the last century, was considerably delayed on the Italian peninsula." In the rural, underdeveloped agricultural *Mezzogiorno*, Jews were rarely seen and often unknown. See Andrew Canepa, "Christian-Jewish Relations in Italy from Unification to Fascism." Unpublished paper presented to the Conference on "Italians and Jews: Rescue and Aid During The Holocaust," Boston University, 6 and 7 November 1986.
4. Prior to 1938, Mussolini himself was wont to distinguish Italian Fascism from Hitler's Nazism on the grounds that the former was free of the anti-Semitism so dominant in the latter. Mario Toscano reports that: "In the 1932 interview with the journalist, Emilio Ludwig, published by Mondadori, Mussolini confirmed the full integration of Jews into Italian society, the nonexistence of anti-Semitism in the country . . . " Mario Toscano, *The Jews in Italy* p. 37.
5. For an interesting personal narrative and historical overview of Jews in the Piedmont region, see: Dan Vittorio Segre, *Memoirs of a Fortunate Jew* (New York: Dell Publishing, 1988), especially chapters 1–4.
6. See: Emily Braun, "From Risorgimento to the Resistance: A Century of Jewish Artists in Italy," in *Gardens and Ghettos,* pp. 137–189; and H. Stuart Hughes,

Prisoners of Hope: The Silver Age of the Italian Jews 1924–1974 (Cambridge: Harvard University Press, 1983).

7. Toscano, "The Jews in Italy," p. 25.
8. Eugenio Zolli, *Before the Dawn: Autobiographical Reflections* (New York: Sheed and Ward, 1954), chapter 1.
9. Johanna Pick Margulies, telephone interview, 2 June 1988. A niece of the eminent rabbi, Ms. Margulies lives in Florence.
10. Zolli, *Before the Dawn,* p. 63.
11. Matrimonial Records of the Jewish Community of Trieste 1913–1925.
12. Rabbi Elia Richetti, personal interview, Trieste, 25 May 1988. Rabbi Richetti, the current Chief Rabbi of Trieste, is the grandson of Rabbi Friedenthal.
13. Nives Castelbolognese, personal interview, Trieste, 24 May 1988. All male offspring born to Jewish parents are expected to be circumcised on the eighth day following birth. However, Jewish religious law permits the postponement of the *brit* or circumcision where the infant is weak and ill and performance of the rite would be hazardous. Along with most Jews in Trieste, Laura Erbsen was married by Zolli. The year was 1935. She has described him as strange, cold, removed, a prima donna who felt he was God. He had no affection for children, according to Erbsen, who recalls the Chief Rabbi yelling at a group of youngsters because supposedly they had no respect for the sanctity of the temple. Laura Erbsen, personal interview, New York, 14 March 1988.
14. Mario Stock, personal interview, Trieste, 31 May 1988. The community leader in question was Riccardo Leipziger.
15. Silvia Suadi Volpi, personal interview, Trieste, 30 May 1988.
16. Clementina Ianni, personal interview, Trieste, 26 May 1988; Giorgio Voghera, personal interview, Trieste, 25 May 1988; Suadi Volpi interview 30 May 1988; Stock interview, 31 May 1988.
17. Ianni interview, 26 May 1988.
18. Guido Spiegel, personal interview, Trieste, 24 May 1988.
19. Stock interview, 31 May 1988.
20. Mario Stock, *Nel segno di Geremia: Storia della comunità israelitica di Trieste dal 1200* (Udine: Istituto Per L'Enciclopedia Del Friuli - Venezia Giulia: 1979).
21. Trieste Synagogue Files, 1928, Letter from Zolli to the Presidency, 18 December 1928.
22. Ibid., letter from J. Capi to Zolli, 20 December 1928.
23. Ibid., letter from Zolli to the Presidency, 27 December 1928.
24. Ibid., 1931, Letters from Fraternità' Israelitica Di Misericordia to Giacomo Seppilli, 21 September 1931 and Alberto Levi to Zolli, 22 September 1931. In this clash Zolli had the support of the Fraternità which sharply criticized Levi.
25. Ibid., 1934, letters from Mario Calimani to Zolli, 29 June 1934 and Mario Calimani to the President, 13 June 1934.
26. Ibid., letter from Zolli to Carlo Morpurgo, 25 May 1934.
27. Ibid., letter from Morpurgo to Zolli, 8 June 1934.
28. Ibid., letter from Zolli to Morpurgo, 10 June 1934.
29. He was accused of joining the Fascist party. See Newman, *A "Chief Rabbi"* . . . , p. 77. This charge was later repeated by Rabbi Gerald Raiskin in a sermon, "Story Of A Convert," delivered at the Stephen Wise Free Synagogue in New York City, 9 April 1954. In contrast, Zolli was credited with being anti-Fascist by

one writer. See Dan Kurzman, *The Race for Rome* (Garden City: Doubleday, 1975), p. 54.

30. Newman, *A "Chief Rabbi . . ."*, p. 77.
31. Raiskin sermon, pp. 2–3.
32. *Il Piccolo Di Trieste*, 8 October 1935. One vitriolic critic later said that Zolli's language was even more objectionable: "He hailed Il Duce and sent hearty congratulations to the 'heroic brave sons of Italy, who are fighting for the glory of the Fatherland in the name of civilization against savages and contemptible enslavement'." See A. S. E. Yahuda, "The Conversion of a 'Chief Rabbi'," *The Jewish Forum* (September 1945): 174.
33. *Il Piccolo Di Trieste*, 8 October 1935.
34. Trieste Synagogue Files, 1935, letter from Zolli to Carlo Perusino, 17 December 1935.
35. Ibid., letter from Felice di L. Ravenna to President of the Trieste Jewish Community, 10 December 1935.
36. *Il Piccolo Di Trieste,* 19 December 1935.
37. Trieste Synagogue Files, 1936, Letter from Riccardo Curiel to the Union of Italian Jewish Communities, 11 November 1936.
38. Ibid., 1935, letter from Giacomo Seppilli to Guido Liuzzi, President of the Jewish Community of Torino, 21 January 1935.
39. Ibid. For example see letter from Zolli to Carlo Perusino, 11 December 1935. In Zolli's letter to Perusino of 17 December 1935 the Chief Rabbi sent his "most distinct Fascist greetings."
40. Zuccotti has written that throughout Italy twelve hundred professors signed. Only twelve refused, three of whom were Jews. All who refused lost their jobs. See Susan Zuccotti, *The Italians and the Holocaust: Persecution, Rescue and Survival* (New York: Basic Books, Inc., 1987), p. 259.
41. One who knew Zolli very well in his Trieste phase has asserted that privately the Chief Rabbi was critical of *La Nostra Bandiera*, a Jewish pro-Fascist, anti-Zionist publication, Speigel interview, 24 May 1988. The precise nature of the relationship between Zolli and Mussolini is unclear. Zolli did tell rabbi Morris N. Kertzer of the United States military that he had protested to Il Duce against the vandalism perpetuated against the synagogue in Trieste (1938). A furious Mussolini supposedly hurled imprecations: "The Nazi Swine! I have always said that when you scratch a German, you get a barbarian." Jacob Hochman Papers, Statement on Zolli by Rabbi Morris N. Kertzer (1945).
42. Israele Zoller, *Letture Ebraiche* (Trieste: Libreria Editrice-Treves Zanichelli, 1922), pp. 72–73.
43. Ibid., *In Memorie Di Ahad Ha-Am* (Trieste: "La Sera," 1927), pp. 7–9.
44. *Il Piccolo Di Trieste*, 11 and 12 and *le Popola D. Trieste*, 12 July 1934.
45. Zuccotti, *The Italians and the Holocaust,* p. 32.
46. Meir Michaelis, *Mussolini and the Jews: German-Italian Relations and the Jewish Question in Italy,* 1922–1945 (Oxford: The Clarendon Press, 1978), pp. 85–87.
47. Joseph B. Schechtman, *Fighter and Prophet: The Vladimir Jabotinsky Story—The Last Years* (New York: Thomas Yoseloff, 1961) p. 550. Jabotinsky saw Italy as a counterpoise, an alternative to Britain as a Mediterranean power and as an ally in his Zionist struggle. Also see Renzo de Felice, *Storia degli ebrei italiani sotto il fascisimo*. (Roma: Einaudi, 1961), pp. 195–203.

48. In 1903, at a time when Palestine was under Ottoman domination and therefore unavailable to the Jews, the British government offered the fledgling Zionist movement an opportunity to establish a Jewish colony in East Africa. The proffered land was in the British East Africa Protectorate, later known as Kenya, but for various reasons is mistakenly situated in neighboring Uganda by Jewish scholars. By 1905 both the British and the Zionists agreed to abandon the project. See Robert G. Weisbord, *Africa Zion: The Attempt to Establish a Jewish Colony in the East Africa Protectorate 1903–1905*. (Philadelphia: The Jewish Publication Society of America, 1968.)
49. Eugenio Zolli, *Christus* (Roma: Casa Editrice A.V.E., 1946), p. 181.
50. Israele Zoller, *Tre milleni di storia* (Firenze: Israel, 1924).
51. Ibid., *La comunita' israelitica di Trieste: Studio di demografia storica* (Ferrara: Casa Editrice, 1924).
52. Ibid., *La vita religiosa Ebraica* (Trieste: Tip. Sociale, 1932).
53. Ibid., *Israele: Studi storico-religiosi* (Udine: 1st delle Ediz Accademiche, 1935).
54. Ibid., *Il Nazareno: Studi di esegesi neotestamentaria alla luce dell' aramaico del pensiero rabbinico* (Udine: Istituto Delle Edizioni Accademiche, 1938).
55. Zolli, *Before the Dawn*, p. 75.
56. Italo Zoller, "A testimonianza per loro," Estratto da *Ricerche Religiose* Vol. 5, N.5.(n.d.).
57. Newman, *A "Chief Rabbi,"* p. 89.
58. Isaac Landman (ed.), *The Universal Jewish Encyclopedia* (New York: The Universal Jewish Encyclopedia Inc., 1941) Vol. 5, 639.
59. Ibid., (1943), vol. 10, 672.
60. Yahuda, "The Conversion of a 'Chief Rabbi,' " p. 175.
61. *New York Times,* 17 June 1944 and 27 July 1944.
62. Eugenio Zolli, "The Status of the State of Israel," *The Catholic World,* Vol. 169 (August 1949): 326. In the *Catholic Periodical Index* (1943–1948) Anton is given as Zolli's middle name. In Volume 3 of the *Guide to Catholic Literature* (1944–1948) he is listed as Israele Anton Zolli. Anton was dropped in Volume 4 (1948-1951).
63. Zuccotti, *The Italians and The Holocaust,* p. 35.
64. S. William Halperin, *Mussolini and Italian Fascism* (Princeton: D. Van Nostrand Company, Inc., 1964), pp. 174–175. For a discussion of the anti-Semitic campaign that led to the passage of the anti-Semitic laws and Mussolini's key role in that campaign see Chapter V of Michaelis, *Mussolini and the Jews* and Michaelis, "The Attitude of the Fascist Regime to Jews in Italy," *Yad Vashem Studies,* IV (1960); 7–41. For many years Il Duce who harbored hostile views toward Zionism and Jewish finance was pro-Jewish in his public utterances.
65. Zuccotti, The Italians And The Holocaust, p. 36.
66. Ibid. and Salvatore Jona, "Contributo allo studio degli ebrei in Italia durante il fascismo" *Gli ebrei in Italia durante il fascismo* (ed.) Guido Valabrega. *Quaderni del Centro di Documentazione Ebraica Contemporanea Sezione Italiana* (Milano: 1962), p. 20. A tendency to abandon Judaism was discernible before 1938 and not just among ordinary Jews. For example, Margherita Sarfatti, the celebrated art critic and biographer of Mussolini, who was also the Duce's mistress, became a Catholic ten years before the adoption of the Racial Laws.
67. Dan Vittorio Segre, *Memoirs Of a Fortunate Jew: An Italian Story* (New York: A Laurel Book, 1988), p. 44.

68. Ianni Interview, 26 May 1988.
69. Stock interview, 31 May 1988.
70. Trieste Synagogue Files, 1939, Letter from President E. Canarutto to Zolli, 10 December 1939.
71. Trieste Synagogue Files, 1939, Letter from President E. Canarutto to Zolli, 27 December 1939.
72. Richetti interview, 25 May 1988.

CHIEF RABBI ZOLLI WITH RABBI MAYER BERMAN (*left*)
AND RABBI JACOB HOCHMAN (*right*).

6

Chief Rabbi Zolli and the Holocaust

As noted in chapter 5, Zolli's legal position as a Jew and as a spiritual leader of Jews was precarious even before his arrival in the city on the Tiber. In January 1943, despite misgivings about the Chief Rabbi, the Jewish community in Rome approved funds to meet the sizeable expenses Zolli was incurring in order to gain recognition as an Italian citizen and as a Chief Rabbi. By then he was already embroiled in internecine controversy.[1]

Almost from the beginning of his tenure as Chief Rabbi in Rome, there was tension between Zolli and members of the *giunta* or Jewish council and, in particular, acrimony in Zolli's relationship with Ugo Foà, the president of the Jewish community. There was strife within the Chief Rabbi's office as early as 1942. In March of that year Zolli was sufficiently agitated to write to Foà that correspondence addressed to him was being opened by others in violation of his right to "epistolary secrecy."[2] Feuding between Zolli and Anselmo Colombo, a member of the *giunta*, bubbled to the surface in April when Zolli complained that Colombo was giving orders in the Chief Rabbi's office and was personally interrogating people who had come to see the rabbi. Colombo was fomenting trouble, was guilty of making obscene gestures, and of maligning the rabbi. On one occasion, the rabbi had to eject Colombo from his office. Zolli dubbed Colombo "*malvagio*" (wicked).[3] For his part, Colombo bemoaned the fact that he had been mistreated in the presence of rabbinical students, of officiants, and even in the presence of the doorman. Enumerating his grievances to Foà, Colombo alleged that Zolli had used vulgar language and had been insolent to the secretary and to the *parnas* (leader or president of the congregation) of the Spanish synagogue. Colombo foresaw a danger to the community and requested a special meeting of the *giunta* to find some recourse. The fundamental problem, he asserted, was Zolli's character.[4] In retrospect, it seems clear that these altercations were a harbinger of future conflicts which would culminate in Zolli's baptism.

Zolli's difficulties were not only with the community's leaders. Almost from the outset, rapport between Zolli and most of his congregants was extremely poor. With few exceptions, they viewed him as icy, distant, reserved, aloof, haughty, and unapproachable. He has been described by many in the community as a not particularly sympathetic figure, a person who had great difficulty communicating with people, adults and youngsters alike. It was Trieste all over again. Zolli conceded in retrospect, "I know how to love better than how to make myself loved."[5]

Although Zolli the scholar was respected, Zolli the man and Zolli the rabbi were not. It was the opinion of an American army chaplain, Rabbi Jacob Hochman, who first met Zolli in the summer of 1944, that "whatever warm and genuine feeling there was in him was for books and their scientific study." Hochman found him "cold and uninspiring."[6] Zolli's younger daughter, Miriam, in a conversation with Hochman and his British counterpart, Rabbi Meyer Berman, asserted that her father never belonged in a synagogue as a rabbi. Rather, his place was with books in an academic hall.[7]

From the very first, Hochman was taken aback by Zolli's deprecation of what he termed the ignorant, rude masses that supposedly constituted the bulk of his community. His learning was wasted on them and, furthermore, they showed him bad manners.[8] There seems little doubt that Zolli saw his congregation on the whole as uncultured and, consequently, undeserving of an illustrious scholar such as himself. It was reported that in October 1942 he told a plenary meeting of the Jewish council, "I consider it an honor for the community of Rome to have me as Chief Rabbi and I do not consider it an honor for me to be Chief Rabbi of the community."[9]

In the aftermath of Zolli's conversion, the community conducted an investigation into his performance as Chief Rabbi. Testimony was taken from sundry individuals who had known Zolli, worked for or with him or studied under him at the rabbinical college.[10] Much of the sharpest criticism came from former rabbinical students. Several faulted Zolli's deportment during religious services, funerals, and circumcisions. They claimed that during worship he slept, read profane, that is, non-religious books, talked, sucked hard candies, or cleaned his glasses with prayer shawls when he should have been saying his prayers. They testified that he tried to accelerate the praying, or departed before the services were actually finished. Furthermore, they accused Zolli of chiding officiants for wailing during prayers and rebuked him for deriding a number of traditions of Judaism as superstitious. One former student remembered that Zolli called the *mezzuzah* (i.e., the small case containing a parchment inscribed with Biblical verses traditionally affixed to a doorpost) a pagan symbol and disparaged the *shofar* which is sounded on Rosh Hashanah as a "little trumpet" which was breaking his eardrums.[11] More than one critic remembered that Zolli often used to urinate in the washbasin located in the rabbi's dressing room instead of walking up the stairs to the bathrooms.[12] If the charge is accurate, the rabbi's practice may well have been explained by his heart condition, but after Zolli's conversion, his former students and congregants were disinclined to be charitable in their analysis of his character.

Laxity in religious observance was a recurring theme in the indictment of Zolli. It was said that he commemorated the dead during a prohibited period and allowed women in that area of the temple reserved for men. He was inclined to offer rational explanations for "miracles" recounted in the Old Testament, e.g., the parting of the Red Sea when Moses led the children of Israel out of Egyptian bondage. Some of his beliefs and practices were probably closer to those which we today associate with Reform Judaism, a movement which did not officially exist in Italy.[13] It is not inconceivable that Lelio Vittorio Valobra, a Jewish attorney from Genoa, was on the mark when he described Zolli to a Dutch journalist as a nonbeliever. Zolli was ". . . an extremely learned man but basically he was an atheist . . . He was a man intensely interested in religion, but not a religious man."[14] Of course, Valobra's assessment is extremely difficult to reconcile with Zolli's own view of himself as a spiritual and mystical soul.

For his part, Zolli also insisted that he had fought against the contamination of authentic Judaism. He explained some of his religious differences with his congregants by saying that the Judaism practiced in Italy had been tainted by superstitious customs borrowed from Italian Catholicism. One bizarre practice so offended him that he thundered against it in the synagogue: on the *yahrzeit*, or anniversary of the date of death of a parent, relative, or friend, the faithful would trek to the cemetery and sacrifice a chicken at the gravestone. Speaking to an American rabbi right after the liberation of Rome, Zolli said that his opposition to this primitive custom had alienated some members of his congregation.[15]

During the inquest, Cesare Tagliacozzo testified that Zolli made several speeches in which he virtually exhorted his students to abandon the rabbinical profession, arguing that it afforded one no satisfaction as rabbis were not held in great esteem.[16] Zolli was also attacked for demeaning rabbinical students in public. One, Angelo Sonnino, observed that Zolli jokingly referred to future rabbis and cantors as ''cardinals'' and nicknamed each of them with the cognomen of a famous prince of the Catholic Church.[17] Zolli's humor is ironic in light of his conversion, as is the following incident. After the liberation of Rome, Zolli had a discussion with Rabbi David Panzieri in front of the holy ark where the books of the law are kept. At one point Zolli cried out, ''My Jesus, save me,'' a very strange choice of language for a rabbi.[18]

By June 1944, when the Nazis had fled before the advancing Allies, the atmosphere in Jewish Rome was permeated by bitterness and recrimination. Zolli had become persona non grata mainly because of what he had done or failed to do during the Nazi occupation of the Italian capital. By April 2 the council had dismissed Zolli as Chief Rabbi.

From the perspective of Ugo Foà and many other Roman Jews, Zolli's actions had been completely reprehensible during the months of Nazi draconian rule. The Chief Rabbi had deserted his post and had become unreachable even before the threat was clearly delineated. As of 9 September 1943, the very day the Germans entered Rome following the Italian surrender to the Allies, Foà wrote that Zolli was not to be found.[19] Not only had he abandoned the faithful in their hour of danger, but he had allegedly failed to safeguard the sacred objects and cultural treasures of the library and college. Foà's scathing bill of particulars included the serious charge that Zolli had been concerned only with his personal safety and had contributed to the disorientation, confusion, and dismay of his brethren. Foà acknowledged that Zolli was in jeopardy, but so were others who did not vanish. He later cited as a case in point the tragic fate of Commendatore Giuseppe Pardo Roques, former president of the Jewish community in Pisa. Roques lived openly and was unmolested by the Nazis until August 1944 when he was murdered by the S.S.[20] Foà's implication was that is was preferable for Jewish communal leaders to die rather than disappear.

Zolli was to contend that he had no obligation to forfeit his life. To Herbert L. Matthews of the *New York Times*, Zolli quoted an old Roman proverb: ''First live, then worship God.''[21] Only the living could praise God as the proverb and a Biblical psalm point out.

It is noteworthy in this connection that during the entire time Rome was under the Nazi jackboot, Rabbi David Panzieri officiated alone at clandestine religious services which were held at the ''Tempietto,'' the little temple then situated on the Tiber Island. Undaunted by the Nazi menace, Panzieri walked openly through the streets of the ghetto.

In October it was Rabbi Panzieri, not Zolli, who appealed to the Holy Father to try to ameliorate conditions for Roman Jews who were en route to camps in Poland. During that horrendous episode Zolli continued to conceal himself.

Even when Zolli emerged from hiding following the liberation of Rome, he showed no interest in the faithful or the temple, according to Foà. He did not even inquire about the well-being of his congregants. He only asked for money to meet his personal needs. Specifically, Foà declared, he demanded stipends for the period when he was underground. Because of what the council interpreted as Zolli's defection and dereliction of duty, those funds were not forthcoming.[22]

Zolli defended his conduct by saying that as a Polish Jew he understood the Nazi menace better than the Roman Jewish leadership which might have believed that their ties to high-ranking Italian Fascists could protect them. Indeed, it is probably true that the Jews in Italy were psychologically unprepared for the catastrophe that was to befall them. Because of pervasive assimilation—they were virtually indistinguishable from Italian Catholics in language, dress, and manners—they found it difficult to conceive of themselves as second-class citizens inferior to their countrymen. As previously indicated, prior to 1938, when Mussolini implemented his anti-Semitic racial legislation, discrimination against Jews had been minimal, not at all comparable to that which was rampant in Eastern Europe in the late nineteenth and twentieth centuries. To Italian Jews, genocide was unimaginable.

But Zolli in the 1930s in Trieste had met Jewish refugees from Germany and they had impressed the reality of the Nazi peril on him. He came to appreciate the fact that the Jews would likely experience a bloodbath.[23] Zolli's behavior was determined at least in part by his awareness of the fate that had befallen other rabbis. He knew that the Chief Rabbi of Copenhagen had been deported, as had the Chief Rabbi of Florence. The Chief Rabbi of Milan had been forced to seek refuge in Switzerland, while the spiritual leader in Genoa, Rabbi Riccardo Pacifici, was beaten, tortured, and eventually sent to his death in Auschwitz.[24]

On this point at least one American rabbi later agreed with Zolli and took his overseas critics to task.

> Who is anyone sitting in a comfortable New York apartment to sit in judgment and suggest martyrdom? To my mind there is little sense to Kiddush Hashem [sacrificing one's life for God] unless it serves a useful purpose. Perhaps if a few more rabbis had not volunteered to march to the death chambers, European Jewry might not be so spiritually impoverished.[25]

Zolli's version of the events that unfolded in the autumn of 1943 is as follows. Because he truly understood the Nazi danger he recommended the total suppression of public Jewish functions, the closing of administrative offices, the dispersion of his co-religionists, the distribution of financial help to those in need, and the reduction of the community treasury to a shadow operation. However, those proposals were rejected by the lay Jewish leadership, Ugo Foà and Dante Almansi, president of the Union of Italian Jewish Communities.[26] With Rome under the dreaded swastika, Zolli compared himself with Jesus on the cross between two thieves. On the one side were the German persecutors and on the other the "Facist" Jewish leadership.

Zolli also made the extremely serious claim that he had strongly urged the destruction of the file cards which contained the names and addresses of donors to the Jewish community, lest that potentially lethal information fall into the murderous hands of the Nazis. But Foà failed to heed his warning and, according to Zolli, even placed the files at the disposal of the German occupiers, thus sealing the fate of Roman Jews when the ghetto roundup occurred on 16 October 1943.[27]

There has been much speculation about the possible source or sources of data used by the Nazis to identify Jews. Giacomo Debenedetti, for one, ruled out the idea that the information was culled from the archives of the Jewish community. He contended that, whereas the community rolls only included the names of contributors, the Nazi lists also included the names of Jews who had never contributed.[28] Census data which doomed ''citizens of the Hebrew race'' in Rome might have come from local Fascists or from Italian government sources in which case Zolli's accusation would have been unfounded.

On September 9, Zolli gave a speech in the Spanish temple and tried to make the gravity of the situation clear, but his words fell on deaf ears. That was his last public appearance for about ten months. Zolli later insisted that his continued public presence would only have spread an illusory sense of tranquility.[29]

For advice, an understandably anxious Zolli turned to the police who told him to make himself scarce as they could not guarantee his safety. One policeman told Zolli on that occasion that an hour after the Nazis marched into Prague they had killed the Chief Rabbi in the Czechoslovakian capital. Zolli claimed that several Jewish community leaders and people in touch with anti-Nazi partisans reproached him for remaining visible. Non-Jews did also. After all, the Gestapo was looking for him, and there was a three hundred thousand lire price on his head. In early October, Zolli's derelict apartment was plundered by two Nazi officers. Papers and books were impounded.[30] The Chief Rabbi's counsel to the Roman Jews over whom a sword of Damocles hung, was to scatter, to leave Rome or to find sanctuary in a convent.[31]

Zolli himself briefly hid in the houses of Jewish friends, but the crucial question is whether he was really incommunicado during that time. To counter Foà's accusations that he was unreachable, Zolli, in his autobiography, reprinted a letter from Ruggero DiSegni, an attorney who was councillor of the community and who is described as a friend of Foà's. DiSegni confirms the fact that at Zolli's request he notified the community that for direct contact with the Chief Rabbi they could telephone the home of Giorgio Fiorentino who was a young Jewish lawyer and a supporter of Zolli's.[32] Dr. Luigi Tagliacozzo, another Roman Jew, also testified that shortly after the Germans invaded Rome, a dishevelled Zolli arrived at his home. It was agreed that the Chief Rabbi would go to the house of a Dr. Angelo Anav where he remained for about fifteen days. Zolli authorized Luigi Tagliacozzo to confidentially communicate his whereabouts to Almansi, which he did.[33] Evidently, Zolli concluded that staying at the homes of fellow Jews was fraught with danger, and he soon relocated to the home of sympathetic Catholics, Amadeo Pierantoni and his family who were engaged in activities aimed at subverting the Nazis. They courageously stored arms and explosives at their premises and prepared flyers urging Italian and German military personnel to desert. Amedeo Pierantoni was both a staunch anti-Fascist and a Communist. His son, Luigi, a physician, was later martyred in the infamous Fosse Ardeatine massacre. To protect his benefactors, the Pierantonis, in the fall of 1943 Zolli had to give his word of honor not to let anyone know his whereabouts.[34] Hunted by the Nazis, Zolli was understandably petrified. Nilda Zaccharia, whose brother had married Zolli's daughter, Dora, recalls delivering a basket of food to the hiding place. Zolli, who had taught Jewish religion to Zaccaria in Trieste, was too frightened to show himself, and she left the food with someone else.[35]

Yet even then, Zolli later maintained, he labored to aid his beleaguered brethren. For example, he cited his role in the harrowing story of the fifty kilograms of gold which the Nazis extorted from the terrorized and helpless Jews of Rome in September, 1943. What are the facts about this much misunderstood incident?[36]

The gold scheme was certainly the brainchild of the German security police chieftain, S.S. Major Herbert Kappler. On September 26, Kappler, who was soon thereafter promoted to the rank of Lieutenant Colonel, summoned Dante Almansi and Ugo Foà to his office at 145 Via Tasso that served as both Gestapo headquarters and a jail in which enemies of the Third Reich were often detained and tortured.[37] There Kappler informed them that the Italian Jews as enemies of his government had to pay a tribute of fifty kilograms of gold which was to be used supposedly to buy new arms for the German army. Failure to pay that amount would result in the deportation of two hundred Jews, he warned, and the leaders had just two days in which to raise the levy.

They acted with alacrity. Word about the dire peril spread rapidly throughout the city and, in short order, a line of donors formed outside the Tempio Maggiore, the main synagogue and the place where the community's offices were located. Of course, most of those contributing gold objects were Roman Jews, denizens of the old ghetto or residents of the Trastevere region, but their ranks were augmented by altruistic Gentiles, including some clerics. The previously cited eyewitness to these events, Giacomo Debenedetti, has provided posterity with a moving description of those anonymous givers who were truly worthy of the name Christian:

> Wary, as if fearing rejection or as if intimidated in offering their gold to the rich Jews, several Aryans came forth. Embarrassed, they entered the designated locale adjacent to the synagogue not knowing if they should remove their hats or keep their heads covered as dictated by well-known Jewish ritual. Almost humbly, they asked if they could . . . if it was acceptable . . . if it was to the Community's liking.[38]

A goldsmith carefully weighed the precious objects that were offered by the Jewish and non-Jewish donors.

Years later Zolli claimed that upon hearing of the grave danger he gave his gold chain and five thousand lire. He had been informed, somewhat mistakenly, that the Jews had but twenty-four hours to raise the fifty kilograms or three hundred hostages would be seized.[39]

Zolli also stated that during these critical hours he slipped out of his haven and, at great personal risk, hurried to the Vatican to seek the Pope's assistance in raising the quota of gold. As told in his 1954 autobiography, Zolli travelled incognito as a Christian engineer whose task it was to inspect walls under construction in the Vatican. He was allegedly accompanied by Giorgio Fiorentino and, according to another account of the adventure, travelled with a Catholic friend as well.[40] At that juncture, Zolli had been told that the Jews had been able to raise only thirty-five kilograms. An additional fifteen kilograms were needed to satisfy the Nazi demand and to forestall a catastrophe.

When he reached the Vatican, Zolli went to see Bernardino Nogara, a layman and an architect, who served as head of the Treasury. From there, he went to the office of Luigi Cardinal Maglione, the Secretary of State, where he pleaded for help and offered himself as surety. "Since I am poor," he promised, "the Hebrews of the whole world will contribute to pay the debt."[41]

In his account of the events in question, Giorgio Fiorentino stated that he accompanied Zolli only as far as the main door of the Vatican. Zolli left him to speak to Nogara, who then went to consult Pius XII. Subsequently, Zolli told Fiorentino that they had received papal authorization for the fifteen kilogram loan which was to be repaid four years after the cessation of hostilities.[42] Zolli purportedly drew up a receipt and sent a letter to Foà apprising him of the details of the loan and offering to be the first hostage in case of a roundup.

In the end, however, because the collection at the synagogue exceeded the fifty kilograms, it was unnecessary for the Jews to borrow anything at all from the Vatican.[43] According to a document published by the Holy See itself, Zolli returned on September 28 to advise Nogara that the loan was not needed. For some inexplicable reason, Nogara in turn wrote to Cardinal Maglione that the fifteen kilograms had been obtained from "Catholic communities" which he did not identify.[44] They have never been identified.

Confusion has enveloped this episode of the gold ever since 1943. A front-page story in the *New York Times* of 17 October 1943 quoting a broadcast on Bari radio, reported that the Pontiff "had joined the Jewish community of Rome in paying a ransom of 50 kilograms of gold which the Germans demanded for the release of 100 Jewish hostages." The *Times* further misinformed its readers when it stated that Pius XII had "contributed a considerable amount." American military personnel who later occupied the capital city also subscribed to the legend of Vatican largesse. Captain Maurice Neufeld of the U.S. Army for instance, labored under the misconception that the Jews in Rome would have been killed "if it hadn't been for gold sent by the Pope."[45]

The inaccurate assertion that the Papacy actually contributed fifteen kilograms or more has been made for over forty years by writers eager to prove the Vatican's philo-Semitism during the Holocaust. In 1945, using the pseudonym "Jane Scrivener," a longtime American inhabitant of the Eternal City, wrote of the extortion that the Jews "appealed to the Pope, who helped them to complete the amount." Scrivener, a Catholic religious also wrongly stated that the Nazi authorities sent for Zolli personally and demanded that he procure "one million lire and fifty kilogrammes of gold." Much more recently, in *La Popessa,* the story of Sister Pascalina, the German-born nun who became housekeeper to and confidante of Pope Pius XII, the authors assert that the Jews turned to the Pope when they could not "acquire the gold." His Holiness did not fail them, readers are assured. Allegedly, in less than a day, the ransom was met through papal efforts. "With the Holy Father's permission Pascalina undertook the responsibility of having numbers of priceless holy vessels melted down to provide the required gold."[46]

Surely it is also disingenuous to imply that the Vatican gold was or would have been donated without expectation of repayment, when it was a *loan* not a gift that was approved. Furthermore, it is less than candid to state, as did Father Robert Leiber, that Pius XII "spontaneously" offered to make up the deficit for the Jews.[47] The gold was solicited by Zolli and also, independently, by Renzo Levi, President of Delasem[48] in conjunction with Dr. Adriano Ascarelli who were acting for the Jewish community. They approached a Padre Borsarelli, Vice Prior of the Convent of Missionaries of the Sacred Heart, who made contact with the Curia about the Jews' desperate need for a loan and who also received an affirmative reply.[49]

Of course, it is inconceivable that the Vatican authorities were unaware of the gold ultimatum issued by the Nazis to the Jews of Rome. All of Rome must have known. In fact, by September 27, the day after Kappler confronted the lay Jewish leadership, the Vatican was informed by Monsignor Antonino Arata that the Jews had to deliver fifty kilograms of gold by the following day.[50]

The drama of the gold collection was enacted virtually on the Pope's doorstep. Yet His Holiness did not take the initiative and seek out the Jewish leaders to proffer succor. They went to him. For the Holy See, it was hardly their finest display of Christian charity.

Roman Jews have often expressed skepticism about Zolli's putative role in the gold matter.[51] After the Nazi occupation ended, Ugo Foà, Zolli's bête noire, denied that he had ever received a note from the Chief Rabbi in which the latter assured the community of the Vatican's willingness to lend fifteen kilograms. Writing in July 1944, Foà would only admit that the rabbi's daughter, Miriam, verbally conveyed a vague promise of eventual help from the papacy. Foà emphatically denied that he had ever received an oral or a written communication from Zolli declaring his readiness to turn himself in as a hostage.

During the entire period of the Nazi persecution, Foà contended, he had received only one handwritten communication from the rabbi—a request in February 1944 for money.[52]

But the preponderance of evidence, notably the testimony of Giorgio Fiorentino and the published Vatican document previously cited, would seem to support Zolli on the gold ransom. Furthermore, an undated document in the Zolli file of the Rome synagogue concedes that Zolli had consulted Nogara and had received a guarantee from the chief of the Vatican Treasury that a loan of fifteen kilograms would be put at the Jews' disposal.

As we have already seen, the final act in the Roman Jewish tragedy was played out on 16 October 1943 when the Nazis besieged the ghetto and rounded up Jews who were quickly dispatched to Auschwitz. In the end Kappler got both the Jews and their gold.

As far as can be determined, except for his effort to solicit gold from the Vatican in September 1943, Zolli, unlike some of his rabbinical counterparts in the peninsula, remained in hiding until the Allies freed Rome from the Nazi yoke. Critics could make invidious distinctions between his conduct and the heroic, but ultimately fatal exploits of Rabbi Nathan Cassuto in Florence. Still in his early thirties in 1943, Cassuto, a distinguished physician and medical researcher as well as a rabbi, was captured by the Nazis, escaped, and then chose to again risk his life in the service of Jewish fugitives instead of simply going underground. Throwing caution to the winds, he formed a committee for the purpose of furnishing fraudulent papers, money, food and shelter, but was betrayed and, in 1945, murdered by the Nazis.[54] In contrast with Cassuto, Zolli pursued a safer, more prudent course of action, one which his detractors thought cowardly and egotistical. They would neither forgive nor forget. Their negative attitude toward Zolli would accelerate his departure from the Jewish world of his fathers.

Notes

1. Tempio Maggiore (Rome) Modern Archives, Zolli file, Letter from Pres. Aldo Ascoli to the Ministry of the Interior; 15 July 1940 and Verbal abstract of Minutes of the Council, 26 January 1943.
2. Zolli file, Zolli to Ugo Foà, 30 March 1942.
3. Ibid., Zolli to Ugo Foà, 30 April 1942.

4. Ibid., Anselmo Colombo to Ugo Foà, 12 June 1942.
5. Eugenio Zolli, *Before the Dawn* (New York: Sheed and Ward, 1954), p. 63.
6. Jacob Hochman Papers. Rabbi Jacob Hochman statement about the Zolli conversion (undated). This statement was made available to the authors by Mary Hochman, Rabbi Hochman's daughter.
7. Ibid.
8. Ibid.
9. Zolli file, statement by Ugo Foà, 12 October 1945.
10. Ibid., testimony by Sergio Sierra, 15 July 1945; Alfredo Ravenna, 25 July 1945; Angelo Sonnino, 12 July 1945; Settimo Di Castro, 12 July 1945; Cesare Eliseo, 26 July 1945; Marco Vivanti, 25 July 1945; Gino Moscati, 25 July 1945; Aldo Bises, 7 July 1945; Nello Pavoncello, 5 August 1945; Cesare Tagliacozzo, 5 August 1945; Mario Sed, 5 August 1945; and Luigi Tagliacozzo, 15 July 1945.
11. Ibid., Sonnino testimony, 12 July 1945, Di Castro testimony, 12 July 1945, and Eliseo testimony, 26 July 1945.
12. Ibid., Moscati testimony, 25 July 1945, Sonnino testimony, 12 July 1945 and Di Castro testimony, 12 July 1945.
13. It has been said that the "Roman Jewish community is Orthodox; Roman Jews are not. They do not quarrel with the orthodoxy, but merely do not practice it, and do not practice it with aplomb." Chaim Bermant, "Rome Report," *Present Tense* (Winter 1978), p. 16.
14. Quoted in Sam Waagenaar, *The Pope's Jews* (Open Court, La Salle, Illinois: A Library Press Book, 1974), p. 447. Valobra was also the national director of Delasem and vice-president of the Union of Italian Jewish Communities.
15. Kertzer, *With an H*, pp. 65–66.
16. Zolli file, Cesare Tagliacozzo testimony, 5 August 1945.
17. Ibid., Sonnino testimony, 12 July 1945.
18. Ibid., Cesare Eliseo testimony, 26 July 1945 and Sergio Sierra testimony, 15 July 1945.
19. La Comunità Israelitica di Roma, *Ottobre 1943: Cronaca di un'infamia* (Roma, 1961), p 31. It is noteworthy that Zolli's conduct was later compared with that of Dante Almansi who concealed himself after deportations began but who remained in touch with those who were helping the Jews with food, money, ration cards, and counsel. See *Israel*, 13 January 1949.
20. Statement by Ugo Foà, 12 October 1945 and Susan Zuccotti, *The Italians And The Holocaust: Persecution, Rescue and Survival* (New York: Basic Books, Inc., Publishers, 1987), p. 198.
21. *New York Times*, 9 July 1944.
22. Statement by Ugo Foà, 12 October 1945.
23. Zolli, *Before the Dawn*, p. 142.
24. Emanuele Pacifici (ed.), *Commemorazione di Riccardo Pacifici—Rabbino Capo di Genova vittima delle persecuzioni naziste* (Genova, 1984) and Emanuele Pacifici, Personal Interview, 21 May 1987. Emanuele Pacifici, the son of the murdered Chief Rabbi, was himself almost mortally wounded in an attack in the Tempio Maggiore carried out by Arab assailants in 1982.
25. Hochman papers, Letter from Morris N. Kertzer to Jacob Hochman, 26 December 1945.
26. Zolli file, Statement by Israele Zolli, 21 June 1944. The statement was actually a letter. However, it is not clear if the recipient of the letter was Foà. Almansi's son,

Renato, has vehemently denied that his father failed to see the danger that loomed ahead. He recalls that his mother frequently quoted her husband to the effect that "the circle is getting tighter." Renato who fled Italy in 1939 insists that his father "put the Union's money and important papers in a safe place." Mass flight for the Jews was not feasible after the Nazi occupation commenced: ". . . until the deportation actually started the practical and psychological circumstances for a successful dispersal of the Jews of Rome did not exist." See Renato J. Almansi, "Dante Almansi: President of the Union of Italian Jewish Communities—November 13, 1939 to October 1, 1944" Unpublished manuscript (15 August 1971), pp. 35–36.

27. Zolli, *Before the Dawn*, pp. 154–155.
28. Giacomo DeBenedetti, *16 ottobre 1943 Otto ebrei* (Roma: Editori Riuniti, 1978), p. 57. Translation by Wallace Sillanpoa.
29. Ibid.
30. Meir Michaelis, *Mussolini and the Jews: German-Italian Relations and the Jewish Question in Italy 1922–1945* (New York: Oxford University Press, 1978) p. 358.
31. Zolli, *Before the Dawn*, p. 148.
32. Ibid., p. 205.
33. Luigi Tagliacozzo testimony, 15 July 1945.
34. Zolli statement, 21 June 1944. After the arrest of Luigi Pierantoni, Zolli found sanctuary with another Catholic family, the Falconieris.
35. Nilda Zaccaria, personal interview, Trieste, 27 May 1988. Zaccaria says that someone other than Zolli gave her the Chief Rabbi's address.
36. The gold episode has been recounted in many places. See for example, Robert Katz, *Black Sabbath: A Journey Through a Crime Against Humanity*, (Toronto: The Macmillan Company, 1969), Part I.
37. Arrigo Paladini, *Via Tasso: Carcere nazista* (Roma: Istituto Poligrafico E Zecca Dello Stato, 1986).
38. Debenedetti, *16 ottobre*, p. 36.
39. Zolli, *Before the Dawn*, pp. 159–160. In a declaration printed in the autobiography, Miriam Zolli says that she turned in "twelve grams of gold and the sum of five thousand lire" as a personal offering from her father (pp. 207–208).
40. The autobiographical narrative makes no mention of the Catholic friend, but in a 1950 interview he is referred to by Zolli. See the Israeli newspaper, *Maariv*, 9 June 1950.
41. Zolli, *Before the Dawn*, p. 206.
42. Zolli file, Giorgio Fiorentino testimony, 16 July 1945. Fiorentino's declaration published in the appendix to Zolli's autobiography states different terms for the Vatican loan. In the 1954 account Fiorentino wrote of a loan of "fifteen kilograms of gold *to be returned without limit of time* in equivalent gold or currency, on the simple guarantee of a receipt signed by the Head Rabbi and by the President of the Israelite Community of Rome" [emphasis ours]. See pp. 206–207 in Zolli, *Before the Dawn*.
43. One account of the ransom episode credits Zolli with playing an active and crucial role in collecting gold objects from members of the Jewish community to meet the German demand. This is pure fiction. See Leboucher, *Incredible Mission*, p. 131.
44. Letter from Nogara to Cardinal Maglione, 29 September 1943 in *Actes Et Documents Du Saint Siège Relatifs À La Seconde Guerre Mondiale*. Vol. 9, (Libreria Editrice Vaticana), 1975, p. 494. The erroneous notion that Catholic

communities provided the fifteen kilograms in the end has been repeated. See P. Dezza, ''Eugenio Zolli: da Gran Rabbino a testimone di Cristo (1881–1956),'' *La Civilità Cattolica'*, I Quaderno 3136 (February 21, 1981): 341.

45. Letter from Maurice Neufeld to Hinda Neufeld, 12 July 1944 in *Library of Congress*, Maurice Neufeld Papers, container 5.
46. Jane Scrivener, *Inside Rome With The Germans* (New York: The Macmillan Co., 1945), p. 31. Paul I. Murphy and R. Rene Arlington, *La Popessa* (New York: Warner Books, 1983) p. 207. Also see Anthony Rhodes, *The Vatican in the Age of the Dictators 1922–1945*. (London: Hodder and Stoughton, 1973), p. 341. The Zolli entry in the *New Catholic Encyclopedia*, Vol. XIV, p. 1128 also says that the Vatican provided financial assistance to meet the German demand as does Joseph L. Lichten, ''Pius XII and the Jews, ''*The Catholic Mind*, vol. 57, no. 1142 (March–April 1959), p. 161. A hagiographic account of Pacelli's life and career extols the pontiff for his ''most Christ-like succor of those of an alien faith'' in having sacred objects melted down to produce the gold demanded of the Jews. See Hatch and Walshe, *Crown of Glory*, p. 168. For still another declaration that the ''pope supplemented the inadequate Jewish holdings with gold from the Vatican,'' see Leonidas Hill, ''The Vatican Embassy of Ernst Von Weizsäcker, 1943-1945,'' The *Journal of Modern History* Vol. 39 No. 2 (June 1967), p. 147. A biographer of Paul VI writes that ''When ransom in gold could not be raised by the Jewish community in Rome, Pope Pius XII personally sent the sum needed.'' John G. Clancy, *Apostle For Our Time: Pope Paul VI* (New York: P. J. Kenedy and Sons, 1963), p. 55.
47. R. Leiber, ''Pio XII e gli ebrei di Roma 1943-1944, ''*La Civilità Cattolica*, 112 Vol. I (4 Marzo 1961) p. 450. The Leiber article was simultaneously published in German in *Stimmen Der Zeit*. Ordained in 1917, Leiber became a professor of ecclesiastical history at the Gregorian University and served for many years as Pacelli's secretary.
48. Delasem stood for Delegazione Assistenza Emigranti Ebrei. It was a Jewish agency which aided refugees.
49. Letter from Lelio Vittorio Valobra to Father Robert Leiber (April, 1961) objecting to various inaccuracies in Leiber's account. This letter was made available to the authors by the Jesuit historian, Father Robert Graham. Based on an interview with Renzo Levi, Robert Katz in his *Black Sabbath* (p. 87) stated that Pius XII had personally authorized a loan with terms similar to those cited by Giorgio Fiorentino. Repayment could be made in installments with the date for the completion of payments left open. See footnote 39.
50. Notes of the Secretary of State, Cardinal Maglione, 27 September 1943, in *Actes Et Documents Du Saint Siège Relatifs* À La *Seconde Guerre Mondiale*. Vol. 9, p. 491. Foà was erroneously identified as the Chief Rabbi of Rome in this Vatican document. Arata was the Secretary of the Congregation for the Oriental Church.
51. A 1968 piece published in a Roman Jewish periodical completely ignores Zolli's approach to the Vatican for gold. See Ariel Toaff, ''Eugenio Zolli e l'oro di Roma,'' *Shalom*, Vol. 2 No. 9 (October 1968): 3–4.
52. Zolli file, Letter from Ugo Foà to Israele Zolli, 4 July 1944.
53. In 1948 Kappler was tried, convicted and sentenced to life imprisonment for the 1944 Ardeatine Cave massacre. Largely on the testimony of Ugo Foà, he was sentenced to an additional fifteen years on a charge related to the gold extortion. In August 1977, Kappler, seriously ill with cancer, was spirited out of a Rome

military hospital and transported to West Germany. Italy's request to have Kappler extradited was rejected, but he died the following year. In 1988 a brouhaha developed in Italy when it was announced that Kappler's widow, Annelise, was planning a trip to promote her book about the onetime Gestapo chief. To the Jews of Rome promotion of the book entitled *I Will Take You Home* was especially odious. The outspoken President of the Union of Italian Jewish Communities, Tullia Zevi, commented, "This book is indecent. But I don't think of this as a Jewish affair. It is more an offense to Italian democracy than to Jews. It is really Italy that is being laughed at." Quoted in Clyde Haberman, "Promotion of New Book Revives Italians' Anger Over Nazi Occupation," *New York Times*, 23 October 1988, p 14.

54. Zuccotti, *The Italians And The Holocaust*, pp. 157–158, 160–161.

PROFESSOR EUGENIO MARIA ZOLLI
A FEW YEARS AFTER HIS CONVERSION.

7

The Baptized Rabbi of Rome

On 4 June 1944, wildly cheering crowds greeted Lieutenant General Mark W. Clark and the Allied 5th Army when they entered the Eternal City as conquering liberators. For war-weary Romans the Nazi scourge had ended. Rome's monuments were intact, its beauty unimpaired, but its economy was shattered and much of its population had been badly traumatized.

The formidable task of ruling over a free but prostrate Roman population fell to a Harvard-educated attorney, Charles Poletti, the son of an Italian granite cutter. Poletti, who had studied in Rome in 1924–25, was put in charge of the Lazio-Umbria region by the Allied Military Government. An affable, industrious, ambitious colonel in his early forties, Poletti had once been counsel to Governor Herbert Lehman of New York. After a brief stint as justice of the New York Supreme Court, he successfully ran for Lieutenant-Governor of the Empire State. Following his 1942 defeat for re-election, Poletti became Governor for one month when Lehman resigned to become United States director of foreign relief. In fact, he was the first Italian-American to become chief executive of any state. Poletti was briefly a special assistant to Secretary of War Henry Stimson before joining the military and serving initially in North Africa and subsequently in Italy.[1]

With food still in short supply in postwar Rome, hungry Romans dreamt up slogans which revealed their impatience and disgruntlement. They needled their new proconsul with the following mocking rhyme: ''Ci dànno Poletti e vogliamo spaghetti'' (They give us Poletti and we want spaghetti). If Roman life in general was austere, conditions for the decimated and factionalized Jewish population were even worse. It had suffered grievously and there was widespread depression of spirit.

Large segments of the Jewish community were impoverished. Many people were chronically hungry. Max Perlman of the Joint Distribution Committee, a relief and rehabilitation agency, described "men, women and children with the typically bloated stomach and sunken eyes that speak of steady starvation."[2] The "Joint" established soup kitchens and distributed clothing throughout war-ravaged Italy, including Rome. Jewish institutions had been shut down. Hospitals, schools, homes for the aged, facilities for children—all had to be re-opened and funded. To make matters worse, the local Jewish leadership was in disarray and involved in acrimonious squabbling. As Captain Maurice Neufeld, Poletti's aide and close friend put it, "The Jewish community is in a mess." Many of the "big shots" were Fascist sympathizers who were indifferent to the community.[3] Personal gossip of a malicious nature was rampant. Arthur C. Greenleigh, the Joint Distribution Committee director for Italy, called the Jewish community "a real headache at present with no recognized leadership and the worst factionalism possible."[4]

On the first Friday after liberation, religious services were held in the Tempio Maggiore. For an American chaplain, Rabbi Morris N. Kertzer, the event was one of the most significant in the two millennia old saga of the Jews of Rome. Never before had he heard Jews reciting a *shehechiyanu*, the prayer of thanksgiving and blessing for life, in such an "atmosphere of painful relief and ineffable joy." Not an inch of space could be found in the synagogue. Rabbi Kertzer shared the pulpit that night with Zolli and at least two other rabbis. In his military memoirs Kertzer has left us with a vivid picture of the emotional outpouring that followed the conclusion of the services.

> Every chaplain had the uncomfortable role of a messiah, being the living symbol of liberation to a people whose hearts overflowed with gratitude. They crushed one another attempting to get close to me, to touch my clothes, press their fingers to my insignia [the Star of David], and place their lips against it. Several elderly ladies kissed my cheek; many young ladies kissed my hands. I cringed with embarrassment. "Multe [sic] grazie, signor rabbino, multi grazie," the people cried. . . . I was an incarnation of the armed forces which had brought light to their darkened world.[5]

Zolli was not the object of such reverence or respect. Many no longer saw him as their rabbi.

To fill the void in spiritual leadership, Colonel Poletti, despite opposition from the community, restored Zolli to his rabbinical office from which he had been dismissed by the *giunta* in the spring. Having heard that the Chief Rabbi was ailing, Poletti wrote to him on June 30 expressing his hopes for a swift recovery that would enable Zolli to resume his activities in full. It was the regional commissioner's desire that, "the direction of all affairs inherent to the rabbinical office as well as the task of presiding over the solemn religious functions should be entrusted to the expert and reliable hands of the religious leader himself."[6] At that juncture, Poletti had not yet met Zolli. He did soon thereafter and was favorably impressed. In late August, while reviewing the Allies' accomplishments in Rome, Poletti remarked that "one of the most thrilling and satisfying experiences" as regional commissioner had been his work with Chief Rabbi Israele Zolli.[7]

On June 30, Colonel Poletti had requested Zolli to personally supervise the preparation of a special divine service of thanksgiving for victory for the numerous Jewish troops under the Rome area allied command. Although he was still ailing, the Chief Rabbi agreed to do so. At that service Zolli was interrupted by his associate, Rabbi Panzieri, when he began to introduce Chaplain Kertzer. Briefly the two Roman rabbis spoke at the same time. Although the tensions between them went unnoticed by most assembled in the synagogue, a humiliated and disappointed Zolli commented to Kertzer, "Now my own people have added to my torment."[8]

When Zolli's turn to speak came, on his own behalf and on behalf of the Roman Jewish community, Zolli offered thanks for their deliverance from the Nazis. With members of the Palestine Brigade present he blessed the Jews in the *Yishuv* (i.e., those residing in the Holy Land) and voiced admiration for their "work of reconstruction in the country of our Ancestors, the country of the Patriarchs, the Prophets and the martyrs." Zolli then spoke eloquently of the European earth soaked with the blood of their brethren. "Everywhere Abel's blood cries from the earth; blood of innocent Abel slain by Cain. Nevertheless, we shall rebuild the ruins and reconstruct upon the ruins." It was insufficient to rebuild towns and factories, he declared. An edifice of universal love had to be erected. It was with this "messianic picture" in his heart that he greeted and blessed the Jewish soldiers from France, Poland, South Africa, Canada, as well as those from the United States, Britain, and Palestine.[9] That night none of them could possibly have imagined that even before the final defeat of Hitler, the Chief Rabbi of Rome would openly proclaim Jesus as the Messiah. Certainly not Captain Neufeld.

Neufeld, a Jew who served as a liaison with the Roman Jewish community, then shared his superior's flattering assessment of Zolli. Not only was the Chief Rabbi a respected scholar well-connected throughout the Jewish world, but Neufeld characterized him as "kindly and tolerant."[10] He essentially accepted Zolli's version of his difficulties with a Fascist-led Jewish community. Apparently, Rabbis Hochman, Kertzer, and Berman were also favorably disposed toward Zolli in the autumn of 1944. Subsequent events would require a drastic reassessment of the Chief Rabbi.

Ugo Foà was removed by Poletti because he was "persona grata with important Fascist officials" and because of his open dealing with the S.S. in Rome. Born in Florence and raised in Leghorn, Foà was a military hero in World War I, studied law, became a member of the Fascist party and served as a magistrate until he was dismissed in accordance with the 1938 racial laws. In justifying his 1944 removal of Foà, Poletti granted that the former President of the Jewish Community may have acted in good faith "believing that such maneuvering with Fascists and Nazis would save the community" during the *anni di piombo* (years of lead), but the consequences for the community had been disastrous.[11] Poletti thought it best to put new faces in office.

One new face belonged to Giuseppe Nathan, an affluent and respected banker whose father, Ernesto, had been in 1907 the first Jew elected Mayor of Rome.[12] Nathan succeeded Dante Almansi who had been forced out of his position as President of the Union of Italian Jewish Communities,[13] a position he had held for almost five years, beginning in November 1939. Rightly or wrongly, the Allied Military Government purged Almansi because of his alleged Fascist past. Born in 1877, Almansi earned a law degree from the University of Parma. He reorganized a number of small municipalities before being called to Rome in 1919. There he functioned as a vice prefect and as a vice director of the police. According to his son, Almansi, to whom politics were a "boring waste of time," viewed the rise of Fascism with misgivings and accepted his Fascist party card with great reluctance. Nonetheless he functioned until the anti-Semitic laws forced him into retirement from the government. Although Poletti, and some who have written about Italian Jews under Mussolini, have regarded him as a committed Fascist, Almansi has had many defenders in the Roman Jewish community.[14]

Nathan had never been an observant Jew, nor was he involved in the community's seemingly interminable internal quarrels. Although his health was poor owing in part to the months he had spent in the infamous Regina Coeli prison, Nathan accepted the post as an obligation to his coreligionists. As he observed in 1946, "I felt myself bound in a special way after the abominable persecutions of which we were the victims."[15]

Another new face belonged to Silvio Ottolenghi, a well-known attorney whom Poletti appointed as extraordinary commissioner of the Jewish community of Rome, notwithstanding the fact that he had not previously been active in Jewish communal matters. Ottolenghi's task was to serve as an intermediary between the Allied military government and the community. From the day of his appointment many Roman Jews believed that Ottolenghi should have resigned rather than accept the Allies' order to restore Zolli to office. Had he opted to do so, Poletti et al. would have understood that the order ran contrary to the sentiments and the best interests of the community. But Ottolenghi did not resign, and the initial suspicion that Ottolenghi was selected by Zolli himself persisted. Indeed, after 20 July 1944 when the extraordinary commissioner made a passionate defense of Zolli making the Chief Rabbi appear to be a martyr and hero, the suspicion deepened.[16]

In point of fact, the suspicion was wholly justified. Both Colonel Poletti and Captain Neufeld explicitly stated that they had chosen Ottolenghi at Zolli's suggestion after consulting a number of people, Jews and Gentiles. Writing to his wife in New York City, Neufeld said that anyone the Allies had selected would have been the target of sniping.[17] Nevertheless, the final choice was a curious one in that Ottolenghi was known to be pro-Fascist, and the military government was obviously hostile to Foà and Almansi whom they viewed as pro-Fascist and whom they fired.

In August 1944, Greenleigh bluntly asserted that Ottolenghi was "once an ardent apologist for the fascists"[18] and Neufeld knew specifically that he had been one of the signers of the May 1937 ''Manifesto of Rifredi'' which declared that Italian Jews were first and foremost Italians who rejected Zionism, Communism, Freemasonry, and other international ideologies and loyalties.[19]

Poletti, who saw Ottolenghi as a man of integrity and ability, pooh-poohed accusations that he was a Fascist. According to Poletti, Ottolenghi joined the Fascist Party ''only because he could not practice his legal profession without a tessera.''[20] In November 1944 Poletti admitted that at the time the appointment was made, he had been unaware that Ottolenghi had singed the Rifredi Manifesto.[21] Neufeld believed that he had picked out ''the most honest and intelligent man I could find with the backing of the Rabbi an important consideration.''[22]

For the time being, Captain Neufeld, Rabbi Hochman, and Rabbi Berman all assisted Zolli and his impoverished family in the post-liberation period, and sometimes did so from their personal resources. Our knowledge of the Zolli affair has recently been significantly deepened by the discovery of relevant letters and papers of the two chaplains.[23] They and other chaplains gave the Zollis money and gifts. Hardly a week passed, Berman wrote, without a food parcel being sent to the Chief Rabbi.[24] Another American chaplain, Rabbi Aaron Paperman, recalls being importuned for cigarettes by Zolli.[25] Almost from the day the military government took over, Zolli bombarded the Allied Command with requests. He was at their premises almost every day and, according to Neufeld, ''pestered the hell out of me.''[26] It seemed that in the fall of 1944, Zolli was reaching the end of his tether, emotionally even more so than financially.

He was in his mid-sixties at the time; fatigued, ill, and embittered. Rabbi Berman painted the following personality portrait: ''He was sour and uncongenial. At times he gave one the impression of much greater age and little vitality and yet at times he appeared the cool calculating self-centered and astute schemer. He was mentally and physically tired and broken.''[27]

Nevertheless, in the autumn of 1944, Zolli conducted religious services on Rosh Hashanah, the Jewish New Year. Two thousand worshipers crowded into the central synagogue while thousands more milled about outside. Their distaste for the Chief Rabbi notwithstanding, the Jewish families of Rome prayed openly, a freedom which was all the more precious because they had not been able to exercise it during the Nazi occupation. Indeed, there was hardly a Jewish household without its dead and the majority of the congregation were mourners who rose at services to say the kaddish or prayer for the dead.[28]

Unpopular with his constituents and consequently insecure about his pulpit, despite the backing of the Allied Military Government, Zolli sought lifetime tenure in his rabbinical position. Using his friends in the Jewish world, he tried to influence the new Italian government. In September 1944, S. H. Hertz, the Chief Rabbi of London, wrote to Ivanoe Bonomi, the Italian Prime Minister, about conditions among Roman Jews. Cognizant of the divisions within the Jewish community, Hertz sided with Zolli whom he knew personally to be an illustrious teacher and a man of great culture. He expressed the opinion that it would be tragic if Zolli's leadership were to become a victim of injustice.[29]

While Zolli fought to retain his rabbinical post, he simultaneously sought an appointment at the University of Rome. In November and December 1944 and January 1945, as his rabbinical fortunes declined, his academic prospects brightened somewhat. He was considered for a chair in epigraphy and Semitic antiquities and the Italian government was disposed to back his candidacy. Documents in the Italian State Archives indicate that some officials in the Interior Ministry had ulterior motives. They were distressed that other nations were ahead of Italy in developing commercial links with Palestine which was still under British control. A November 1944 memorandum noted that Zolli had many important contacts and could be useful in fostering business connections between Italy and Palestine.[30] The Prime Minister's office also wanted Zolli to teach modern Hebrew to those preparing for diplomatic and consular careers, and to do so without compensation.[31]

As the new year approached, Zolli must have seen himself as decreasingly isolated from the Jews of Rome. In failing health, he faced a bleak future, at least as a rabbi. In December 1944, Zolli had told Ottolenghi confidentially that he wanted to retire for health reasons.[32] A medical certificate signed by Dr. Augusto Calonzi, Zolli's own physician, citing the Chief Rabbi's cardiovascular condition and recommending avoidance of physical and psychic stress, was submitted in January 1945.[33] Dr. Augusto Fiorentini, a second physician who was appointed by the community, examined Zolli and confirmed his appreciable physical deterioration. Dr. Fiorentini also referred to cardiovascular problems and a hernia. In addition, he noted that Zolli was suffering from severe psychological depression. As the rabbi was in need of physical and emotional rest, Dr. Fiorentini concluded that Zolli could not carry out his activities as Chief Rabbi.[34]

Ottolenghi, in all likelihood, secretly welcomed Zolli's decision to step down as Chief Rabbi. The extraordinary commissioner had long labored in vain to reconcile the strong desire of many Roman Jews to recall ex-chief Rabbi David Prato from Palestine with his own concern for providing Zolli with a livelihood. Ottolenghi's compromise solution was to appoint Zolli the director of the rabbinical college. Therefore, on January 26 Ottolenghi honored Zolli's request for retirement as spiritual leader of the community effective February 1. Simultaneously, Guiseppe Nathan decreed the reopening of the rabbinical college with Zolli as its head. Zolli's income in that capacity plus his pension to be shared by the Trieste and Roman communities would have guaranteed him an income slightly in excess of what he had been receiving as Chief Rabbi.[35] Zolli temporarily accepted the offer, but on February 6 he notified Ottolenghi that he would not take the headship of the rabbinical college as he had other possibilities for his "scientific career." Explaining his decision to Cesare Eliseo, a twenty-five year old former student at the rabbinical college, Zolli said in early February that wider horizons that went beyond university teaching were opening before him. He gratuitously added that he regretted spending so many years of his life with Jews.[36]

An angry Zolli was convinced that his supporters in the Roman Jewish hierarchical structure had not adequately upheld his cause. In Zolli's judgment, Nathan had shown himself to be weak and without influence. Zolli was even more bitter about Ottolenghi who, he believed, had betrayed him. The Chief Rabbi thought that the extraordinary commissioner had sacrificed him to curry favor with the populace. They had offered Zolli the job as head of the rabbinical college, virtually a nonexistent institution, to sidetrack and delude him. Rabbi Hochman tried to probe Zolli's troubled psyche: "They [Ottolenghi et al.] thought they were smart. But he was nobody's fool. He would show them." Hochman went on to compare Zolli with an animal brought to bay—frustrated, humiliated, infuriated.[37]

At the beginning of February, Neufeld wrote to Zolli that both he and Colonel Poletti regretted that the Chief Rabbi was resigning from the post in which he had served with distinction for so many years. He thanked Zolli warmly for his work in resolving the most difficult and delicate problems besetting the Jewish community. Neufeld then wished that Zolli in his new position at the rabbinical college would derive all the satisfaction that his learning and his honesty merited. Furthermore, the captain hoped that Zolli would be able to contribute to the moral and spiritual reconstruction of the Italian Jewish community.[38]

On February 8, Zolli wrote to Captain Neufeld telling him that he was declining the tendered post at the rabbinical seminary. He explained that, given his less than robust health, he lacked the inner strength to live and work in so "hot" an atmosphere. Moreover, as head of the college, he would have to work under the jurisdiction of Rabbi Prato who, Zolli hinted, had Fascist tendencies. The somewhat paranoid Zolli seemed envious of Prato's greater popularity and remarked that he, Zolli, had always been cast as a *guastafesta* or spoilsport in the community. Zolli was not forthcoming about his plans. His less than candid letter to Neufeld was silent on the impending conversion which occurred just five days later.[39]

On 13 February 1945 Israele Zolli and his wife, Emma Majonica Zolli, were baptized in a small chapel of Santa Maria degli Angeli. Located near the Piazza della Repubblica, the church was built on the ruins of the Baths of Diocletian and was designed by Michelangelo. Perhaps a dozen people, among them several prominent Jesuits, an order for which Zolli (and Pacelli) had a special affinity, were present for the ceremony. They included the future Augustin Cardinal Bea, Father Paolo Dezza who was Pius XII's tutor in Ignatius Loyola's *Spiritual Exercises*, and Father Pietro Paolo Boccaccio who had known Zolli since the rabbi taught Hebrew language and literature at the University of Padova in the prewar period. One of the Catholic couples that had sheltered Zolli during the Nazi occupation was also in attendance. Baptism was administered by Monsignor Traglia whom *L'Osservatore Romano* identified as the Vicegerente of Rome. Not surprisingly, the official Vatican newspaper, in an article entitled "The Baptism of Professor Zolli," found it significant that the erstwhile Chief Rabbi had assumed the name of Eugenio Maria in homage to Pope Pius XII.[40]

Readers were also informed that Monsignor Cosimo Bonaldi, pastor of Santa Maria degli Angeli, and other Jesuits had instructed the Zollis in the Christian religion. Apparently, Zolli had been thoroughly prepared for the conversion, that is to say, he already knew Catholicism well when he took the sacrament.[41] Unbeknownst to those witnessing the baptism, the event took place almost ten years after Zolli, with Jewish converts to Catholicism in mind, had written to Angelo Sacerdoti, then Chief Rabbi of Rome, that the "souls of the patriarchs, Moses, the prophets, the martyrs, and rabbis down through the ages trembled before the degrading spectacle of those deserters who repudiate the Tora, fatherland of their spirits and inheritance of their fathers."[42] We can only wonder if on 13 February 1945 Zolli himself remembered what he had written in March 1935.

It was announced that in a few days the newly baptized Zollis would be confirmed and would receive communion. Indeed, shortly thereafter, Bishop Fogar of Trieste, Zolli's old friend, confirmed him, and the former Chief Rabbi received his first communion from Father Dezza in a chapel of the Gregorian University.

Dezza had known of Zolli's intention to convert for some time. Zolli had informed him back in August 1944 that he wished to become a Catholic.[43] On the fifteenth Zolli had gone to see Father Dezza at the Gregorian University and had asked for the water of baptism. His request had been an unconditional one. He wanted nothing in return, Father Dezza was later to write. The Nazis had taken everything from him and he expected to die poor.[44] During the intervening months while Zolli secretly planned to join the Catholic Church and while he surreptitiously prepared for his new faith, he continued to serve as the titular spiritual leader of Rome's Jews. As late as two days prior to his momentous trip to the baptismal font, Zolli, functioning as president of a rabbinical tribunal, pronounced a divorce between two Yugoslav Jews. Given the fact that his baptism was imminent, this act on Zolli's part was regarded retrospectively as duplicitous. In fact, more than one Jewish critic of Zolli found his behavior in the matrimonial matter hypocritical because of the Catholic Church's vehement opposition to divorce. For a fee of a thousand lire, he had trod upon both Jews and Catholics and carried out a most deplorable act.[45]

To the Jews of Rome still recuperating from the Nazi persecution, the news of Zolli's conversion struck like a bolt of lightning. They were incredulous. A flabbergasted community almost immediately vented its hostility on the apostate rabbi and subjected his entire family to what his daughter, Miriam, remembers as terrible and inhuman treatment.[46] There were threatening phone calls and letters and insults galore. In an autobiographical note dated 22 February 1945 Zolli claimed that an anonymous caller, whom he described as a "young Jewess," telephoned and expressed a wish to see him and his entire family soon buried in tombs marked by crosses.[47] Frightening graffiti such as "Down with the Zollis—Death to the traitor" were reportedly painted on ghetto walls.[48] Miriam painfully remembers being spat upon in the streets.[49] Zolli soon abandoned his apartment at 19 Via S. Bartolomeo de' Vaccinari on the fringes of the ghetto and took up residence at the Gregorian University.

Just two days after the baptism, *Israel*, the weekly newspaper of Roman Jewry, hastily published an unsigned editorial entitled "Una clamorosa defezione" (a clamorous defection). It acknowledged that Zolli's action had caused a general shock and stated that the Jewish community was rightfully indignant. Aggravating the defection were the means and the moment of the conversion which came after Jewry had passed through one of the most tragic periods in its entire history. *Israel* commented that most of the Jews had previously detached themselves from Zolli for he lacked the qualities of heart and character required in a religious teacher. Others, those who still considered him their rabbi, would observe the traditional seven days of mourning and weep for Zolli as for a deceased person.[50]

On the Friday evening following Zolli's baptism, a huge crowd gathered at the Great Synagogue for the traditional Sabbath service. Their primary purpose was to reaffirm their fidelity to Judaism and the Jewish people. Their presence was a restatement of their trust in the historic, moral and spiritual vitality of Israel. A few thousands Jews—estimates run as high as four thousand—went to give their impassioned response to their former leader's defection.

David Panzieri, the revered assistant rabbi at the Great Synagogue, officiated and spoke. He was very elderly, diminutive, frail, and deaf. Nevertheless he spoke inspiringly of the ancient traditions of Italian Jews and of their significant contributions to the ethical and spiritual legacy of world Jewry. He implored the congregants to subordinate their differences to the common good. Panzieri referred neither to Zolli nor his deed, although in the future, he would refer to the ''fu'' Rabbi Zolli, that is, the *late* Rabbi Zolli.[51]

Chaplains Berman and Hochman also addressed the assemblage that Sabbath evening. Never had Jewry ''been more broken or tortured than it is now in Europe, and in Italy, as a result of the Nazi-Fascist years,'' the latter stated. But, it was a fact, ''proven in countless centuries of history, that our people never permitted itself to remain broken because of its sufferings. Rather by a dauntless spirit it ever rose above the conditions that would hold it down, to emerge a purer, stronger, more creative community.'' Hochman assured his audience that the Jews of Britain, the United States, Palestine, and everywhere else were deeply concerned and stood ready to give aid and comfort. Although the spectre of Zolli hovered over the assemblage, Rabbi Hochman did not mention him by name.[52]

Dr. Umberto Nahon as a representative of the Jewish Agency[53] spoke forcefully, even fiercely. Over the millennia many had betrayed Israel and departed the fold. Their names had been expunged from memory and they were forgotten. But Israel, despite the most horrible persecutions including that of the Nazis, had survived. It was now incumbent upon Rome's Jews to reconstruct their community and to rid themselves of the Fascists.[54]

Even Ottolenghi, Zolli's erstwhile ally, had been alienated by the rabbi's deed. Writing to Major Berman, he said that the Zolli case had not even grazed the body of Roman Jews. Indeed, the community had become reinvigorated and strengthened as always happens whenever useless and harmful things are jettisoned.[55]

By March 1945 Berman regarded Zolli as an ''egotist of the first order with a mania for himself.''[56] Hochman concurred. Both concluded that he was concerned only with himself and not with communal problems. Hochman called him a ''man without integrity of character.''[57]

When the Italian rabbis gathered in Genoa they issued a blistering statement on Zolli for his act of apostasy. By a unanimous vote, they recorded with bitterness the unheard of act carried out by Zolli in abandoning Israel. There was no justification for his behavior. The timing of his baptism was especially reprehensible to his former colleagues because it occurred not right after Zolli's emergence from hiding but several months after he had resumed his rabbinical ministry. Divine justice would be meted out to Zolli, the assembled rabbis confidently asserted.[58]

At that time the Italian rabbinate was experiencing an acute crisis. No fewer than six rabbis had been deported by the Nazis and, in the words of Rabbi David Prato, "one has vilely and shamefully abandoned us." Prato had reluctantly decided to return to his former Roman pulpit from Israel because "so few of us remained."[59]

Roman Jews, in particular, were greatly embarrassed by Zolli's conversion which, in the opinion of one, gave the Catholic world an advantage over Jews. Piero Modigliani vividly remembers people asking him in the wake of the conversion if he, too, wanted to embrace Catholicism. After all, his spiritual leader had done so. Modigliani was offended by the question and replied that he would continue in the faith of his forefathers.[60]

Clara Della Seta, who had worked for Foà as a secretary and then sought refuge from the Nazi scourge in a convent, also recalls Catholic friends telling her in 1945 that she should reconsider the possibility of converting to Catholicism given the fact that her rabbi had done so.[61] She too remained a Jew.

Diasporan Jewish leaders, especially those in the United States, were very apprehensive about the possibility that Zolli's action would prove contagious among his coreligionists.[62] Author Meyer Levin wrote, quite inaccurately, that several thousand Italian Jews were reported to have followed a converted rabbi into the Catholic Church.[63]

The Reconstructionist, a liberal periodical, stated that to avoid wholesale desertion it was necessary to build a new, vital and relevant Judaism. To keep Jews loyal to Judaism in good and bad times, "one must give them a clear conception of Judaism and a compelling conviction of its worth."[64] Only then could the blandishments of the more "glamorous" and "successful" faiths be resisted.

Similar discomfort about the boost that the Zolli incident might have given to proselytizing was expressed in *New Palestine*, an American Zionist publication devoted to Jewish affairs. Daniel Frisch, a prominent Zionist, wrote an open letter to his daughter, Hadassah, a university student who had written to him about campus discussions sparked by Zolli. Ostensibly, she had remarked that the conversion underscored and tacitly sanctioned the inclination on the part of many young Jews to flirt with Catholic mysticism. For her father, the answer lay in the "sustaining power of your rich Jewish background." Frisch reassured his daughter that there was no element of happiness in other faiths that was absent from Judaism.[65]

Dr. A. S. E. Yahuda, a Jerusalem-born Biblical scholar, added his voice to the Jewish chorus of scathing criticism. Yahuda painted Zolli as a chameleon character, "cynical, essentially negative, changing his convictions according to circumstances" and belittled his academic credentials. Zolli, he wrote, had contributed little to Hebrew scholarship and that opinion was shared by both Jewish and Gentile authorities. Yahuda also charged that in 1945 the Director of the Papal Relief Mission touring newly liberated concentration camps, was conducting an objectionable campaign to convert former Jewish inmates. Allegedly, the Director hinted that conversion to Catholicism was warranted because the Church had saved many Jews. But, according to Yahuda, the Pope was not responsible for the proselytizing effort. Rather, it sounded to him, "more like a message coming from the converted 'Chief Rabbi.' "[66]

Perhaps it was fear of other defections from the Jewish fold that prompted the United Synagogue of America to sponsor a national speaking tour by Rabbi Hochman upon his return to the United States. Hochman's topic was the case of Rabbi Zolli.

Apprehension that Zolli's "appalling example" would have disastrous consequences for Italian Jewry as a whole was also evinced by Cecil Roth in England. Conversion was already common in Italy and ignorance epidemic there, he wrote to the *Jewish Chronicle*, the organ of British Jewry. Zolli's apostasy "with its suggestion of long-continued insincerity is likely to undermine the convictions of very many more."[67] Professor Roth foresaw "rapid and widespread disintegration" in the community, but events proved him much too pessimistic.

In its review of the year 1945, the American Jewish Year Book seemed relieved that Zolli's trip to the baptismal font had found few imitators among Italian Jews.[68] The much feared ripple effect never materialized. Because Zolli was held in contempt by so many in Rome's Jewish community prior to his conversion, it was unlikely that they would follow his example. Indeed, Zolli's baptism may have confirmed their long-held negative appraisal of him. It proved that he was worthless. Rabbi Hochman even averred that the "act served to clear the air." It awakened them to the critical condition of their communal life, and of the urgency to unite for its reconstruction.[69]

In Rome, Rabbi Bernard Casper, the Senior Chaplain of the Palestinian Jewish Brigade, in an open letter published by the Roman Jewish newspaper, *Israel*, wrote that news of Zolli's baptism let loose a storm of indignation among Jewish troops. Zolli's act was a "stab in the back." To the Jewish soldiers who had come to fight for Jewish honor under the Jewish flag it was an "unimaginable act of villainy."[70] His desertion was still more shameful because Jews had just suffered under Nazi slavery.

Apart from pledges of support, most reactions from Jews outside Italy were derisive to the ex-Chief Rabbi. They flayed him for abandoning his people and for the timing of his abandonment when Jews were still utterly supine in the wake of the Nazi genocide. Telegrams and letters, several passionately worded, have been preserved in the Zolli file of the Rome synagogue's modern archives. A Mrs. E. S. Schweig who was living in Kew Gardens, Queens expressed almost uncontrolled rage towards Zolli. In a letter addressed to the Chief Rabbi himself she called him a "disgrace to humanity." Given the suffering of the Jewish people, Zolli could not have chosen a worse moment to convert. He had done incalculable damage to the Jewish cause, and his behavior served to show that the persecutors were justified. She then expressed the view that Zolli had lived long enough.[71]

A missive to the President of the Jewish community of Rome came from Dr. Kalman Friedman, then the rabbi of Temple Emanuel in Newton Center, Massachusetts. Dr. Friedman, who had left the rabbinical chair in Florence in 1939, said that his first impulse on hearing the news of the conversion had been to return to Italy to help his people, but he contented himself by expressing deep sympathy to Rome's Jewry which had been "orphaned by its spiritual leader" in that difficult moment. He also severely condemned Zolli's "nefarious" deed which he branded "high treason." In his judgment, Zolli had shown a very weak character and a "not very lucid mind."[72]

Equally disparaging was the New York Board of Jewish Ministers 1945 Passover letter which denounced Zolli's "act of desertion and apostasy" and accused him of "abandoning his people when he should have been sharing their faith and fate."[73]

Still stronger language was employed by Louis I. Newman, a rabbi in the United States, who compared Zolli with Marshall Pétain and Pierre Laval, the traitorous leaders of Vichy France, and with Vidkun Quisling of Norway whose surname has become synonymous with treason since the end of World War II. In his 1945 book about the conversion, Newman proclaimed that "even as Revolutionary America had its Benedict Arnold, Israel in Rome has had its Zolli."[74]

Rabbi Stephen S. Wise, perhaps the preeminent rabbi of the time, echoed the twin themes of desertion and betrayal in his initial comment on the conversion: "If it be the duty of a private to stand at his post, what shall we say of a General, the man in highest command."[75] Rabbi Wise was the author of an unsigned editorial, "Zolli's Apostasy," which appeared in *Opinion*, a journal of Jewish life and letters, of which he was the chief editor. Declaring that there are "crimes too terrible for punishment" and "acts too lamentable for tears," Wise opined that "when the Chief Rabbi of a great community such as Rome, forsakes his faith and enters into the communion of another Church, he does not merely repudiate his faith but he deserts his people."[76]

Zolli's conversion also elicited comment from fringe organizations, some little known at the time and long since forgotten. A Jewish group described variously as the International Committee of Action and the International Union of Antifascist Emigrants and Refugees tried unsuccessfully to exploit Zolli's defection. From its headquarters in Rome the group proposed the establishment of an independent Jewish state in German territory, preferably in northwest Prussia, as an alternative to Zionist efforts to create a Jewish homeland in Palestine. It was worried about the absorptive capacity of Palestine, about Arab opposition, and about the reluctance of European emigrants to the Levant to become "Asians." In March 1945, the International Committee wrote to the United States State Department regarding Zolli's baptism and warned:

> This is an alarm signal! When the man most authorized to win people of other faiths to the Jewish faith looses [sic] his nerves and goes himself over to another faith, this can mean really the beginning of the end of the Jewish nation. . . . We have

> said from the beginning . . . that we must act quickly if we are to save the remainder of the Jewish nation.[77]

Zolli also drew critical reaction from *The European Jewish Observer*, a London-based publication. Although the *Observer's* principal focus was on the horrifying events unfolding in Poland during the war years, it also editorialized about happenings in strife-torn Jewish Rome. Two months before Zolli's "rebirth" in February 1945, the *Observer* reviled him for trying to save his own skin when the Nazis became masters of the Italian capital. In general, Jewish spiritual leaders had established an admirable record of sharing the destiny, good or bad, of their congregations. Indeed, the *Observer* had no knowledge of any rabbis in Poland who had preserved their own lives by escaping and hiding. It was apparent that they had fulfilled their obligations to "remain with their people to administer such consolation and comfort as they could."[78] By his example, Zolli should have fortified his flock for whatever fate held in store for them. In the *Observer's* opinion, the rabbinical calling required Zolli to stand up, to combat evil and, if necessary, even to make the supreme sacrifice.

On 23 February 1945, in an editorial entitled "The Deserter," the *Observer* excoriated Zolli for his treachery which occurred in such "unsavoury circumstances." While the paper conceded a person's prerogative to change his religion, it found Zolli's timing objectionable. He had opted to trade the synagogue for the church when Jews were in "most grievous need of his spiritual support and undergoing the bitterest trial in their history."[79]

In addition, Zolli's "despicable" actions caused the *Observer* to question whether it was really necessary for Diasporan Jewish communities to have Chief Rabbis. In Eastern Europe, the office had been eliminated in Warsaw and elsewhere. Personal rivalries had been sharpened and public disunity fostered by a rabbinical selection process that stressed the political rather than the spiritual. Moreover, the occupant of the coveted Chief Rabbi's office was unrealistically expected to be both quintessentially erudite and quintessentially virtuous. Unsuitable men had often been appointed, for instance, in the case of Zolli. Consequently, the *Observer* concluded, "Rome should make a clean sweep now and follow the example of Warsaw by abolishing the office of Chief Rabbi altogether, and . . . other communities should seriously consider whether they should not do likewise.''[80] The shattered Roman Jewish community never considered abolishing the Chief Rabbi's office after Zolli's surprising departure. It simply found a preferable replacement in the person of Rabbi David Prato.

A second London-based periodical, *The Jewish Standard*, published an editorial entitled ''A Strange Conversion'' about what it called ''a most painful episode in modern Jewish history.'' Long before his baptism Zolli had deserted his post and supposedly taken refuge in the Vatican. Not since the Spanish Inquisition had a rabbinical luminary forsaken his faith to find physical safety, the *Standard* asserted. As to Zolli's supposed reason for embracing Catholicism, i.e., to thank the Vatican for saving Jewish lives, the weekly commented caustically: ''Time was when the Catholic Church destroyed the bodies in order to save the souls. Now it seems the saving of the body has become an excuse—by an Ex-Chief Rabbi—for the surrender of the soul.''[81]

Much of the *Standard's* animus towards Zolli, it appears, was based on what it perceived as his hostility towards the ''New Zionists'' whose cause the *Standard* championed. Led internationally by Vladimir Zev Jabotinsky, the New Zionists, or Revisionists as they were generally known, offered an alternative to the rival Labor Zionists who long dominated the World Zionist Organization. *The Standard* charged Zolli with being ''one of the bitterest persecutors of the New Zionists in Italy.'' Supposedly he used his influence to curtail their activities and endeavored to get their branches closed down. Furthermore, ''he did not hesitate to employ the usual slanders.''[82]

Zolli's baptism did not pass unnoticed by the local, vocal Italian press. Several Roman newspapers tersely announced the event and commented on it, not all favorably. For example, *Avanti*, the Socialist daily, stated in a clearly sarcastic tone ''Already ex-Zoller, already ex-fascist, Prof. Israel Zolli is now ex-rabbi. This thing of 'ex' is therefore a special calling like music and mathematics.'' It had little sympathy for Zolli whose conduct during the Nazi period was ridiculed. His spiritual leadership was carried out at a distance, *Avanti* wrote.[83]

If Zolli was denigrated by his former co-religionists and by anticlericals for joining the rival camp, he was lionized by Catholics who were exhilarated because of the new highly esteemed addition to the Church. After all, Zolli was not only a Jew, but a rabbi, not simply a rabbi, but *the* Chief Rabbi of Rome. When he gave a lecture at the Gregorian University shortly after his conversion, it was to a jubilant overflow crowd which gave him a deafening, seemingly interminable ovation. A modest Zolli declared that the applause was not for him personally, but rather for the glory of God.[84]

While Catholics in general unconditionally welcomed Zolli's momentous decision to cross the religious Rubicon, a few found it difficult to divest themselves of deeply ingrained physical stereotypes of Jews. In 1947, a Spanish padre, Father Ortiz de Urbina, wrote approvingly of Zolli's conversion. He then described the former Chief Rabbi as a man who did not possess overly Semitic features except for a somewhat prominent nose and fleshy lips.[85]

Although Catholics the world over were understandably delighted by the "great conversion," they tried not to gloat. They were inclined to see the baptism as the logical end product of a rational intellectual comparative analysis of Judaism and Catholicism on Zolli's part. One article appearing in the American Catholic press found some newspaper commentary about Zolli "insolent." What the author of the article, A. B. Klyber, himself a Jewish convert who became a missionary priest, had in mind were newspaper headlines such as "Voices, Rays, Convert to Catholicism." Those headlines which apparently originated in an Associated Press dispatch, smacked of poor sportsmanship, Klyber thought. In addition, to refer to the conversion as a "religious switch" was offensive and disrespectful to millions as it failed to note that Zolli's decision followed a prolonged period of thought and study.[86]

An editorial comment published in the Catholic *Journal of Religious Instruction* compared Zolli to no less a personage than Cardinal John Henry Newman and noted that 1945 marked the centennial of that nineteenth-century English theologian's conversion from Anglicanism to Catholicism. After briefly describing Zolli's maltreatment as a traitor and a heretic at the hands of his former Jewish associates, the unsigned piece observed, "Far be it from Catholics to reproach the Jews for their treatment of Zolli; rather we shall pray for them, as Zolli and his wife now do, that the light of faith may shine in their hearts."[87] Zolli had bravely trod the path laid out by St. Peter, the "Prince of Apostles," who acknowledged that it is Jesus who "hast the words of eternal life." In other words, Roman Catholicism had *the truth*. Zolli had discovered that incontrovertible fact, and other Jews would be fortunate to do the same.

Monsignor John M. Oesterreicher's deeply felt views were expressed in a 1946 review of Rabbi Louis I. Newman's book on the Zolli conversion. Oesterreicher said that he could appreciate that the Chief Rabbi's baptism was a "bitter blow to many Jews," especially after the events of the preceding decade. He could tolerate some fiery responses to Zolli but he could not permit Newman's interpretation to go unchallenged. To Oesterreicher, the rabbi's book had to be "called by its proper name—downright abuse."[88]

Oesterreicher, who was born and raised a Jew himself, took sharp issue with the declaration about converts that "what falls off is offal."[89] In rebuttal, he quoted Franz Rosenzweig, the German Jewish theologian, philosopher and writer,[90] to the effect that baptism deprived Jews of the best, not the worst among them. In Oesterreicher's judgment, Newman's motive was to dishonor those who had already left Judaism and those who were considering doing so.

More than forty years later Oesterreicher still believes that Newman had been unfair and that his book was an attempt to curtail Zolli's influence among Jews. The monsignor underlines the fact that in the wake of Zolli's much heralded conversion, the leakage from Judaism to Catholicism was minimal.[91]

Notes

1. See Joe Fromm, "Cleanup Man for the AMG," *Coronet* (November 1944), *The Stars and Stripes*, 23 February 1944 and Fiorenza Fiorentino, *La Roma Di Charles Poletti* (Roma: Bonacci Editore, 1986). Additional information may be obtained from the entry for Poletti in *Current Biography: Who's News and Why, 1943*, ed. Maxine Block (New York: The H. W. Wilson Co., 1944): pp. 599–602.
2. American Jewish Joint Distribution Committee Papers, Address given by Max S. Perlman, AJDC Representative in Italy, at Southern Regional Meeting, 14 January 1945, Atlanta, Georgia and File 716, Memo from Inter-Governmental Committee On Refugees, Headquarters Allied Control Commission to American Joint Distribution Committee, 22 September 1944. Initially founded in 1914, the Joint Distribution Committee worked tirelessly to rescue and succor the Jews of Europe during the Holocaust. After the Allied victory, it provided desperately needed money, food, medical supplies, child care and vocational training to survivors.
3. Neufeld Papers, container 5, letter from Maurice Neufeld to Hinda Neufeld, 10 September 1944.
4. American Jewish Joint Distribution Committee Papers, File 716, Letter from

Arthur Greenleigh, 20 August 1944. It is not clear to whom Greenleigh was writing.

5. Morris N. Kertzer, *With an H on my Dog Tag* (New York: Behrman House Inc. 1947).
6. Neufeld Papers, container 21, letter from Col. Poletti to Chief Rabbi Zolli, 30 June 1944.
7. Ibid., remarks by Col. Poletti made at a Regional Commissioners Conference, 22 August 1944. The Israeli historian, Meir Michaelis, is of the opinion that the American authorities were ignorant of Italian Jewish affairs and saw Zolli as a martyr because the Italian Jewish Fascist leaders despised him. See Meir Michaelis, "Rabbi Eugenio Zolli and Italian Jewry," Unpublished manuscript (in Hebrew), p. 3.
8. Kertzer, *With an H*, p. 63.
9. Hochman Papers, "Message From Chief Rabbi I. Zolli, Rome" (n.d.)
10. Neufeld Papers, container 5, letter from Maurice Neufeld to Hinda Neufeld, 12 July 1944.
11. Ibid., container 21, Memo from Col. Poletti to Lieut. Carl E. Fehr, Security Division, Allied Commission, Headquarters, 24 November 1944.
12. Zuccotti, *Italians and the Holocaust*, pp. xiii–xv.
13. Constituted in 1930, the Union served as liaison between the Italian government and the Jewish populace. It had responsibility for meeting the religious needs of the community, including the training of rabbis. It operated Jewish institutions, sponsored cultural enterprises and combatted anti-Semitism.
14. Both Almansi and Foà were praised for their dignity and courage during the Nazi era by Sergio Piperno and Giorgio Sierra. See *Shalom*, (July–August 1973): pp. 20–21. For several years the defense of Almansi has been spearheaded by his son, Dr. Renato J. Almansi, a physician who has long resided in New York City. Dr. Almansi has prepared an unpublished manuscript, "Dante Almansi, President of the Union of Italian Jewish Communities, November 13, 1939 to October 1, 1944" (1971) which offers details about his father's career and a rebuttal of charges leveled against him by Robert Katz and others.
    Dante Almansi's daughter, Dr. Elena Nunberg, has described her father as essentially non-political, a bureaucrat who never really supported Fascism but rather had to join the party for pragmatic reasons. Personal interview, Rome, 28 May 1987. After his death in 1949 Dante Almansi was eulogized in the Roman Jewish periodical, *Israel* (13 January 1949). Additional praise for Dante Almansi may be found in Renzo De Felice, *Storia degli ebrei italiani sotto il fascismo* (Roma: Einaudi, 1961): pp. 478–485 and in Meir Michaelis, "Rabbi Eugenio Zolli and Italian Jewry," p. 2 Michaelis describes Almansi as talented, effective, experienced, honest, devoted and practical.
15. AJDC Files, summary of report Giuseppe Nathan, 27 March 1946 at the Convention of the Union of Jewish Communities in Italy, Rome.
16. Zolli file, observations of Signor Maggior, 25 March 1945. Of course, it was Poletti and Neufeld as well as Berman and Hochman not Ottolenghi who insisted on Zolli staying on as Chief Rabbi. See Neufeld Papers, container 5, letter from Maurice Neufeld to Hinda Neufeld, 8 April 1945.
17. Neufeld Papers, container 5, letter from Maurice Neufeld to Hinda Neufeld, 10 September 1944.
18. AJDC, Arthur Greenleigh letter, 20 August 1944.

19. Neufeld Papers, container 5, letter from Maurice Neufeld to Hinda Neufeld, 10 September 1944.
20. Memo, Col. Poletti to Lieut. Fehr, 24 November 1944.
21. Ibid.
22. Letter from Maurice Neufeld to Hinda Neufeld, 10 September 1944. In March, 1945 Neufeld made it clear that his opinion of Ottolenghi was a high one. Neufeld saw him as "an honest citizen not seeking personal power and a gentleman to boot, who has taken more unjust abuse than anyone else I know around here." The captain added that Rabbis Berman and Hochman were also great admirers of Ottolenghi. Letter from Maurice Neufeld to Hinda Neufeld, 1 March 1945.
23. While in North Africa and Italy, Rabbi Meyer Berman corresponded regularly with his wife, Judith, in London. Those letters are in the possession of Mrs. Berman, his widow, who has made them available to the authors. Rabbi Hochman's papers, while skimpier, have been shown to the authors by his daughter, Mary Hochman, a medical student at the University of Pennsylvania.
24. Berman papers, letter from Rabbi Berman to Judith Berman, 20 March 1945.
25. Rabbi Aaron Paperman, telephone interview, 23 June 1987. A major in the U.S. Army, Rabbi Paperman attended the yeshiva in Telshe, Lithuania and became a Talmudic scholar of note. He received a Bronze Star for his military service in Europe.
26. Maurice Neufeld, telephone interview, 2 March 1987.
27. Berman papers, letter from Rabbi Berman to Judith Berman, 20 March 1945.
28. Hochman papers, talk by Chaplain Jacob Hochman over National Broadcasting Company, 12 November 1944 as part of the "Eternal Light" program.
29. Italian State Archives, Interior Ministry, Cabinet 44–46, Envelope 56, Letter from Chief Rabbi Hertz to Prime Minister Ivanoe Bonomi, 22 September 1944. Neufeld claimed credit for getting Bonomi to recognize Zolli's citizenship and his tenure as Chief Rabbi. Letter from Maurice Neufeld to Hinda Neufeld, 15 February 1945.
30. Ibid., Ministry of Interior memorandum, 3 November 1944.
31. Ibid., letter from Prime Minister's office to the Ministry of Public Instruction, 15 November 1944. Zolli's candidacy for a teaching post was also pressed by Capt. Neufeld. See Neufeld Papers, Letter from Maurice Neufeld to Hilda Neufeld, 15 February 1945.
32. Zolli file, letter from Ottolenghi to the Prefecture of Rome, 27 December 1944 and Ottolenghi statement, 26 January 1945.
33. Ibid., statement of Dr. Augusto Calonzi, 19 January 1945. Enclosed in letter from Zolli to Ottolenghi, 19 January 1945.
34. Ibid., statement of Dr. August Fiorentini, 21 January 1945.
35. Neufeld Papers, container 21, report of the Extraordinary Commissioner of the Jewish Community, Silvio Ottolenghi, for the Administration Council, elected on March 18, 1945, p. 2.
36. Zolli file, Eliseo testimony, 26 July 1945.
37. Hochman Papers, Hochman statement (undated).
38. Neufeld Papers, letter from Neufeld to Zolli, 1 February 1945.
39. Ibid., container 21, letter from Zolli to Neufeld, 8 February 1945.
40. *L'Osservatore Romano*, 15 February 1945.
41. Father Paolo Dezza, personal interview, Vatican City, 22 May 1987.

42. Quoted in Ettore Ovazzo, *Il problema ebraico-Risposta a Paolo Orano* (Roma: Casa Editrice Pinciana, 1938), pp. 181–182.
43. Dezza interview, 22 May 1987. Dezza later became confessor to two Popes: Paul VI and John Paul I. He was also the temporary Superior General of the Jesuits.
44. Dezza, "Eugenio Zolli," *La Civiltà Cattolica*, p. 340.
45. Zolli file, undated statement of the Jewish Council.
46. Miriam Zolli-deBernart, personal interview, Rome, 23 May 1987. Even Miriam's daughter, Maura, who was born after her grandfather's conversion, reports being the target of verbal abuse over the years. Maura de Bernart, personal interview, Rome, 23 May 1987.
47. Eugenio Zolli, *Christus* (Roma: Casa Editrice A.V.E., 1946), p. 155.
48. *Palestine Post*, 18 February 1945.
49. Miriam Zolli-de Bernart interview, 23 May 1987.
50. *Israel*, 15 February 1945. It is curious that *Halachah* (Jewish religious law) rejects the possibility of a bona fide Jew forsaking his faith. He can renounce Judaism. He can go through the prescribed initiation ceremonies of another religion. He is still a Jew according to *Halachah*, although one who has transgressed.
51. Neufeld Papers, container 21, letter from Maurice Neufeld to Hinda Neufeld, 15 February 1945.
52. Hochman Papers, statement by Chaplain Jacob Hochman, Rome Synagogue, 16 February 1945.
53. Under the British mandate for Palestine, the Jewish Agency had the responsibility for supervising the creation of a Jewish homeland. Both Zionists and non-Zionists were members.
54. Letter from Maurice Neufeld to Hinda Neufeld, 15 February 1945.
55. Zolli file, letter from Ottolenghi to Berman, 9 March 1945.
56. Berman papers, letter from Rabbi Berman to Judith Berman, 4 March 1945.
57. Hochman statement (undated).
58. Zolli file, Report of the Meeting of the Rabbinical Assembly in Genoa, 1 and 2 August, 1945.
59. Trieste Synagogue Archives, letter from David Prato to Clemente Kerbes, Commissioner of the Israelite Community of Trieste, 29 November 1945.
60. Piero Modigliani, personal interview, Rome, 28 May 1987.
61. Clara Della Seta, personal interview, Rome, 1 June 1987. Nello Povencello, a former rabbinical student, recently asserted that after Zolli's conversion, priests and nuns went to the Great Synagogue to proselytize. Personal interview, Rome, 27 May 1987.
62. See, for example, Newman, *A "Chief Rabbi,"* pp. 19–20.
63. Meyer Levin, "What's Left of the Jews," *The Nation*, 28 July 1945, p. 75.
64. "The Challenge of Rabbi Zolli's Conversion," *The Reconstructionist*, No. 2 (March 9, 1945): 4–5.
65. Daniel Frisch "Another Letter by the Layman to His Daughter," *New Palestine*, 36 (October 12, 1945): 19–20.
66. A. S. E. Yahuda, "The Conversion of a 'Chief Rabbi,' " *The Jewish Forum* (September, 1945): 174–175, 177.
67. *Jewish Chronicle*, 23 February 1945.
68. *American Jewish Year Book, 5707* (1946–1947) Volume 48. (eds. Harry Schnei-

derman and Julius B. Maller). (Philadelphia: The Jewish Publication Society of America, 1946), p. 298.

69. Hochman statement (undated).
70. *Israel*, 22 February 1945. After the war Casper enjoyed a distinguished career as a rabbi and an educator in Britain and in Israel. Beginning in 1963 he served for almost a quarter of a century as chief rabbi of Johannesburg. He died in Jerusalem in 1988.
71. Zolli file, letter from Mrs. E. S. Schweig to Zolli, 16 February 1945.
72. Ibid., letter from Dr. Kalman Friedman to President of the Jewish Community Rome, 14 March 1945.
73. Quoted in Newman, *A Chief Rabbi of Rome Becomes A Catholic*, p. 80.
74. Ibid., p. 4.
75. *Jewish Telegraphic Agency*, 15 February 1945.
76. "Zolli's Apostasy," *Opinion*, 15, no. 5 (March, 1945): pp. 3–4."
77. National Archives, Suitland, Md., RG84 Records of the Foreign Service Posts of the Department of State, Rome Embassy and Consulate, General Records 1945: 840.1-841.5 Box 154, Letter dated 15 March 1945. Also see 1944 American Embassy-Rome correspondence-Kirk, File #824 Continued 843, Vol., XXV, Letters 18 November 1944 and 7 December 1944.
78. *The European Jewish Observer*, 15 December 1944.
79. Ibid., 23 February 1945.
80. Ibid. Rabbi Morris Kertzer minimized the significance of the conversion of a Chief Rabbi. He graded as mediocre the rabbinate in Italy, France, and North Africa. As scholars they were generally not exceptional, as speakers they were almost all poor and, in general, they lacked warmth in their interaction with people. Moreover, he concluded that the appellation "Chief Rabbi" was empty of real meaning given the fact that the Roman Chief Rabbi led a congregation no larger than that of Des Moines, Iowa. Kertzer, *With an H*, p. 65.
81. *The Jewish Standard*, 23 February 1945.
82. Ibid.
83. *Avanti*, 15 February 1945. Also see *Risorgimento Liberale*, 14 February 1945, and *Il Quotidiano*, 15 February 1945.
84. Dezza, "Eugenio Zolli . . . ", pp. 344–345.
85. Cited in the prologue to Eugenio Zolli, *Mi Encuentro Con Cristo*. trans. Jose Maria Gonzalez Ruiz (Madrid: Ediciones RIALP, 1948) p.vii. The prologue was written by Francisco Cantera Burgos who held the chair in Hebrew language at the University of Madrid.
86. A. B. Klyber, "The Chief Rabbi's Conversion," *The Catholic Digest* (September 1945), p. 92.
87. "From Synagogue to Christianity," *Journal of Religious Instruction*, 16 (October 1945): 173–174.
88. John M. Oesterreicher, review of *A "Chief Rabbi" of Rome Becomes a Catholic: A Study in Fright and Spite* by Louis I. Newman, *Catholic World*, 163 (April 1946), p. 86.
89. Ibid., Newman quotes an American to the effect that "these prospective apostates are no loss to the community" (p. 174).
90. Franz Rosenzweig (1886–1929) retreated from the brink of baptism to become a committed Jew.
91. John M. Oesterreicher, telephone interview, 11 January 1989.

8

The Zolli Conversion: Background, Motives, and Legacy

Since February 1945, Zolli's reason or reasons for becoming a Catholic have been the subject of much speculation. What really motivated him? Perhaps there is no monistic, no single, simple explanation for Zolli's decision to join the Catholic Church, but it is almost certain that revenge against the Jewish community for what Zolli perceived as its shabby treatment of him, especially after the liberation, was one major factor. Support for this thesis comes from various quarters, not all unfriendly to Zolli. For example, in a conversation in September, 1944 with Giorgio Fiorentino, one of his few staunch supporters, Zolli talked of the Jewish community's iniquitous attitude and threatened that if he were thrown into the streets after dedicating forty years of his life to Judaism, the community would pay dearly. Fiorentino was overwhelmed by the rabbi's words and cautioned Zolli about doing anything that would justify the conduct of Rome's Jews.[1]

On 11 February 1945, two days before Zolli's baptism, Rabbi Hochman encountered him leaving his rabbinical office where he had just presided over the divorce proceedings previously alluded to. They chatted for a while and Zolli cryptically commented, "Now I'm happy . . . they will now see what a mess they've gotten into by forcing my resignation."[2]

Shortly after being informed by a midnight telephone call that the Chief Rabbi had been baptized, Rabbi Berman telephoned the Zolli household to determine if the shocking information was accurate. He spoke to Miriam Zolli who neither confirmed nor denied the story but asserted that if her father had converted she could well understand it as he had received such bad treatment at the hands of the community.[3]

Zolli's estrangement from his congregation was also the central theme of his conversation with the Allied chaplains who visited him for two hours shortly after his conversion was announced by the Italian press. Berman, the senior Jewish chaplain in the Central Mediterranean force and a recipient of the MBE (Member of the British Empire) for his gallantry and distinguished service in Italy, meticulously recorded the conversation in a letter to his wife. Zolli explained at length how much he had suffered since he had been in the service of the Jewish community, first in Trieste and afterwards in Rome. There had been scant recognition of his scholarly qualities in Trieste in the nearly three decades he had spent there. But the treatment meted out to him in the Italian capital was even worse. From the outset he had encountered obstruction and an absence of appreciation. A litany of grievances tumbled from the ex-Chief Rabbi's lips. Animosity directed to Zolli when he reappeared after the Nazis departure had made him sullen. On the very first day he came out of hiding, he had been the target of violence.[4]

Echoing the erstwhile Chief Rabbi's sentiments, Berman wrote that Zolli was fatigued, ill, and under considerable strain. Furthermore, he was hungry and he bemoaned the fact that his salary was inadequate to meet his basic needs. Zolli told the chaplains that at the age of sixty-four he was being abandoned, notwithstanding the fact that he had worked long and faithfully, toiling from morning until night, day in and day out. It was obvious to Zolli that he was a pariah in the community which wished to recall his predecessor, Rabbi David Prato, from Palestine.[5] What was he to do? Where was he to go? It is highly significant that during this long discussion the embittered Zolli used the Hebrew term *meshummad lehachis*, a convert out of spite, more than once.[6]

Berman who had allowed Zolli to bare his soul without interruption, then said that he appreciated all the suffering and hardship that the Chief Rabbi had undergone and felt great sympathy for him. Perhaps in the hope of convincing Zolli to renounce his conversion, Berman granted that Zolli had made a persuasive case of communal ingratitude, but was that enough to make him a Catholic?[7]

The Polish-born Hochman, a graduate of the Jewish Theological

Seminary, who had served as a chaplain in the American army for two and a half years in Algeria, Tunisia, and finally in Rome, reminded Zolli of a conversation they had had four or five months earlier in which the Chief Rabbi had declared the following: "How beautiful Catholicism is on the outside. Everything is so orderly. The authorities receive so much respect. But on the inside—nothing. And Judaism, how shabby on the outside—but on the inside so rich."[8]

Zolli brushed Hochman's recollections aside and replied that he did not wish to engage in any polemical discussions. He did add that he had thought about the subject of Christianity for a long time and found the figure of Christ very appealing.[9]

It is noteworthy that when Rabbis Berman and Hochman spoke to Zolli's wife that same morning she spoke of her husband as a "great man who was not understood by his people; a tired, old man who had been abused by them." In the new milieu, she said, obviously referring to the Catholic Church, "his capacities were appreciated."[10] Apparently that day neither Rabbi nor Mrs. Zolli mentioned any personal religious experience they had recently undergone. This oversight takes on considerable importance in the light of Zolli's later explanation for the fateful step he took in February 1945.

Rumors have long circulated that Emma Majonica, whom Zolli had wed after the death of his first wife in 1920, was not Jewish by birth. Indeed, one Zolli detractor wrote that the 13 February 1945 baptism was a "reconversion" for Emma because she was actually a "Catholic girl" to begin with. In order to marry a rabbi, she had to become a Jew. After twenty-five years of Judaism, "he simply brought the lost sheep back to the fold of her shepherd."[11] Father Pietro Paolo Boccaccio, an eyewitness to the baptism, also suspected that Zolli's consort was originally Catholic, for he observed her holding a crucifix and an old dogeared prayer book which, he assumed, had long been in her possession.[12] However, Miriam Zolli de Bernart has stated that her maternal grandfather was a Jewish archaeologist and her maternal grandmother a Catholic who had embraced Judaism.[13] Birth records of Gorizia show that Emma Majonica was born into the Jewish faith.[14] In any case, there is no evidence suggesting that Zolli's decision to join the Catholic Church was influenced by his second wife who seems to have followed her husband's lead in most matters.

Rabbi Berman posed the puzzling paramount question in the following terms: was this conversion "a case of treacherous traitorship or calculated fraud" or, alternatively, was it an act that sprang from "genuine affection for the Catholic faith" engendered by Zolli's scholarly studies of Christianity?[15] Berman himself came to the conclusion that the community was not blameless, that money which had been a large bone of contention between it and Zolli had provided the catalyst for the conversion. Berman had not the slightest doubt that had the community decided to retain Zolli and had it offered him an "honorable salary," he would not have taken the sacrament. For Berman, one of the most painful experiences of his entire life was hearing Commissioner Ottolenghi try to prove his loyalty to the Jews of Rome by explaining that he had sought a way to pay Zolli the smallest possible pension upon his retirement.[16]

In contrast, Rabbi Hochman ascribed the ex-Chief Rabbi's "strange act" to a personality disorder, an aberration. Zolli's personality was a sick one, the American chaplain thought.[17] For Rabbi Louis Newman, Zolli was sure to prove a "fertile subject for psychiatrists."[18] It sorely strained Jewish credibility to accept the idea that Zolli's conversion was rooted in his sincere espousal of Jesus as the messiah.

Yet in his 1954 autobiographical remembrances entitled *Before the Dawn*, Zolli asserted simply that his "conversion was motivated by a love of Jesus Christ."[19] His mystical attraction to Jesus was traceable to childhood experiences. By the time Zolli was five or six years of age, his family had moved from Brody to Stanislavia, another city in the Austrian-controlled region of a partitioned Poland. There on the wall of a friend's home was a wooden crucifix with an olive branch over it. Whenever young Israel gazed at it he felt his spirit stirring. He found that Christ awakened in him a sense of great compassion.[20]

In retrospect, it is difficult not to be skeptical of Zolli's account of his initial encounter with a crucifix. Given the melancholy history of anti-Semitism in Poland and the late nineteenth century recrudescence of Jew-baiting in Austria, an association between the figure of Christ and the quality of mercy was most unlikely for a Jew in that era. For almost two millennia, Jews had been persecuted in Christ's name. They had been maimed and killed because their forefathers had supposedly been guilty of the crime of deicide, of murdering God's only begotten son. Pogroms had often been carried out during Easter by mobs with Christ's name on their lips. Yet Zolli would have the readers of his autobiography believe that a Jewish child educated in Jewish schools and nurtured in a Jewish home would equate Jesus with compassion.[21]

According to Zolli, the seeds of the future conversion sown in his Galician childhood would ripen half a century later in Rome. During the intervening years, Zolli remained haunted by the mystery and meaning of Jesus' passion on the cross.

Sometime during World War I—probably in 1917—he underwent what he claimed was the first in a series of intensely personal religious experiences. Seated alone in his house, Zolli, "as if in a trance, began to invoke the name of Jesus." He then saw Jesus "as if in a large picture without a frame, in the dark corner of the room." Zolli stared at him " . . . without feeling any excitement, rather in a perfect serenity of spirit."[22] Other apparitions allegedly followed in 1937–38. With hindsight Zolli wrote that "Jesus had entered into my interior life as a guest, invoked and welcomed."[23] Jesus was present in him and he in Jesus, but he did not contemplate formal conversion because he had not yet heard the call to convert. That came only after the searing ordeal of Nazism and its appalling carnage.

In his memoirs, Zolli recounted a final, very profound religious experience which he underwent on Yom Kippur, the day of atonement, in 1944. During the last service on that holiest of days in the Jewish calendar, Zolli described himself as withdrawn from the ritual, conscious of neither sorrow or joy and devoid of thought and feeling. His heart was lifeless, he wrote. Then suddenly came a vision of Christ whom the Chief Rabbi was soon to embrace as the savior. Here is Zolli's verbatim account as published in a chapter entitled "The Triumph of the Rising Sun."

> I saw Jesus Christ clad in a white mantle, and beyond His head the blue sky. I experienced the greatest interior peace. If I were to give an image of the state of my soul at that moment I should say: a crystal-clear lake amid high mountains. Within my heart I found the words: "You are here for the last time." I considered them with the greatest serenity of soul and without any particular emotion. The reply of my heart was: So it is, so it shall be, so it must be.[24]

Zolli elaborated on the events that occurred in the wake of Jesus' Yom Kippur manifestation. Later that evening, after he had broken the obligatory Yom Kippur fast, Zolli's wife informed him that she too had had a vision of Christ. She claimed that when her husband had stood before the Holy Ark she had seen a white figure of Jesus place his hands on the rabbi's head as if to bless him.[25]

Indeed, in his autobiography Zolli contends that his daughter, Miriam, reported that she too had been dreaming that she saw a "very tall, white Jesus."[26] However, Miriam Zolli-de Bernart, a psychoanalyst in Rome, has categorically denied having had any religious experience in the fall of 1944. She insists that she is the least mystical of people and is not a practicing Catholic. "If you squeeze me like a lemon you would not find a drop of mysticism" are her exact words.[27] Although Miriam did convert after her parents, she retrospectively explained her conversion in terms of filial piety and love. She has explicitly stated that she would have followed her father to hell. Moreover, at that time she was confused and under considerable stress and did not want to feel isolated.

Curious indeed is the fact that autobiographical reflections Zolli penned just weeks after his February 1945 incorporation into the Roman Catholic Church do not contain a word about his recent Yom Kippur mystical experience in the synagogue which spelled finis to his career as a Chief Rabbi. Nor is there even a syllable about the apparitions of his wife and daughter Miriam. There is a very vague reference to "a time not long ago when Jesus appeared before the eye of the spirit."[28] Zolli heard the stride of his light foot, but declared that after his baptism he no longer saw nor heard anything as Jesus was in him. How could the former Chief Rabbi have completely overlooked such a profound religious adventure, such a life-changing event as his vision of Jesus in the Tempio Maggiore which he was able to narrate in vivid detail in 1954?

Perhaps that omission is even more bizarre in that his 1945 diary does include an allusion to a 1917 mystical experience which occurred, he said, at a time when he felt alone, fragile and broken, when he was unsure of who he was. He compared himself at that juncture in the midst of the Great War to a last piece of dust in the immense space of the universe. Life seemed meaningless. "Christ, save me," he cried out.[29]

Surely it is not coincidental that the foregoing occurred in 1917 in the wake of the death of Zolli's first wife. Other visions supposedly took place in 1937–38, a critical moment in Italian Jewish life, and in the fall of 1944 when Zolli was under assault by the Roman Jewish elders who wished to oust him.

In February 1945, Zolli wrote somewhat contradictorily that he could not speak of mystical raptures. Reason had always been his faithful companion. He had always reasoned things out without being a rationalist. His historical-religious studies, once an impediment on the path toward the gift of faith, came to assist him in those latter times. The gift of faith matured slowly in him, but finally the "light of thought harmonized with the heat of faith."[30] For such he thanked the Lord. Staying with Judaism, he concluded, was a dishonest thing to do for it meant proceeding on a road which was no longer his. Consequently he renounced everything.

Miriam Zolli-deBernart, who is still devoted to her father, believes that he had two sides to his nature—one scholarly, which enabled him to do rigorous Biblical exegesis, and a second, mystical aspect. After the tumultuous Nazi era, the latter came to dominate.[31]

Mysticism has often gone hand in hand with almost medieval asceticism. If Zolli was indeed a mystic, there was certainly not even a scintilla of self-denial in his makeup. Unlike, for example, Simone Weil, the French Jewish writer and mystic who, in the end, became a "slave" to Jesus,[32] Zolli never renounced worldly pleasures. His critics considered him unduly materialistic, even mercenary. Nor like Weil did Zolli identify with or toil for the downtrodden of society. Unlike Weil he showed no saintly concern for fellow human beings. He certainly never sought martyrdom as did Weil who deliberately starved herself to death in 1943. Zolli's quite normal self-protective conduct during the Nazi occupation was aimed at avoiding what he regarded as a pointless sacrifice.

The conflict between mysticism and rationalism within Zolli's soul was also commented on in 1945 by Giuseppe Bertel who claimed that he had known Zolli well during his own residence in Italy. Bertel acknowledged the cold, rational trend of Zolli's thinking, but he also discerned an opposing facet of the Chief Rabbi's character and thought in a lecture Zolli delivered in Modena, perhaps in 1934. Zolli's ideas dealt with the meaning and importance of prayer and how it generated emotional ecstasy. The talk brought vividly to Bertel's mind the words of St. Catherine and he became convinced that "at bottom Rabbi Zolli was a mystic."[33]

This curious amalgam of analytical detachment and intense mystical fervor that Bertel speaks about must be taken into account when trying to interpret and explicate a scholarly book written by Zolli when he was yet Chief Rabbi of Trieste's Jewish community and a professor of Semitic studies at the University of Padova.

Published in Udine by the Institute of Academic Editions in 1938[34], one year before Zolli was called as Chief Rabbi to Rome, *The Nazarene* is subtitled *Studies in New Testament Exegesis in the Light of Aramaic and of Rabbinical Thought*. In *The Nazarene*, Zolli demonstrates his impressive skills as a master philologist and biblical exegete through a series of interconnected essays focused on the figure of the Christ of the Gospels. At various intervals throughout the book, Zolli reminds readers of his stated goals first mentioned in the preface, that is, to present several essays on the contribution that ''the science of Judaism'' can offer towards the clarification of certain New Testament problems.[35] For a rabbi to devote an entire volume to the Christ of the Gospels may appear, at the very least, rather unusual; for a professor of Semitic philology and rabbinical thought at a State-run, secular university to do so seems perfectly in keeping with professional conduct and scholarly pursuits. Even prior to an assessment of *The Nazarene's* contents, then, Zolli's reader is placed in the uneasy position of trying to balance fairly these two seemingly irreconcilable conditions. What Zolli says about Christ, personally and theologically, can always be explained as pronouncements filtered through ''the science of Judaism.'' Nevertheless, the scientific detachment of the philologist and exegete does not necessarily rule out possible protests by readers, especially Jewish ones, who believe that Zolli ultimately appears to affirm Christ's divinity, and who does so in a conventional Christian manner: by underscoring the validity of the Gospel narration through recourse to Old Testament prefiguration and prophecy.

Admittedly, an impartial appraisal of *The Nazarene* and the debate to which it gives rise cannot be arrived at easily. Zolli's text abounds with statements that, when extrapolated from context, could support either a charge of Jewish heterodoxy or a defense on the grounds of dispassionate scholarship.

The books's opening chapter details the philological roots of the appellation, ''Nazarene'', as applied first to Christ and then to his followers. Citing extensively from Greek, Latin, German, French, and Italian scholarship, as well as from his own familiarity with Aramaic and Hebrew sources, Zolli argues that there is no reason to claim that the figure of the Nazarene and his geographical origins are merely mythological, or that the term was applied to Christ and his followers solely to distinguish one from any number of religious sects.[36] Instead, Zolli insists that, philologically and historically, the term Nazarene was coined by Christ's enemies who employed the term, Jesus of Nazareth, as polemic irony suggesting someone from nowhere important.[37]

Using an editorial "we," Zolli asserts that what remains essential is the fact that "It was Jesus—according to us—who rendered Nazareth famous and not Nazareth which made Jesus rise to the everlasting glory of Nazarene."[38] To these observations, Zolli adds his own philological contribution to New Testament exegesis when he concludes that Jesus and his followers received from everyone—from friends, from admirers, from adversaries—the name, "Nazarenes" which signifies "preachers."[39]

Even so cursory an assessment of this first chapter should substantiate the claim made earlier that Zolli's text can be evaluated in two distinct manners. The text may be cited as simply the scholarly research of a professional philologist and historian of religion. At the same time, however, the author's interest itself in resolving an exegetical debate centered on a proper designation of Christ as Nazarene could arouse the suspicions of any reader, especially a Jewish one, that Rabbi Zolli is very close to disclosing his own theological and personal inclinations to treat the Christ of the Gospels in a manner far removed from those usually associated with a more orthodox Jewish approach.

Subsequent chapters of *The Nazarene* seem to bolster these suspicions, though, once again, the controlled discourse of philological analysis serves to modulate outright declarations of faith. When describing the nature of Christ's doctrine, for example, Zolli—in a manner typical of most of the text's early chapters—adopts a manner that reveals personal conviction through implication alone: "Jesus speaks as one who has exousia, that is, not as one who represents an earthly power, but as one who has received religious and moral authorization from God himself."[40] Such use of introductory qualifiers abounds throughout the text[41] and leaves the reader to speculate on the exact nature and degree of Rabbi Zolli's innermost sentiments and convictions.

As the reader draws near to the end of the text, however, ambiguities dissolve and detached scientific discourse gives way to pronouncements of a more direct temper. When addressing the Gospel narrative of Christ's last hours, Zolli uses parallelisms and precedents from Hebrew scripture to confirm, in effect, that Christ is the fulfillment of Old Testament prophecy. Zolli first cites Christ's ability to predict the unfolding of his betrayal, passion, and death as proof of "the divine force of the foresight possessed by Jesus."[42] Then calling attention to the ritual of Christ's washing of his followers' feet at the last Seder, Zolli states that: "The washing of the feet therefore results—according to the conception we have exposed—in a charismatic act that elevates the disciples precisely to the level of apostles, *eo ipso* to the level of angelic beings."[43] From this observation, Zolli moves next to declare that: "The fundamental idea is that to receive Christ, be it purely through one of his emissaries, means to receive God. Everywhere it ensues: Christ is God."[44] On the very next page, Zolli's syllogism is finally brought to a decidedly christological conclusion: "Christ is the Messiah and the Messiah is God: therefore Christ is God."[45]

One could argue that Zolli is merely adopting here the logic of the Gospel text itself. Nevertheless, a close reading makes clear the unequivocal ring of the pronouncements. Indeed, it would be difficult to dismiss these assertions as simply dispassionate exegetical clarifications.

Moreover, it would be equally difficult to overlook as mere exegesis or impersonal philological explication a number of declarations Zolli enunciates in the book's closing pages. Intellectual allegiance, not mere reporting, seems to fire Zolli's assertion that

> The definition of Jesus's sacrifice that St. Augustine gives is most exact from the historical-religious point of view. It is perfectly situated on the line of development of that process of the human soul that we have just now analyzed, a line of development that begins in its primordial inception with the concept of *kippuru* and which arrives, by means of various phenomena, right up to the figure of Christ.[46]

And persuasion, not philological inquiry, would appear to support Zolli's declarations that

> Jesus and Jeremiah are the two great misunderstood figures in the history of Israel. . . . Jesus foretells a kingdom that is not of this world; not of this earth.[47]
>
> Jesus represents a turning of heaven towards earth. Jeremiah is an attempt at ascension, a desperate invocation that the earth rise to heaven. Jesus wants to found a new kingdom; Jeremiah wants to save a kingdom about to collapse.
>
> Jeremiah wants to rescue; Jesus wants to redeem. . . . [48]
>
> Like the blood of Abel, the blood of Christ screams toward heaven.
>
> Ezekiel promises a resurrected earthly Jerusalem. Jesus promises the kingdom of heaven, a celestial Jerusalem.[49]

Subsequently, in less epigrammatic, more discursive language—and despite similes that poorly conceal the author's adhesion—Zolli proclaims:

> Jesus appears as the strong one who accomplishes prodigies without equal (neither Jeremiah nor the e b h e d J. [Servant of Yahweh] accomplish miracles) with the help of his Father in heaven, Jesus is like the man who, having died amid earthly pain, reappears following ascension into eternal glory. Jeremiah and the e b h e d J. are both vanquished; Jesus is the unvanquished and triumphant victor.[50]

Finally, assertions in the book's concluding pages seem to provide a possible interpretative key to Zolli's attachment to the Christ of the Gospels, although seven years will pass before Zolli publicly avows his allegiance to the Christ of the Roman Catholic Church. Twice on the last page, in summary fashion, Zolli indicates that it is the transcendental nature of the union between the transient and eternal as embodied in Christ that speaks to his own thirst for the mystical. This personification of mystical union likewise satisfies a longing present beneath the surface of Jewish religious history:

> Rabbinical teaching, despite the fact that it was widespread and popular, was never within easy reach of everyone. By now the bloody cult no longer satisfied that instinctive need to sacrifice that a people so profoundly religious as Israel feels. And the eternal, imperishable thirst for mystical sensations lived yet beneath the surface of the Hebrew soul. A people who have produced the sublime figure of the e b h e d J. can not have completely forgotten it. The desire to sacrifice for reasons of catharsis, for reasons of finding again the way to reconciliation with the Lord,

> cannot be extinguished in the soul of Israel. All that is reflected in the figure of Christ . . . the nostalgia for mystical communion with the Absolute.[51]

Having posited this mystical thirst for the Absolute within the Jewish tradition from its very inception through to Christ, Zolli universalizes the experience in language that can only be described as rhapsodic. It is hard to imagine the rabbi as distinct from the detached Biblical scholar making such pronouncements as the following:

> These remembrances, these desires, these aspirations form a synthesis which is personified in Jesus. The kippuru is accomplished, and it is the sacrifice of one's own self, and it is the blood that flows, and it is the blood freely shed, and it is the act of reconciliation by which God is glorified and sanctified, and it is the mystical union with the Absolute.[52]

Given such statements open to public scrutiny, it is curious, indeed, that a cry of protest—or at least a demand for explanation—did not arise from the Jewish community. This is true especially in regard to the community in Rome where, just a year later, its representatives would call Zolli from Trieste to serve as Chief Rabbi at Italy's most prestigious synagogue. Instead, *The Nazarene* became the subject of violent attack only seven years later, after the rabbi's conversion to Catholicism. Within days of the conversion, the *Daily News Bulletin* of the Jewish Telegraphic Agency, an international wire service specializing in Jewish affairs, reported on the Zolli affair on 20 February 1945. When informing its readership on the Zolli conversion, the "Bulletin" unleashed a scathing condemnation of *The Nazarene*. According to the report, Zolli allegedly replied to the demands of journalists for an account of his conversion by stating that: "This has been going on in me for years, for tens of years."[53] This admission on the part of Zolli that his conversion was the result of a long incubation is what prompted the editors of the *News Bulletin* to revive debate on Zolli's 1938 publication.

In a terse but biting critique of *The Nazarene*, the editors of the *News Bulletin* quote directly from the text to intimate that Zolli's pronouncements on the nature of Jesus and the soundness of Christ's doctrine were, from the start, antithetical to Jewish teaching. A careful check of the quotations reveals that, indeed, all do appear in *The*

Nazarene, though the editors of the *News Bulletin* provide only snippets wrenched from context, most likely because of the constraints imposed by its telegraphic format. Nevertheless, after reading the entire text of *The Nazarene*, one must concur with the polemical thrust of the editor's indictment. That indictment charges Zolli's book with promoting an acceptance of Christ as Messiah despite its scholarly facade. In 1945, Zolli himself quoted an unnamed archbishop's evaluation of *The Nazarene*: "Everyone is susceptible to errors, but so far as I can see, as a bishop, I could sign my name to this book."[54] Zolli's personal testimonial to the Christ of the Gospels remains all the more remarkable since its author was about to preside for six years as Chief Rabbi of Europe's most ancient Jewish community.

Jews in Italy and abroad found it implausible that Zolli, whose intellectual stature had never been in question, had sincerely relinquished Judaism for Catholicism. To believe that the conversion was genuine was to somehow admit that in the doctrinal competition between the two faiths, Judaism had been found wanting. Jews therefore attributed Zolli's baptism to psychological quirks, to personality shortcomings, or to a vendetta against the Roman Jewish community which, in effect, had dismissed him as Chief Rabbi. Jews were eager to believe that they had rebuffed Zolli before he rejected them.

The truth appears to be more complex. At least on some level of his being, Zolli had intellectually and emotionally crossed the line—some would say it was a gulf—that demarcated Judaism from Roman Catholicism even before the onset of World War II. However, it was the envenomed relations between Zolli and the Jews of Rome after June 1944 that provided the proximate cause, the spark and the incentive for the formal conversion, that determined its timing and its circumstances.

If Rabbi Zolli thought as a Catholic by 1938, if he accepted Christ as the messiah foretold in the Old Testament, why did he not have himself baptized then instead of waiting seven years? Perhaps we will never know the answer to this intriguing question. Cynics would postulate that his concern with career advancement discouraged him from doing so. After all, he had devoted a lifetime to the rabbinate. To be sure, his position in Fascist Italy would not have been improved by baptism inasmuch as the Racial Laws promulgated in November 1938 defined as Jewish a convert whose mother and father were both

Jewish. It was a "biological" definition to which the Catholic Church took strong exception.

Flight from Italy was also an option open to Zolli at that juncture. Supposedly, in 1938 Zolli was offered an opportunity to teach at Dropsie, a Jewish college in Philadelphia, but he declined the offer. Why? His daughter Miriam explains that he could not take his fellow Jews with him and he was unwilling to abandon them.[55] So he stayed in Trieste, a Marrano in reverse. Unlike the Marranos of old who were outwardly Catholic and inwardly Jewish, Zolli remained Jewish, even rabbinical on the outside, but covertly Catholic within.

Given Zolli's romance with Catholicism even before he took up residence on the banks of the Tiber, is it conceivable that Zolli's "rebirth" was the consequence of a deliberate seduction by the Holy See? Captain Neufeld who was stunned when informed of Zolli's conversion by a late night phone call from the chaplains, suspected that the Vatican had enticed Zolli: "The Pope had made it known, through the devious means the Church is adept at, that the Pope would grant Zolli an audience if he desired one."[56] According to Neufeld, the Swiss Guard, the pontiff's colorfully attired bodyguards, then performed their "fancy gyrations" and Pius XII told Zolli that while he might not be fully appreciated by his own denomination, it was readily apparent that he was highly valued by the Catholic Church. Assurance of a post either as a teacher or a librarian was also part of the seduction.[57] Neufeld further speculated that the conversion which took place just before Lent, might have been encouraged by the Church to embolden upper middle class Jews already predisposed to Catholicism to take the final step away from Judaism. This thesis has not been corroborated and no proof was cited by Neufeld at the time. While it may be safely assumed that the Church did not discourage Zolli's desire to embrace Catholicism, it is almost certain that the Chief Rabbi, not the Vatican, was the first to make overtures.

Although Zolli undoubtedly chose Eugenio as his baptismal name in order to honor Pius XII—this has been confirmed by his daughter Miriam and by Father Dezza[58]—he unequivocally denied that he converted out of gratitude to the Pope.[59] Despite persistent rumors to the contrary, Zolli did not seek nor did he enjoy sanctuary in the Vatican when the Nazis occupied Rome. Nevertheless, within two weeks of the liberation of Rome, Zolli, speaking in his temple, expressed appreciation for what the Catholic Church, particularly the Pope, had done for persecuted Jews during the Nazi occupation. Thanks to Pius XII's indefatigable efforts Jewish lives had been saved. Because of his intercession harsh penalties had been mitigated.[60] Five weeks later, the Chief Rabbi was granted a twenty-five minute private audience with the Pontiff. Zolli's purpose in going to the Vatican was to formally voice his thankfulness to Pius XII for the material and moral succor the Vatican had provided the Jews of Rome. It was reported that Pacelli modestly commented, "What we did was nothing more than what was to be done."[61]

In Zolli's autobiography he wrote at length about Pacelli's magnanimity during the Holocaust in Italy. An entire chapter is devoted to his generosity and altruism in Zolli's autobiography.

> Like a watchful sentinel before the sacred inheritance of human pain stands the angelic Pastor, Pius XII. He has seen the abyss of misfortune towards which humanity is advancing. He has measured and foretold the greatness of the tragedy. He has made himself the herald of the serene voice of justice and the defender of true peace. He took into his heart the pain of all the sufferers.[62]

In Zolli's eyes, the Holy Father's charity was manifold. He even credited the pontiff with sending "by hand a letter to the bishops instructing them to lift the enclosure from convents and monasteries, so that they could become refuges for Jews."[63] There is no gainsaying the fact that countless Jews, perhaps thousands, found asylum in Italian churches, monasteries, and convents. The courage and humanity of many Catholic clergy in Italy who risked their lives to save the lives of Jews has been amply documented, but there is only the flimsiest evidence of a papal letter ordering or even encouraging them to do do so. As mentioned in Chapter 4, one priest in Assisi recalls seeing a letter in 1943 from the Vatican Secretary of State which supposedly requested bishops to go to the aid of endangered Jews. If such a letter existed in the voluminous Vatican archives it would surely have been produced by Vatican authorities to counter those beginning with Rolf Hochhuth in *The Deputy* who have pilloried Pius XII for his dereliction of moral duty.[64] To be fair to the pope, one cannot exclude the possibility that instructions to assist Jews were conveyed verbally.

* * *

Ever since 1945 there has been much conjecture about the depth of Zolli's Catholicism. Four decades after the conversion, Father Dezza remembered Zolli as a man of great intellectual honesty. Interviewed in the Vatican in 1987 when he was eighty-six years old, Dezza commented that the former Chief Rabbi impressed everyone with his warmth and modesty. He was very sympathetic, very human, Dezza told two American academics. At the Gregorian University where Zolli lived after his baptism, Zolli went to mass every morning and stayed afterwards to pray. There were times when he actually had to be summoned to breakfast. It was good to be with the Lord, Zolli reportedly told the Jesuit priest.[65]

It has been alleged by Father Dezza that Zolli at the Gregorian received visits from American Jews including Rabbi Hochman who wanted him to repudiate his conversion. They offered him whatever sums of money he desired, but he was unmovable. Even Protestants approached him to convince him that as a Biblical authority, he should understand that the primacy of the Pope was without any Scriptural basis. They too were snubbed.[66] Zolli had become a loyal son of the Catholic Church.

Zolli rejected the suggestion that the Jesuits or anyone else in this world had converted him. It was Jesus who had taken him sweetly by the hand. Zolli wrote that he profoundly and insatiably loved the Cross. He loved Jesus and opined that if everyone felt likewise all men would be brothers. Sooner or later, everyone does arrive at the throne of divine majesty, at the foot of the cross of Christ. Many are the ways, the destination only one, Zolli observed less than two weeks after his baptism.[67]

But the change from Judaism to Catholicism was a difficult one and Zolli actually founded a center for converted Jews under the auspices of the Sisters of Sion in Rome. The main purpose of the center was to ease the transition for converts like himself. Zolli attended on a regular basis.

Zolli insisted that he was steadfast in his loyalty to the Church. In 1950 he agreed to be interviewed by a reporter from the Israeli daily, *Ma'ariv*. Seeing a crucifix and a madonna on Zolli's walls, the journalist asked the former rabbi if he were an observant Christian. Zolli's reply was that he was ''religiosissimo,'' that is, extremely religious and added that he scrupulously observed all Catholic practices. The visiting Israeli then asked Zolli as the product of a pious family who for six and a half decades observed Jewish tradition if the holy days didn't elicit any desire to recite a Hebrew prayer or cause some Jewish sentiments to vibrate. Zolli's answer was unambiguous. It was as if the entire period of his life spent as a Jew had never existed. He felt as if he had been born Catholic.[68]

Zolli conveyed the same ideas to others. He told Sofia Cavaletti, his former student at the University of Rome who later became his assistant, disciple, and close friend, that he had really been a Christian since childhood without knowing it. He didn't know why he had waited so long to convert. Cavaletti was to write in 1956 that, after having shared with his race the dangers, suffering, and sacrifices of the Hitlerian persecution, Zolli "gathered unto himself the light of Christ."[69] She still views the erstwhile Chief Rabbi through rose-tinted glasses. Cavaletti is but one of those in the Catholic world who has described Zolli in the most positive, even glowing terms. Interviewed in her Roman apartment which, coincidentally, is located in the same building in which Pius XII was born, Cavaletti remarked that Zolli was a self-effacing man who did not like to talk about himself. He was truly devout. Indeed, religion was his life. Prior to his baptism, Cavaletti said, Zolli had no problem with the Jewish community as such, only with its president.[70] On that point Cavaletti is surely in error.

A reviewer of Zolli's autobiography in *Commonweal* also uncritically accepted the thesis that Zolli's conversion was an authentic one and that, "under the influence of the love of Christ" he was "well on his way to conversion long before he encountered the wonderful charity of Pius XII." In the reviewer's estimation, *Before the Dawn* was written "humbly and simply" and Zolli himself was "a man who wanted to love all, and from the first tended to love all."[71]

The autobiography earned kudos from virtually all Catholic reviewers none of whom entertained any doubts about Zolli's sincerity. One anonymous reviewer called the book much more than the "mere record of growing conviction under the impact of exposure to Christian doctrine." Every single page was characterized by "profound scholarship." In addition, as the saga of a soul it belonged "unashamedly with such texts as Augustine's and Teresa's."[72]

Although Zolli would not acknowledge any causal link between the conflict with some of his erstwhile coreligionists between 1943 and

1945 and the fact that his Catholic religiosity reached its apex at the same time, the available information clearly suggests otherwise. Perhaps Zolli thought it necessary to ingratiate himself with Catholic Church authorities, to convince them of the sincerity of his theological metamorphosis. A convert out of spite would not be so warmly welcomed into the bosom of the Church. In addition, his conversion, if spawned by anger and a thirst for revenge, would pain the Jews less than a bona fide change of heart. The latter would unmistakably imply that Judaism and its adherents are somehow deficient.

Many converts, including the modern-day "Jews for Jesus," insist that in espousing Christianity they are not forsaking Judaism. After his baptism, Zolli told Catholics that his conversion was not a rupture with his past but a continuation of it. For him Isaiah, the prophet, the servant of God, deserved to be nicknamed the fifth evangelist. It was Isaiah who had shown Zolli the path that took him to Christianity. Zolli had not denied his Jewish past. Was not the God of Jesus and Paul also the God of Abraham, Isaac, and Jacob, he asked rhetorically. When Paul converted he did not abandon the God of Israel, Zolli asserted. Neither had he.[73]

Zolli declared that the church—Christianity—was the completion, the crown, the integration of the synagogue. Judaism promised. Catholicism, true Christianity, fulfilled that promise. Christianity presupposed Judaism. Indeed one could not exist without the other.[74]

In sharp contrast, Judaism views itself as complete, perfectly capable of an independent existence without Christianity. It is not a prologue to Christianity. Furthermore, Jews see conversion as both treason to one's people and to one's faith and perceive converts as traitors. Because of Zolli's eminence and his high visibility, because he surreptitiously studied for his baptism while simultaneously serving as Chief Rabbi, Jewish animosity towards him was profound. Of course, the timing of the conversion which came on the heels of the Nazi cataclysm only deepened that animosity.

After Zolli's baptism, he had virtually nothing to do with his former coreligionists in Rome. However, in an autobiographical note written just days after his baptism, Zolli protested that he still loved the Jews from the bottom of his heart in the name of the Lord, and feelingly denied that he was a serpent burning in the breast of the Jewish community, one journalist's derogatory appellation. Zolli spoke of the many tears he had shed for the persecuted and barbarically slaughtered Jews. ''Your people are my people,'' he stated. They were of the same stock, but his God was not their God. His was the God of pity, of suffering, of pain. His was the God who had revealed himself in the world after Moses and the prophets in Jesus.[75]

As for the Jews, they scorned him before the conversion. They loathed him afterwards and he, in turn, continued to feel that he, not they, had been ill-treated. A furious Jewish Council had decided in the wake of the baptism that because of Zolli's ''deplorable'' and ''disgraceful'' behavior, the promised pension was no longer due him. Zolli appealed that decision to the civil authorities until May 1946. But, fearful of incurring heavy legal fees, he finally opted to forego the pension altogether.[76]

It is most improbable that Zolli expected his spartan standard of living to be markedly improved by joining the Church. While his life as a Catholic was far from luxurious, his appearance certainly changed for the better. A photograph of Zolli taken some time after his conversion, probably in 1953 or 1954, reveals a clean-shaven, somewhat portly man seated at his desk on which a cross is prominently displayed. The photograph contrasts sharply with several photographs taken of him in rabbinical garb after the liberation of Rome. Those portray a bearded, thin, even emaciated man with a dyspeptic expression on his countenance. It is hard to believe that the earlier and later photographs are of the same individual. Of course, Zolli's almost cadaverous appearance in 1944 may have been due to nutritional deficiencies in his wartime diet. An alternative explanation is that the born-again Zolli no longer forced to function as a closet Catholic, was a man at peace with himself.

As far as can be determined, after February 1945, Zolli had little or no contact with his far-flung rabbinical colleagues in the Jewish world to whom he had become a pariah. He had exchanged his Jewish cosmos for a Catholic cosmos. Instead of heading the rabbinical college and training future rabbis, he taught seminarians at the Pontifical Biblical Institute.

Zolli's scholarly research and writing continued unabated. Between 1945 and his death eleven years later he was as prolific as he had been prior to his baptism. His volume on anti-Semitism appeared in 1945 followed quickly by *Christus*. In 1950 an American publisher brought out his *Nazarene*, a new revised edition in English of Zolli's 1938 book on Jesus.[77] No longer was there any ambiguity. The author's Catholicism was readily apparent from the beginning. Three years later there was *L'Ebraismo*[78] and in 1954 his autobiography, *Before the Dawn*. The latter published in the United States in English with a foreword by the apostolic delegate in Washington, D.C. has never been translated into Italian. Consequently it is little known and unavailable in Italy. In 1956 Zolli's guide to the Old and New Testaments appeared.[79] Posthumously published was his *Talmud Babilonese*.[80]

On rare occasions after his conversion he saw the Pope, his namesake, but they never discussed his conversion, Zolli stated in 1950. When they met, they dwelled upon the Bible and the psalms. How did the Pope regard him, the previously mentioned Israeli newspaperman inquired of Zolli. The ex-Chief Rabbi smiled and replied, "As a Jew," and added that one time at the end of a conversation, the Pope invoked God's blessings on his family and "his people."[81] Perhaps Zolli's reply was actuated by a desire not to be viewed as a betrayer of Jews and Judaism.

The journalist was unsuccessful in luring Zolli into a discussion of Pius's sympathies or lack thereof for the Jews in the fledgling Jewish state. "We never discuss politics," Zolli stated laconically.[82] Of course, the Vatican had not established full diplomatic relations with Israel. Indeed it has never done so. Zolli who, as already noted, had visited Palestine in 1930 when he was still a rabbi in Trieste and had been favorably impressed, vehemently denied that he had been used for anti-Israeli propaganda on the issue of control over the holy sites there. At the time the internationalization of Jerusalem, the venue of most of those holy places, was a cardinal principle of Vatican Middle Eastern policy. Zolli even declared that he wished to pay a second visit but was fearful that the Jews in Israel would attack him as a turncoat.

Despite his bitter altercation with the Jews of Rome, Zolli *supposedly* tried to alleviate theologically based anti-Semitism after he became a Catholic. Once, a few days after the Zollis had received communion and had been confirmed, Father Dezza took them to see Pope Pius XII. Zolli wanted to express his devotion and to personally thank the pontiff. Mrs. Zolli, emotionally moved by the audience, said that she wanted to forgive those Jews who had insulted and threatened her, that after her baptism, she loved everyone and was incapable of hatred.[83] For some time the ex-Chief Rabbi and the reigning Pope spoke privately. Zolli later told Dezza that he had entreated the pontiff to remove references in the solemn Good Friday liturgy to "perfidious Jews." Pius refused to do so and explained to Zolli that the adjective "perfidious" which is ordinarily defined as "deliberately faithless" or "treacherous" or "deceitful" actually meant "incredulous" in the context of the Catholic prayers.[84] Nevertheless, on Good Friday in 1959, Pope John XXIII, Pius XII's successor, declared that henceforth the term "perfidious" with its pejorative connotation would be deleted from the traditional prayers for the Jews.[85] There is not a scintilla of proof that Zolli, directly or indirectly, brought about that change.

There has also been some speculation that Zolli may have influenced the 1965 Declaration on the Jewish People which was issued by the Second Vatican Council convened by John XXIII.[86] That declaration, a milestone in the friction-filled chronicle of Catholic-Jewish relations, stated that Christ's crucifixion "cannot be charged against all the Jews, without distinction, then alive, nor against the Jews of today."[87] It did not forgive the Jews. Rather, it disavowed the erroneous notion of collective Jewish guilt for the crucifixion, a notion so deleterious to Jewish well-being over the centuries. Furthermore, the declaration decried expressions of anti-Semitism and the hatred and persecution of Jews.

The architect of the declaration was Augustin Cardinal Bea who had been appointed president of the Vatican Secretariat for Promoting Christian Unity by John XXIII. A German Jesuit, whose father was a Bavarian woodcutter, Bea had once served as confessor to Pius XII.[88] A versatile linguist and a biblical scholar of high repute, Bea, in the 1920s, taught at the Pontifical Biblical Institute located near Rome's famous Trevi Fountain. In 1930, he became the rector there and for years worked indefatigably to modernize Catholic scriptural scholarship. Bea became Zolli's superior at the institute after the Chief Rabbi's conversion, but the nature of the relationship between the two men—both biblical exegetes—is not known. It is likely, according to Father Dezza, that if Zolli influenced Bea on the deicide issue, he did so very minimally and indirectly.[89]

There is some evidence that after World War II Bea as a German cardinal felt personal responsibility for the mass murder of Europe's Jews. He told Elio Toaff, Chief Rabbi of Rome since 1951, that he bore a large burden for the genocide of the Jews on his own shoulders.[90] If anyone had significantly shaped the Pope's and Bea's exculpation of the Jews for the passion of Christ, it was Jules Isaac, the French Jewish historian.[91] It was he, who had at Bea's request, documented the history of Jewish-Catholic contacts, especially the Church's traditional portrayal of the Jews as a "deicidal people." Consequently, in all likelihood, Vatican II's long overdue conciliatory gesture to the children of Abraham cannot be regarded as part of the Zolli legacy.

At least one of Zolli's Catholic disciples saw him as uniquely qualified to build bridges between the Church and the Jews. In a preface to one of Zolli's last books which was published the year of his death, Sofia Cavaletti wrote that the main function of Zolli's life was to demonstrate that from the Old to the New Testament there is no fracture of discontinuity, but rather a slow proceeding of spirit towards higher goals.[92] Cavaletti is of the opinion that Zolli, a biblical scholar who approached the Scriptures as a living document and who felt that both the Old and the New Testaments were for him, was the ideal person to explain the Jewish faith to Christians. But, in her judgment, the Catholic Church did not fully appreciate his value. It is true that during the summer of 1953 Zolli came to the United States and taught a course on Christian liturgy at Notre Dame University. While he was in South Bend, Indiana, Zolli corresponded with Cavaletti. In his lectures, Zolli was able to furnish his students with important information about the Jewish roots of Christianity. For instance, at Notre Dame he could teach about the Jewish background of the Last Supper which was actually a Passover *seder*.[93]

At that time Jewish fears that Zolli, the ex-Chief Rabbi, the biblical authority, would be used by the Church as a proselytizer, were heightened. History is replete with cases of Jewish converts to Catholicism who spearheaded evangelizing efforts among benighted Jews, writing and speaking of the many blessings of Catholicism. In Zolli's case, Jewish apprehension proved groundless.

In his 1945 book, *Antisemitismo*, Zolli wrote that forced conversions were nugatory and, in general, he avoided using a proselytizing tone. Jews and others, he said, were entitled to follow their consciences in the field of religion.[94]

Nevertheless, from the Jewish perspective, Zolli's apostasy is unforgivable. Among Roman Jews, it has never been forgotten. After his baptism, until his death in 1956 every year on the occasion of his birthday, Zolli received a greeting card from Rabbi Alfred Ravenna who had known Zolli at the rabbinical college. On the card Ravenna wished him ''tanti auguri'' and expressed hope that his eyes would be opened, the same sentiment and words long used by Catholics in their efforts to convert Jews.[95]

From Rabbi Ravenna's vantage point his eyes were never opened, or reopened to be more precise. Zolli died on 2 March 1956 and was interred in Rome's Campo Verano, the cemetery where the Pacelli family members had been laid to rest. In that mammoth, overcrowded burial ground there is a Jewish section, but Zolli was laid to rest with those of his adopted Catholic faith. His plain, inconspicuous tomb located next to that of his wife who died four years later bears only a simple cross and the following inscription on its facade: ''Prof. Eugenio Zolli'' and the dates of his birth and death. Inexplicably, although Zolli throughout his lifetime stated numerous times that he had been born in 1881, the tomb puts his date of birth in September 1885. Why is there this four year discrepancy over his year of birth? That is only one of the conundrums that confront those who would fathom the enigmatic former Chief Rabbi whose tortuous spiritual odyssey calls to mind an observation made in 1938 by a remarkable Afro-American, Paul Robeson. Robeson said, ''There can be no greater tragedy than to forget one's origins and finish despised and hated by the people among whom one grew up. To have that happen would be the sort of thing to make me rise from my grave.''[96] While the notion that the one-time Chief Rabbi *forgot* his origins is debatable, Robeson's observation, which he made with blacks in mind, applies no less to Jews in general and Eugenio Zolli né Israele Zoller in particular.

Notes

1. Zolli file, Giorgio Fiorentino testimony, 16 July 1945.
2. Hochman Papers, Hochman statement (undated). In his 1945 book, *Antisemitismo*, Zolli wrote that in history external intolerance or anti-Semitism had induced some Jews to convert. Others turned to Christianity because of internal intolerance, i.e., intolerance on the part of Jews towards other Jews. Such behavior was a centrifugal force within the bosom of Judaism.
3. Berman Papers, letter from Meyer Berman to Judith Berman, 18 February 1945.

4. Ibid., letter from Meyer Berman to Judith Berman, 21 February 1945.
5. Prato, who was born in Leghorn, had served as a cantor in Florence and as a rabbi in Alexandria before becoming Chief Rabbi in 1936. A passionate supporter of the Zionist cause, he was active in Italian Jewish organizations working for the creation of a Jewish state. In 1938 he emigrated to Palestine. Some believe that Prato was forced to retire from his Roman post because of his anti-Fascist activities. Certainly upon his return to Rome in 1945 he was recognized by the United States Embassy as one who had "a genuinely anti-Fascist background and holds the respect of the community." Alexander Kirk to Secretary of State, 23 February 1945, *National Archives*, American Embassy in Rome. Correspondence, File No. 840.1–841.5, Vol. 51.
6. Letter from Meyer Berman to Judith Berman, 21 February 1945.
7. Ibid.
8. Hochman statement (undated). One day after Zolli emerged from hiding, a mere two months before he opted to become a Christian, he manifested parochialism, even animosity towards Christians. He was visited in his old apartment by Rabbi Morris Kertzer. Zolli commented about a young man who was present on that occasion, "He's a fine man, even though he's a goy [Gentile]." Quoted in Kertzer, *With an H*, p. 61.
9. Ibid.
10. Ibid.
11. A. S. E. Yahuda, "The Conversion of a 'Chief Rabbi,' " *The Jewish Forum* (September 1945), p. 175.
12. Father Pietro Paolo Boccaccio, personal interview, Rome, 22 May 1987.
13. Miriam Zolli de Bernart, personal interview, 23 May 1987.
14. Trieste Synagogue Files, *Comunità israelitica di Gorizia-Registro di nati negli anni*.
15. Berman Papers, Letter from Rabbi Berman to Judith Berman, 21 February 1945.
16. Ibid., letter from Rabbi Berman to Judith Berman, 4 March 1945.
17. Hochman statement (undated).
18. Newman, *A "Chief Rabbi" of Rome Becomes A Catholic*, p. 80.
19. Zolli, *Before the Dawn*, p. x.
20. Ibid., p. 24.
21. This point was also made by Rabbi Gerald Raiskin in a sermon entitled "Story Of A Convert" which was delivered at the Stephen Wise Free Synagogue, New York City on 9 April 1954.
22. Zolli, *Before the Dawn*, p. 72.
23. Ibid., p. 73.
24. Ibid., p. 183.
25. Ibid., p. 184.
26. Ibid.
27. Miriam Zolli-de Bernart, personal interview, 23 May 1987.
28. Zolli, *Christus*, p. 179.
29. Ibid., pp. 162–163.
30. Ibid., p. 157.
31. Zolli-de Bernart, personal interview.
32. Robert Coles. *Simone Weil: A Modern Pilgrimage* (Reading, Mass.: Addison-Wesley Publishing Co., 1987), pp. 117–121.

33. Giuseppe Bertel, "The Case of Rabbi Zolli," *Congress Bi-Weekly* 2 March 1945, pp. 11–12. St. Catherine of Siena, a fourteenth century figure, was a popular blend of humanitarianism and mysticism. Canonized in 1461, in 1939 she was declared one of Italy's chief patron saints along with St. Francis of Assissi by Pope Pius XII.
A dichotomy also existed in the personality of Pius XII who was a cool, calculating rationalist and, at the same time, was mystical and otherworldly. Pacelli is known to have had visions, especially in the last decade of his life. In 1950, for example, while in the Vatican garden, he witnessed the reenactment of the famous miracle that occurred in Fatima, Portugal. There in 1917, it is said that the Virgin Mary appeared to three Portuguese children and imparted several prophecies. Again, in 1954 when he was gravely ill, Pacelli saw an apparition of Christ by his bed. Although the pontiff was at death's door, he was told by the Christ figure that he would not die then. According to the authors of a worshipful biography of Pius XII, *Crown of Glory*, not since St. Peter had a pontiff been blessed with a vision of Jesus. Alden Hatch and Seamus Walshe, *Crown of Glory: The Life of Pope Pius XII* (New York: Hawthorn Books, Inc. Publishers 1958) p. 6. Also see Corrado Pallenberg, *The Vatican From Within* (London: George G. Harrap & Co., Ltd., 1961), pp. 43–46 and "Tre Soli I Papi Che Videro Cristo E Come Lo Videro" in *Le Ore*, 1 December 1955.
34. Zolli, *Il Nazareno-Studi di esegesi neotestamentaria alla luce dell aramaico e del pensiero rabbinico* (Udine: Istituto delle Edizioni Accademiche, 1938 XVI).
35. Ibid., p. 221. Also: ". . . and desirous in this essay, as in the others that make up this volume, of interpreting correctly the Gospel text in light of Old Testament and rabbinical thought, we wish to say only that, both the Master himself in his predictions and in his prophecies, as well as the ancient source from which the evangelist has drawn, could have had in mind the shepherd of souls of Deuteronomy-Zechariah, the messianic figure, vilified, tortured, pierced and bemoaned as a god." Ibid., p. 302.
36. Ibid., pp. 24–25.
37. Ibid., p. 10.
38. Ibid., p. 18.
39. Ibid., p. 36.
40. Ibid., p. 55.
41. Compare this with "Jesus therefore gives the impression of a return of the Holy Spirit of prophecy in the midst of Israel." Ibid. p. 57; "He [Christ] finds himself in splendid isolation; his teaching has all the characteristics of a prophecy; he gives the living impression of singularity." Ibid., p. 42; "Here the Last Supper appears as a true and proper mystical communio between the Master and his disciples, between the Messiah and the heirs to the kingdom of God." Ibid., p. 218.
42. Ibid., p. 268.
43. Ibid., p. 269.
44. Ibid., p. 270.
45. Ibid., p. 271. Also, in discussing Christ's Sermon on the Mount: "However, if all the meek faithful are the adoptive sons of God, Jesus is the direct son, first and only begotten; he is the son of the covenant, like Isaac (and not Ishmael) was for Abraham, as Jacob (and not Esau) for Isaac; he is the 'Son of the Most High.' This

thought leads to a consideration of the Man-God, that is, or a man [who is] the chosen son and 'heir' of God.'' Ibid., p. 122; also: ''In the Gospels—as far as I know—no passage can be found that alludes to the 'God of Jesus,' but Jesus declares himself son of God, not like any other human creature, not in the sense of the biblical *banimattem* . . . , but in a completely particular manner. . . . Jesus is the son of God because of the particular relations that flow between the Lord and him (John XVI), because he alone offered himself to God [and] has carried out the great K i p p u r u in a completely personal way. Only such a figure could arise in the consciousness of millions of men to the level of an edifying and consoling divinity.'' Ibid., p. 352.

46. Ibid., p. 347.
47. Ibid., p. 349.
48. Ibid., p. 352.
49. Ibid., p. 353.
50. Ibid., p. 352. Also: ''. . . the singer of Psalm CXXV, in view of the sufferings endured by the righteous, is concerned with the reputation among peoples of the Lord's justice. Job puts in evidence the incompatibility between divine justice and human woes. One exalts and glorifies in the figure of the *ebhedj.*, and in the person of Jesus Christ human suffering is deified.'' Ibid., p. 330.
51. Ibid., p. 355.
52. Ibid.
53. See *Daily News Bulletin* of the Jewish Telegraphic Agency (New York) Vol. XII, no. 42, 20 February 1945. When *The Nazarene* appeared in English in 1950 five years after Zolli's conversion, it was abundantly clear that Zolli was thoroughly Catholic in his thinking. See Eugenio Zolli, *The Nazarene: Studies in New Testament Exegesis*. Trans. by Cyril Vollert (St. Louis: B. Herder Book Co., 1950).
54. ''Rabbi Zolli Explains,'' *Ave Maria*, 6 October 1945, p. 211.
55. Miriam Zolli-de Bernart interview, 23 May 1987.
56. Neufeld Papers, Container 21, Letter from Maurice Neufeld to Hinda Neufeld, 15 February 1945.
57. Ibid., and letter from Maurice Neufeld to the author, 2 December 1987 and Maurice Neufeld, telephone interview, 2 March 1987. When he returned to civilian life after the war, Neufeld enjoyed an outstanding academic career as a professor of industrial and labor relations at Cornell University.
58. Miriam Zolli-de Bernart interview, 23 May 1987 and Dezza interview, 22 May 1987. Zolli was of the opinion that the sanctity of Jesus Christ was reflected in the sanctity of the Pope. See Eugenio Zolli, *Christus*, p. 173.
59. Zolli, *Before the Dawn*, p. 189.
60. *New York Times*, 17 June 1944.
61. Ibid., 27 July 1944.
62. Ibid. and Eugenio Zolli, *Antisemitismo* (Roma: Casa Editrice, A.V.E., 1945).
63. Zolli, *Before the Dawn*, pp. 140–141.
64. Mae Briskin, ''Rescue Italian Style,'' in *The Jewish Monthly* (May, 1986), p. 22.
65. Dezza interview, 22 May 1987.
66. Ibid. and Dezza, ''Eugenio Zolli,'' p. 344.
67. Zolli, *Christus*, pp. 154, 156–157, 160–161.
68. *Ma 'ariv*, 9 June 1950.

69. See her preface to Eugenio Zolli, *Guida all'antico e nuovo testamento* (Milano: Garzanti, 1956).
70. Sofia Cavaletti, personal interview, 24 June 1985.
71. Leo R. Ward, "Conversion Story," *Commonweal*, 59, no. 26 (2 April 1954): 652–653.
72. *The Sign*, 33 No. 11 (June 1954), p. 71. Also see reviews in *Dominicana* 39 No. 386 (December 1954), p. 86; *Catholic World*, 179 No. 160 (May 1954), p. 160; *Integrity* 8 (June 1954), p. 8 and *The American Benedictine Review* 4 No. 365 (December 1953), pp. 365–366.
73. Dezza, "Eugenio Zolli," pp. 345–346. The question of "Who Is A Jew" has long bedeviled world Jewry. In December 1989, the Supreme Court of Israel ruled that so-called messianic Jews who accept Jesus as the Christ are not entitled to automatic Israeli citizenship under the Law of Return. By embracing Jesus as the messiah they have separated themselves from the Jewish nation. The high court's decision was consistent with the 1962 ruling in the renowned Brother Daniel case. Brother Daniel, a Polish Jew, assumed a Christian identity during the Holocaust, worked for a time as an interpreter for the Nazis, but leaked vital information about impending roundups to a nearby ghetto and thereby saved the lives of many of his co-religionists. After his true identity was revealed, he found sanctuary in a Carmelite nunnery where he converted to Catholicism. Eventually he became a monk and, in 1958, migrated to Israel where he petitioned the judiciary to recognize him as a Jew after the Minister of Interior refused to do so. The Supreme Court rejected his petition. Brother Daniel continued to live in Haifa and became a naturalized Israeli citizen. There are rabbinical authorities who believe that according to Halachah, apostates do remain Jews. See Norman L. Zucker, *The Coming Crisis in Israel—Private Faith and Public Policy* (Cambridge: The MIT Press, 1973): 179–188; Jacob Greenstein, "The Story of the Amazing Oswald (Shmuel) Rufeisen," *They Fought Back: The Story of the Jewish Resistance in Nazi Europe* ed. by Yuri Suhl (New York: Schocken Books, 1975): 246–252; Brother Daniel, personal interview, 14 October 1980.
74. See A. B. Klyber, "The Chief Rabbi's Conversion," *The Catholic Digest* (September 1945): 92–96. Klyber, himself a converted Jew, became a missionary priest.
75. Zolli, *Christus*, pp. 152, 154.
76. Waagenaar, *The Pope's Jews*, pp. 455–456.
77. Eugenio Zolli, *The Nazarene: Studies in New Testament Exegesis*, trans. by Cyril Vollert (St. Louis: B. Herder Book Co. 1950).
78. Zolli, *L'Ebraismo* (Roma: Editrice Studium, 1953).
79. Zolli, *Guida all' antico e nuovo testamento*.
80. Zolli, (ed.) *Talmud Babilonese: Trattato delle benedizioni* (Bari: Editori Laterza, 1958).
81. *Ma'ariv*, 9 June 1950.
82. Ibid.
83. Dezza, "Eugenio Zolli," p. 344.
84. Dezza interview, 22 May 1987. Cardinal Bea also wrote that, "Although to modern ears, this adjective has a pejorative ring, in the medieval latin [sic] of the time of the prayer's composition it simply meant 'unbelieving.' " See August Cardinal Bea, *The Church and the Jewish People: A Commentary on the Second*

Vatican Council's Declaration on the Relation of the Church to Non-Christian Religions. trans. by Philip Loretz (New York: Harper and Row Publishers, 1966), p. 22.

85. Following Vatican II Pope Paul VI renamed the old Good Friday prayer which had been "For the Conversion of the Jews." Henceforth it was simply "For the Jews." See Eugene J. Fisher, "The Roman Liturgy and Catholic-Jewish Relations Since the Second Vatican Council", *Twenty Years of Jewish-Catholic Relations*, ed. by A. James Rudin and Marc H. Tannenbaum (New York: Paulist Press, 1986), p. 137.
86. For example see Dan Kurzman, *The Race for Rome* (Garden City, N.Y.: Doubleday, 1975), p. 425. The same point was made by Fritz Becker, the representative in Rome of the World Jewish Congress, Fritz Becker, personal interview, 13 June 1985.
87. Bea, *The Church and the Jewish People*, p. 152.
88. Peter Hebblethwaite, *In the Vatican* (London: Sidgwick and Jackson, 1986), p. 148. Also see Bea's obituary in the *New York Times*, 18 November 1968. Though physically small, Bea was a tireless worker and emerged at the time of the Second Vatican Council as the Church's chief spokesman for the cause of ecumenism.
89. Dezza interview, 22 May 1987.
90. Elio Toaff, personal interview, 29 May 1987. Also see Malachi Martin, *Three Popes and the Cardinal* (New York: Farrar, Straus and Giroux, 1972), chapter 2.
91. Jules Isaac, *The Teaching of Contempt: Christian Roots of Anti-Semitism* (New York: Holt, Rinehart and Winston, 1964).
92. See her preface to Zolli, *Guida all'antico e nuovo testamento*.
93. Cavaletti interview, 24 June 1985.
94. Zolli, *Antisemitismo*, pp. 229–230.
95. Toaff interview, 29 May 1987.
96. Susan Robeson, *The Whole World In His Hands: A Pictorial Biography of Paul Robeson* (Secaucus, New Jersey: Citadel Press, 1981) p. 248.

9

Epilogue—the Vatican and the Jews since the Holocaust

On an April Sunday in 1986, Pope John Paul II took the unprecedented step of visiting the Tempio Maggiore in the Italian capital city. Located in the old ghetto close to the Ponte Garibaldi, the synagogue is a large stately structure. It has been described by one writer as "perhaps the most magnificent synagogue in Europe."[1] It is the same edifice in which Rabbi Zolli had held services and the one in which he allegedly had a vision of Jesus in the autumn of 1944. Of course, his name would not be mentioned on that Sunday in April 1986.

As far as can be determined, no reigning pontiff except for Peter perhaps, had ever previously set foot in a synagogue in Rome or anywhere else. John Paul II, Bishop of Rome, and Elio Toaff, the Chief Rabbi of Rome, embraced and silently prayed for a moment before entering the central synagogue to thunderous applause from a capacity crowd. A male chorus provided a stirring rendition of the 150th psalm as the two religious leaders walked to the front of the impressive domed Tempio to participate in what the Pope called an "historic celebration."[2]

In his address John Paul II expressed abhorrence of anti-Semitism over the centuries and of the genocide committed against the Jews in the Second World War. He reiterated *Nostra Aetate's* landmark repudiation of ancestral or collective Jewish guilt for the death of Christ, and also stated that Judaism was intrinsic to Catholicism. "With Judaism," he asserted ". . . we have a relationship which we do not have with any other religion. You are our dearly beloved brothers."[3]

To mark this memorable visit, the Vatican struck a medal which portrays the synagogue and St. Peter's basilica side by side on a bridge which spans the Tiber River. Above the two houses of worship is the date of the Pope's visit. On the obverse side of the medal there are three coats of arms, that of the synagogue, Pope John Paul's, and that of Vatican City along with a Star of David and a cross. In addition, there are two inscriptions, one in Latin, the other in Hebrew.[4]

Numerous Catholic leaders, lay and clerical alike, especially in the United States, extolled the papal visit as a meaningful symbol of improving Catholic-Jewish relations. Joseph Cardinal Bernardin of Chicago believed that it indicated "on the church's part a clear end to centuries of discrimination and persecution of the Jews and a deeper appreciation and affection for our Jewish brothers and sisters."[5] Dr. Eugene J. Fisher, director of Catholic-Jewish relations for the National Conference of Catholic Bishops, prophesied that the Pope's call on the Chief Rabbi would abate anti-Semitism and any condescending or superior notions Christians might harbor about Judaism.[6] Ecumenism was fostered by the pontiff's initiative in the judgment of Jean-Marie Cardinal Lustiger, the Jewish-born, Yiddish-speaking Archbishop of Paris who is himself a convert to Roman Catholicism. Cardinal Lustiger's mother died in Auschwitz because she was Jewish. Whether the synagogue summit was the watershed that some thought it to be, only time will tell.

What we do know for sure at this point is that since the defeat of Nazism in 1945, the Vatican has displayed somewhat greater appreciation of Jewish concerns. The issue of coercive conversion is illustrative and the little known Finaly affair provides a case in point.

With the Nazi menace ever present, Dr. and Mrs. Fritz Finaly, Jewish refugees who had fled Austria in 1939, were living quietly in La Tronche on the outskirts of Grenoble in France with their two small sons, Robert Michael and Gerald Pierre. However, in February 1944, the parents were seized by the Gestapo, summarily dispatched to the Drancy concentration camp near Paris and from there to a death camp in eastern Europe where they perished. Prior to their arrest, the Finalys found sanctuary for their sons in a Catholic nursery. As told by M. Keller of Grenoble, with a premonition of impending doom, the Finalys informed the mayor of La Tronche that should they not survive the Holocaust, it was their wish that one of Dr. Finaly's sisters rear the boys.[7] Ostensibly, the same wish was expressed to various friends.

By war's end the Finaly children were in the hands of Mlle. Antoinette Brun, the devout Catholic director of the municipal nursery in Grenoble who had sheltered the youngsters for some time at considerable peril to herself. When Dr. Finaly's elder sister, who was living in New Zealand, sought custody of her nephews, Mlle. Brun balked. She remained refractory even when approached by the Red Cross. In addition, she had Robert and Gerald baptized, although it was illegal under French law for a guardian to change the religion of a child without the consent of a family council. After protracted and complicated legal wrangling, there was a surprising turn of events in early 1953 when they were kidnapped and spirited across the Pyrenees into Spain by a coterie of priests and nuns.

As had been the case with Captain Alfred Dreyfus more than half a century earlier, France was deeply fissured over the Finaly affair. Francois Mauriac, the Catholic writer, entered the lists on behalf of Mlle. Brun and asked rhetorically which of two competing allegiances would emerge victorious in the hearts of the Finaly youths:

> The allegiance to their fathers, to the ashes of martyrs, or the allegiance to that son of David who was crucified for them, too, who has marked them with his sign, and who since their baptism, knows them by their first names? Perhaps they themselves will know how to effect a synthesis between these two allegiances. Is not Christianity, for a baptized Jew, the fulfillment of the word given to Abraham, our father.[8]

And a Father Gabel writing in the organ of the Roman Catholic Church in France, *La Croix*, echoed the papal sentiments heard at the time of the Mortara abduction, when he dogmatically declared: "The Church is a perfect society that has authority over those men who have become its members by baptism."[9]

In early March 1953, it seemed that the Vatican was adamantly opposed to delivering the war orphans to Jewish authorities or providing them with a Jewish education. A Vatican Under Secretary of State told the head of France's Liberal Jewish movement that the Finaly brothers were Catholic, period. Their baptism was valid and they were entitled to select their own faith "without moral pressure from the Synagogue."[10]

Outraged Jews argued that the Catholic Church stood before the historical bar of justice. Pius XII had the power to bring the Finaly catastrophe to a happy and just conclusion. "Dare we hope his Holiness will rise to the occasion?"[11]

At long last the impasse was broken. A French court granted guardianship of the Finaly brothers to an aunt, Mrs. Moshe Rosner, a sister of Dr. Finaly's, who resided in Israel. In the spring of 1953, amidst an international furor over their kidnapping, an agreement calling for their return to France from Spain was worked out by the Chief Rabbi of Paris and the French Catholic Church.[12]

In the end, the Church was unable or unwilling to exercise sole authority over the Finaly youngster's lives as it had over Edgardo Mortara's life. In the final act of the drama the Church relented and the Finaly boys made their way to the Jewish state.

By the 1950s the relevant provisions that had been invoked in the Mortara case were absent from the code of canon law and the Vatican understood that Benedict XIV's policies would, in the perceptive words of Father Edward Flannery, "cause grave scandal among non-Catholics and great uneasiness among Catholics" if applied to the Finaly matter.[13] The virtually monolithic support the faithful gave Pius IX in the Mortara *cause célèbre* could not be replicated in the Christendom of the post-Holocaust era. For one thing, civil authority and clerical power were no longer inextricably linked in an increasingly secular world. For another, the suffering undergone by Jews from 1933 to 1945 had fortified Jewish moral claims on the Christian world. Thus, a new set of circumstances compelled the Vatican to surrender its prerogative in such cases of the unsanctioned baptism of Jewish children and to accept the basic idea that the natural rights of the family superseded the "supernatural," "divine rights" of the Church.[14]

Conversion under duress is now happily relegated to the scrapheap of history, but what of the *meshummad*, for example, Chief Rabbi Zolli, the apostate who, of his or her free will, decides to exchange Judaism for Catholicism? Voluntary conversion is a different matter altogether and has presented a different set of problems. It may well be the most painful issue in Jewish-Catholic relations. Although it is regarded as perfidy by Jews, that brand of conversion, undertaken freely, it would appear, cannot reasonably be used to assail the Roman Catholic Church. After all, freedom of religion guarantees the individual the right to choose among faiths according to the dictates of his or her conscience. However, Jews can expect such conversions to be interpreted with sensitivity and understanding. That is not always the case, as the Tomasi incident and the matter of Edith Stein have dramatically demonstrated in recent years.

A scant six months after Pope John Paul II's journey to the Rome synagogue, a canonization occurred which, according to some Italian Jews, violated the spirit of the nascent Christian-Jewish dialogue calling for mutual respect of religious convictions.[15] At issue was a seventeenth-century figure, San Giuseppe M. Tomasi, a Sicilian noble who became a member of the Theatine Order. Visitors to Rome's Basilica of Sant' Andrea della Valle where his body is contained in a precious urn will also find there a picture of Tomasi embracing Rabbi Mosé 'da Cave whom he had converted to Catholicism. Indeed, the 1698 conversion of da Cave, Tomasi's teacher of Hebrew, was cited in the canonization process as the third and last miracle performed by the saintly Sicilian.

A book published in support of Tomasi's sainthood had argued that he had wanted to determine if the rabbi's stubborn mind could be opened to the truth. Da Cave saw the light, did a religious volte-face, and realized that among Christians there were good people such as Tomasi. In contrast, he concluded that all Jews were "carrion." He eventually left the ghetto in which the Jews were cooped up and undertook a study of Christian doctrine.

Italian Jewish critics in particular were irked that Popes who were responsible for the demeaning ghetto conditions from which a rabbi such as da Cave would want to flee are ignored in the book. The current pontiff is chastised for canonizing Tomasi who converted a rabbi under those appalling circumstances and for not taking a stand in the present-day dialogue on the errors, the guilt, the enormous burden of the Catholic Church for shaping Jewish destiny.[16] In light of the Tomasi—da Cave "miracle," it is not difficult to conjure up a scenario in which a Father Dezza or even a Pope Pius XII would have his canonization cause buttressed by the miraculous conversion of another rabbi in Rome, indeed the Chief Rabbi of Rome!

Edith Stein, the last of eleven children in a devout Jewish family, was born on Yom Kippur in 1891, in Breslau, then a part of Germany and since the end of World War II, a Polish city. Either because she was inspired by the sixteenth-century Spanish mystic, St. Teresa, as she herself claimed, or because of the influence of the philosopher, Edmund Husserl, who was her mentor, or for other more mundane reasons which her niece has recently suggested, Edith, who possessed a brilliant and independent mind, converted to Catholicism in 1922.[17] Eleven years later, shortly after Adolf Hitler became Chancellor of Germany, she lost her teaching position at the Catholic Pedagogical Institute of Muenster owing to the pernicious racial policies of the Nazis.[18]

Still in her early forties, she abandoned academia and the life of a lay Catholic and embarked upon the life of a religious. In April 1934, the Carmelite Order admitted her. Thus, Edith Stein became Sister Teresa Benedicta of the Cross, but anti-Semitism dogged her even after she donned the habit of the Discalced Carmelites. Her doctoral dissertation in philosophy was unpublishable because of her ancestry.[19] Indeed, her personal safety was put in jeopardy. To spare her sister Carmelites the ire of the Nazis, she relocated to the Carmelite convent in Echt, Holland where she was joined by her sister, Rosa, who had also been baptized following the death of their mother. However, in August 1942, the S.S. seized both Rosa Stein and Sister Benedicta. Within days they were interned in the Dutch transit camp at Westerbork.[20] From there, it is believed, both were transported to Auschwitz. According to the Dutch Red Cross, Edith died on August 9 only a week after her arrest "for reasons of race and specifically because of Jewish descent."[21]

Two facets of the tragic Stein saga have lately engendered strife between Jews and the Catholic Church. One has to do with her explanation for the Nazis' persecution which Edith *putatively* ascribed to God's displeasure with the Children of Abraham for having rejected Jesus as the Messiah.[22] The evidence that Stein ever offered such an explanation for the Holocaust is fragmentary and inconclusive. Of course, this kind of interpretation of the Holocaust is deeply offensive to many Jews, as it absolves the Nazis who become instruments of divine will. Simultaneously, it blames the Jewish victims for their victimization. It has also been alleged that Stein even "offered her life for the conversion of the Jews to the Catholic faith."[23]

A second delicate aspect of the Stein story which has produced no little Vatican-Jewish friction is the argument that her death in Auschwitz was due to Nazi hatred of Catholicism. In other words, she died as a Catholic martyr. Some Catholics have argued with justification that Stein's arrest and deportation were triggered by the pastoral letter issued by the Dutch bishops protesting the Nazi "resettlement" of Jews.[24] Seizure of Jewish converts to Catholicism was supposedly Nazi retribution for the bishops' outspokenness. Skeptics have noted that in the absence of miracles which can be credited to Stein, proof that she was a martyr to the Catholic faith would substantially strengthen her chances of beatification and, ultimately, of achieving sainthood. In May 1987, Pope John Paul II raised Sister Benedicta to the status of blessed at a mass in Cologne. The stage has therefore been set for her canonization.

Jews are convinced that Edith Stein perished in the gas chambers not because she was a Catholic or a nun, but because she was born a Jew. For the Nazis, biology, not theology, determined one's fate. Emphasizing Stein's Catholicism, therefore, trivializes the horrific sacrifice of the Jews of Europe and constitutes insensitivity to Jewish feelings. When plans were revealed to construct a Carmelite convent at Auschwitz of which Edith Stein would be the major symbol, they unleashed a torrent of rage in the Jewish world for Auschwitz stands chiefly as a monument to Jewish, not Catholic anguish.

Eager to minimize the damage done to interfaith harmony by the Edith Stein debate, Dr. Eugene J. Fisher has stated that the beatification of Sister Benedicta was a "unique occasion for joint Catholic-Jewish reflection and reconciliation." Dr. Fisher has contended that in paying tribute to Stein, the Roman Catholic Church wished "to honor all six million Jewish victims of the Shoah." While Jews cannot gainsay Stein's right to espouse Catholicism, they can and do argue that a convert to Catholicism is an inappropriate role model in the Catholic-Jewish dialogue. Nor is she an appropriate symbol of the six million.[25] Jews may appreciate Dr. Fisher's feelings, but most are likely to question the Vatican's intentions and its sensitivity in this touchy matter.

Jewish cynicism, coupled with annoyance, had previously greeted another Holocaust-connected canonization campaign, that of Father Maximilian Kolbe, a Polish Franciscan who was made a saint by his countryman, Pope John Paul II, in 1982. Back in 1941, Father Kolbe had selflessly offered himself as a surrogate for a fellow Auschwitz inmate, Francis Gajowniczek, a Polish army sergeant who had been condemned to die by the Nazis. After a period of starvation, Kolbe's agony was ended by a lethal injection. As was the case with Edith Stein, his martyrdom obviated the need to show that miracles had occurred due to his intercession, thereby expediting the canonization process.

About Father Kolbe's suffering and humanitarianism in the hell that was Auschwitz, there is no disagreement. However, because it is known that he had voiced some anti-Semitic sentiments before the outbreak of World War II, there was consternation when he was first beatified in 1971. In October of that year, at a ceremony held in St. Peter's basilica, Pope Paul VI labelled Father Kolbe "perhaps the brightest and most glittering figure" to come out of the era of Nazi immorality.[26] Jewish hackles were raised again.

A passionate devotee of the Virgin Mary, Father Kolbe had published a weekly paper called the *Knight of the Immaculate* which occasionally reflected his stereotypical thinking about an international Zionist-Jewish conspiracy that he said guided anti-Church Masonic and Communist movements. Father Kolbe clearly subscribed to nefarious anti-Semitic views which were rife in Poland during the inter-war era, but did not align himself with the most fervent nationalist groups that persecuted Poland's sizeable Jewish minority.[27]

While the Vatican was declaring the Auschwitz martyr a saint, some Jews and a few Christians were branding him a notorious anti-Semite.[28] One critic caustically commented on the Vatican's motive in the Kolbe matter, "The Church needs a Holocaust saint, because whenever and wherever it could it helped Nazis and Fascists into power."[29] Perhaps the Pope hoped to neutralize some of the Jewish negativism about Kolbe when he used the canonization ceremony to express his revulsion over the October 1982 Arab surprise assault on Rome's Tempio Maggiore which left a two year old child dead and more than thirty worshipers injured, some very seriously. John Paul voiced his solidarity with the Jews of Rome. However, the Vatican's credibility was called into question because in the month prior to the synagogue incident, the Pope had received Yasir Arafat, chairman of the Palestine Liberation Organization, which many people held responsible for the bloodshed. Evidence of residual Jewish bitterness toward the Vatican harking back to the Second World War was provided by a spokesman for the Israeli government who assailed the Pope for meeting Arafat. Given the fact that the Church had been silent at the time of the Holocaust and many Jews believed, rightly or wrongly, the PLO leader wanted to finish the genocide begun by the Nazis, the spokesman thought the meeting "indicative of a certain moral standard."[30]

In 1984, Auschwitz was again at the epicenter of a Catholic-Jewish tremor. Salt seemed to have been poured onto unhealed Jewish wounds when plans were divulged to establish a Carmelite convent in a building on the periphery of the sprawling Auschwitz death camp complex. The exact site was to be a building in which the Nazis had once stored the deadly Zyklon B gas that had, four decades earlier, asphyxiated a few million Jews. For many Jews, the Auschwitz killing center epitomized the *Shoah*, the destruction of European Jewry. Although Catholics, including priests such as Father Kolbe, had been murdered there, most of the victims were Jews whose only crime had been their Jewishness. Thus, the creation of a Carmelite nunnery appeared to be a Catholic attempt to appropriate the Jewish martyrdom. Some Jews viewed it as part of an overall pattern, most evident in Poland and the Soviet Union, to play down and minimize the uniqueness of Hitler's war against the Jews, to make of the Jews just one of many ethnic groups persecuted by the Nazis. On the other hand, there were non-Jews who believed that it was historically inaccurate and unfair for Jews to monopolize Auschwitz as a symbol of Jewish suffering given the slaying of Poles and other Christians there.[31]

Aggravating the dispute was a campaign to collect money to install the would-be convent, a campaign carried out by the Belgian branch of Aid to the Church in Distress. That conservative organization's fund-raising literature rubbed many Jews the wrong way by what it said and by what it failed to say. Conspicuous by its absence was any allusion to Jews, the primary victims of Hitler's madness.

Conspicuous by its presence was a reference to the Carmelites' constructing a sacred sign which will witness the "victorious power of the Cross of Jesus."[32] Potential contributors were told that the convent would "become a spiritual fortress, a token of the conversion of brothers from various countries who went astray."[33] To critics, Jews and even some Catholic prelates, it was highly inappropriate at best and downright offensive at worst to utilize an Auschwitz memorial to reinforce proselytizing efforts.

A particularly acid response to the Auschwitz convent came from Chaika Grossman, a one-time ghetto fighter who emigrated to Israel at the end of the war and is today a well-known leftist member of the Knesset. Grossman charged the Catholic Church with nothing less than "annexing" the death camps. Furthermore, she said that Church documents made it clear that the convent was established to convey a specific theological message, namely that the souls of Christians who perished at Auschwitz, including the souls of Jews who converted to Christianity, had been saved. Salvation was not readily available to the souls of the multitudes of unbaptized Jews who were put to death there. However, Carmelite sisters would pray to atone for the transgressions of the latter. For Grossman, the Catholic Church had embarked on a campaign to posthumously "convert the Jewish victims of the Holocaust to Christianity."[34]

According to the fund-raising text of the Aid to Church in Distress, the convent was also to serve as a "sign of good will to erase the outrage of which the Vicar of Christ is so often the object." It was not made clear whether the pontiff they had in mind was John Paul II, who had just been given a somewhat frosty reception in the Low Countries or another, the earlier and more controversial Pope, Pius XII.

An accord hammered out in Geneva in February 1987 temporarily defused the volatile situation. It was agreed that within two years, in place of the convent, an educational center would be established in the nearby town of Oswiecim to inform the public about the Polish sacrifice and the Jewish *Shoah*.[35] Specifically, its job would be "fighting disinformation on, banalization of and revisionism concerning the Holocaust."[36] However, implementation of the accord did not move forward. In fact, when a Jewish delegation spoke to the Mother Superior of the Auschwitz convent in April 1988 it was told that the Jews no longer owned Poland![37] In the meanwhile, the number of nuns at the original convent site increased. Poland's hierarchy, not to mention the Vatican, were either unable or unwilling to intervene in this matter.

A conference of Jewish and Catholic representatives scheduled for Zurich in February 1989 was cancelled because of the lack of progress in moving the Carmelite convent beyond the perimeter of Auschwitz. The International Jewish Committee on Interreligious Consultations announced in New York on 25 February 1989, that until there was implementation of the so-called Geneva II agreement of February 1987, signed by Jewish leaders and several European archbishops, discussion with the Vatican on the painful topics of the Holocaust and anti-Semitism would be fruitless.[38]

In May 1989, Cardinal Johannes Willebrand, President of the Vatican's Commission for Religious Relations with Jews, guaranteed Jewish representatives that the convent would be relocated. However, he declined to set a deadline for the move, stating that the issue was one which fell under the purview of Franciszek Cardinal Macharski of Cracow.[39]

Meanwhile, construction of a twenty-three foot high crucifix on the convent site further poisoned the atmosphere. In Israel, the organization of Holocaust survivors appealed to the Vatican which had "remained silent at that time" to "remove the shadow of the cross from Auschwitz." At a ceremony held at the Holocaust memorial at Jerusalem's Yad Vashem on Yom Hashoah, the Holocaust memorial day, a spokesman for the group minced no words: "In Auschwitz, Jews were murdered for being Jews. No church or convent and no cross at the entrance to Auschwitz will atone for that horrendous crime, nor will it distort the identity of those who were murdered."[40]

On May 29, some three hundred Jewish women from more than a score of nations participated in a demonstration close to the convent site. They protested against tampering with the memory of the Jewish millions who were put to death at Auschwitz. One of their banners read "Don't De-Judaize the Holocaust." Another demanded "Get the Carmelite Convent Out of Auschwitz!"[41]

Other Jewish protests occurred in rapid succession. One involving American Jews who climbed over a fence around the convent drew a violent reaction from Polish workers and led to dissension among Jewish leaders.[42]

In July, Rabbi Marvin Hier of the Simon Wiesenthal Center in Los Angeles told Agostino Cardinal Casaroli, the Vatican secretary of state, in Rome that the Holy Father had an obligation to order the relocation of the convent. Casaroli said the matter had to be handled by the Polish hierarchy, meaning Cardinal Macharski. In August, Cardinal Marcharski in high dudgeon over the embarrassing Jewish demonstrations, said publicly that he could not continue efforts to build a center for Jewish-Christian dialogue close to the convent site.[43]

Just when the cause of Jewish-Catholic reconciliation appeared to have reached its nadir, the Polish primate, Jozef Cardinal Glemp, delivered what the *New York Times* dubbed a "surly sermon." Cardinal Glemp charged Jews with inciting hostility towards Poles and Polish sovereignty by challenging the Auschwitz location of the convent. He hinted that the aim of one Jewish protest at the convent site had been to murder some of the Carmelite sisters. He admonished Jews not to "talk with us from the position of a people raised above all others" and referred to Jewish access to the power of the mass media in many lands, notions which have long been staples of anti-Semites. In condemning Glemp's astringent comments, Jewish organizations were joined by the Solidarity movement and by Cardinal O'Connor in New York City. Initially, the Vatican indicated that it still deferred to local Polish prelates on this troublesome issue.[44] However, on September 19, under considerable pressure, the Vatican reversed its stand. A statement which appeared in the *Vatican Bulletin* endorsed the plan to relocate the Carmelite convent and to establish an interfaith center for information, dialogue, and prayer. Financial support for the center would be given by the Holy See.[45] Hovering above the convent quarrel as it hovers over the broader still unresolved issue of the Vatican's role in the Holocaust is the ubiquitous ghost of Eugenio Pacelli. Analogies were drawn between Pius XII's silence when confronted with Auschwitz and John Paul II's silence in the face of the Auschwitz convent.

Despite the foregoing altercations, there is no gainsaying the fact that considerable improvement has been recorded in Catholic-Jewish relations since Vatican II. Indeed, Rabbi James Rudin of the American Jewish Committee is surely correct when he writes that "there have been more positive encounters since 1965 than in the first 1900 years of the Church."[46] Nevertheless, in the 1980s, there remain significant bones of contention such as the Vatican's unwillingness to accord Israel full diplomatic recognition, differing views of the Holy See's role during the Holocaust, Catholic efforts to proselytize, and the Church's tendency to view Judaism essentially as prologue to Christianity which makes the former obsolete. Jewish chagrin was evident when the Vatican, in 1985, two decades after *Nostra Aetate*, issued its "Notes on the Correct Way to Present the Jews and Judaism in Preaching and Catechesis in the Catholic Church." Although the "Notes" contained much that was gratifying to the Jewish community, e.g., a denunciation of anti-Semitism and an acknowledgement of Christianity's Jewish roots, they also offended. Short shrift was given the Holocaust, the apocalyptic event in modern Jewish history.

Jews were also angered because the "Notes" stated that the uniqueness of the Jewish historical role lay in preparing the coming of Christ. Two American Jewish Committee specialists in interreligious affairs complained in the pages of *Commonweal*, a Catholic periodical, that, "by implication, Judaism is presented as a failed religion. Judaism fails to save its adherents, fails to understand its adherents, fails to understand its Scriptures, fails to accept its Messiah. Its central and formative events (e.g., the Exodus) are incomplete."[47]

Jews were further rankled because the "Notes" did not unequivocally repudiate evangelizing among Jews. Ambivalence and vagueness had marked the "Declaration on the Relationship of the Church to Non-Christian Religion" issued twenty years earlier. In that momentous declaration, the Second Vatican Council asserted with anticipation that the "Church awaits that day, known to God alone, on which all peoples will address the Lord in a 'single voice and serve him with one accord.' "[48] An earlier draft of the document had contained an allusion to the "conversion" of Jews but it was deleted because the Church leaders were primarily concerned with defining a mutuality of interests between the two monotheistic faiths. Consequently, the euphemism "with one accord" was used lest the Jewish world be upset. Jews have been upset periodically ever since because they contend that all talk of mutual esteem and reciprocal respect is empty rhetoric, and irreconcilable with conversion efforts.

Papal pronouncements raised many of the same concerns in 1986. References to a "New Covenant" or a "New Israel," nomenclature which implies that the Jewish religion is incomplete without Christianity, that Catholicism has supplanted Judaism, and that salvation is only obtainable through faith in Jesus as savior, caused Jews to fume. Such ideas were implicit in John Paul II's sermon delivered on 16 February 1986.[49] A week later, in a second Lenten homily, the pontiff observed that the call to renew the covenant with God originated in Abraham's time. "Nevertheless," he continued, "it is gradually clarified; gradually realized in salvation history. In the cross of Christ it receives its full illumination and final fulfillment."[50]

In 1987, this thorny "triumphalist" issue arose again when Joseph

Cardinal Ratzinger, who is the Vatican's theological watchdog by virtue of his lofty position as head of the Congregation for the Doctrine of the Faith, gave an interview to the conservative Italian weekly, *Il Sabato*. Inasmuch as the Cardinal is the chief guardian of orthodoxy, is thought by some to be the second most powerful man in the Vatican, and is known to be close to the pope, the published interview ignited a controversy between the Vatican and international Jewry.

According to *Il Sabato*'s text, Cardinal Ratzinger stated that the Holy Father's speeches, particularly his homily on the occasion of the beatification of Edith Stein, communicated an important message. Precisely because Jews did not wholly agree with the Pope, a true discourse was possible said the cardinal. On the pope's side, respect and esteem for the opinion of the other faiths is offered, but also a "theological line." Ratzinger continued: "It implies constantly our union with the faith of Abraham, but also the reality of Jesus Christ, in whom Abraham's faith finds its fulfillment."[51] Edith Stein was described as an agnostic who afterwards became a Catholic. By so doing, she not only acquired once again her faith in God, but found her faith in Christ, through which she entered *into the full inheritance of Abraham*" [emphasis mine]. "The Christ-event," said Ratzinger was the revelation of the "deep truth of the religion of Abraham."[52]

Several Jewish leaders reacted indignantly to the published interview which Tullia Zevi, President of the Union of Jewish Communities in Italy, averred was not a call to Catholic-Jewish dialogue, but an invitation to Jews to convert. If Judaism achieved validity only by pouring faith into Christianity, there was no discourse between equals. So long as Judaism was denied acceptance as a faith deserving of respect and reciprocal dignity, meaningful dialogue was not possible.[53]

Rabbi Marc Tannenbaum of the American Jewish Committee opined that Ratzinger failed to acknowledge "the vitality and autonomy of Judaism," adding that the cardinal "simply provides no place for Judaism and hence no space for dialogue."[54] Rabbi Mordechai Waxman, Chairman of the International Jewish Committee for Interreligious Consultations, was so exercised by Ratzinger's views that he cabled Cardinal Willebrand asking for a postponement of the International Catholic-Jewish Liaison Committee's December 1987 meeting scheduled for Washington, D.C. His request was made "in light of recent developments," an obvious allusion to the Ratzinger interview.[55] In January 1988, a number of disgruntled influential American rabbis boycotted a meeting with Cardinal Ratzinger arranged in New York City by Cardinal O'Connor.

Arthur Hertzberg, a prominent rabbi and scholar, thought Cardinal Ratzinger's remarks had cured Jews of the illusion that they and the Vatican could reach agreement on a new liberal theology. Hertzberg saw the remarks as an indication that "the church of John Paul II is unhappy with much of the legacy of John XXIII."[56]

In the hope of minimizing the damage done to the ever-fragile church-synagogue entente, Cardinal Ratzinger issued a clarification of his views. His remarks, uttered in German, his mother tongue, had nuances not rendered in the Italian by *Il Sabato*. Ratzinger insisted that by deleting key phrases such as "for us" and "as we see it" before the assertion Jews found unpalatable, *Il Sabato* distorted his meaning. He was conveying or trying to convey Catholic thinking, not theological beliefs that undergirded Jewish-Catholic colloquy. In his judgment, when a Jew such as Edith Stein becomes a Christian, that person should never forget his/her Jewish heritage. Respect for the Jewish people in their own faith and expectation was also expressed by the cardinal.[57]

In the Catholic world, meaningful religious tolerance and a positive relationship of reciprocal respect with Jews, are most objectionable to the now schismatic movement led by Archbishop Marcel Lefebvre who condemns the liberal and modernist Vatican II as a devil-inspired betrayal of traditional Roman Catholicism. Its Declaration of Religious Liberty exemplifies a spirit of adultery. Lefebvre sees Catholicism alone as the true religion. All other faiths are false. Therefore, attempts to better relations with them are misguided. Non-Catholics should be converted to the truth, not accorded the status of equals.

Lefebvre opposes the idea that "the man who believes in . . . and professes any religion whatsoever is just as worthy of respect as the man who says he professes the true religion."[58] When he consecrated several priests in 1983, the archbishop declared unambiguously that the Roman Catholic Church ". . . cannot admit of there being any other true religion outside of her, she cannot admit that one may find any way to salvation outside of her . . ."[59] Consequently, he continued, "she has a horror of any communion or union with false religions, with heresies, and with errors which put a distance between souls and her God who is the one and only God.''[60] Aberrant ecumenism, he charged, induced Cardinal Bea to enter into relations with ''the Masonic Jewish Lodge of B'nai B'rith of New York in the United States.''[61]

What one sees in Lefebvre's thinking is unadulterated, unconcealed ''supersessionism,'' the concept that Judaism has been superseded by Roman Catholicism. For the apostles of Lefebvre, by virtue of their rejection of the one true faith, most Jews are consigned to hell for eternity. As Bishop Richard Williamson, one of Lefebvre's chief spokesmen in the United States, explained recently, Jews cannot build bridges to heaven. Such bridges, which would be built on falsehoods, are bound to collapse. Bishop Williamson denies that Catholics and Jews worship the same god. Jews worship the god of the Talmud who is ''a devil, an absolute devil.''[62] Whoever rejects Jesus is an anti-Christ, says Williamson. Lefebvre was formally excommunicated in July 1988 after he consecrated four bishops without papal authorization. Consequently, it is unjustified to see his atavistic outlook as reflective of today's Vatican. It definitely is not, but, on the other hand, it is reasonable to say that his pre-John XXIII thinking about fraternal ties with the Jews has not been completely expunged from the Vatican mentality, as the Ratzinger incident reminds us.

To be sure, no modification or clarification by Ratzinger could dispel all Jewish suspicion of the Vatican's real intentions. Jews view the whole question of conversion through a special filter of history, a history replete with persecution and coercive conversion. In addition, because Jewish suffering at the hands of the Nazis was so horrific, because six million Jews—men, women and children—were consumed in the flames of the *Shoah*, and because many, Jews and non-Jews, believe that the Vatican under Pius XII was derelict in its moral duty to save Jews, prickliness about proselytizing which would further diminish the Jewish community is markedly heightened.

* * *

The furor over Kurt Waldheim helped to dramatize the presence of Pius XII's specter three decades after that pope's death. Throughout the Diaspora and in Israel, dismay, shock, incredulity, and anger were the typical Jewish responses to Pope John Paul II's invitation to

Austrian President, Kurt Waldheim, to pay a state visit in June 1987. While Waldheim was Secretary General of the United Nations, disturbing rumors had circulated that he had somehow been implicated in Nazi war crimes in Greece and Yugoslavia during World War II. His personal involvement was a matter of much speculation and debate when he successfully campaigned for the largely ceremonial post of President in June 1986.

Waldheim, who was pro-Nazi as a university student, had always been less than candid about his wartime activities. Indeed, he had initially lied when he wrote in his memoirs that he was a law student, not a soldier, when the atrocities in question were committed in the Balkans. Subsequently, he denied having knowledge of Nazi reprisals in Yugoslavia, or of the deportation of Greek Jews. However, an international commission of historians has concluded that he was culpable, morally if not legally, in the sense that he was in the vicinity when war crimes were carried out and opted not to protest.[63]

Despite the vehement objections of Jews and some non-Jews, the pope on 27 June 1987 became one of the first world leaders to officially greet Waldheim. According to news reports, on that occasion the pontiff lauded the Austrian for his work on behalf of peace. Nothing was said about his service in the German army.[64]

Many Jews could see no worthwhile purpose in the Vatican receiving Waldheim except, perhaps, to hear his confession of unconfessed sins committed more than forty years earlier. They sought to make him an international pariah, for he has been totally unrepentant about his behavior.[65] Like so many Germans and fellow Austrians of his generation, Waldheim has long portrayed himself simply as an obedient soldier who did his duty in extremely trying times and circumstances.

As might have been expected, the incident revived the unresolved controversy over Pope Pius XII's policies during the Holocaust. On the very day that the Pope granted Waldheim his audience in Rome, an event that produced picketing outside St. Peter's Basilica,[66] the American Jewish Congress published an open letter to John Paul II. Revenge was not the Congress' objective. Rather it wished to perpetuate the memory of the Nazi genocide which had claimed millions of lives. Waldheim, it declared, stood for the very opposite of memory. He symbolized evasion and denial. The Congress said that the principles that underlay the Vatican's decision to receive Waldheim were political, not moral. "Is it possible," the Congress inquired, "that in Waldheim's forgetfulness there is an echo, however distant, of the Church's forgetfulness as well? Has Your Holiness dealt with the indifference of the Catholic churches in Europe to the fate of the Jews during World War II?"[67] While acknowledging the heroism of many individual Catholics, the Congress propounded the notion that the "official churches" had abandoned the Jews to their agony.

Papal guilt in the Holocaust era was also the central theme of a syndicated editorial cartoon which was published in the *Boston Globe* and elsewhere. It showed a figure, obviously Waldheim in a Nazi uniform, outside the Vatican. "I have wartime sins to confess," he says. From St. Peter's came the reply, "Yours or ours?"[68]

Stung by the outcry over the Waldheim visit, and concerned about a meeting with Jewish leaders scheduled for September in Miami, the pope, in August 1987, penned a conciliatory letter to the Jewish community. "We Christians," the Polish-born pontiff wrote, "approach with fearsome respect the terrifying experience of the extermination, the Shoah, suffered by the Jews during the Second World War, and we seek to grasp its most authentic, specific and universal meaning."[69]

On September 1, meeting with representatives of Jewish organizations, predominantly American, at his Castel Gondolfo summer residence, the pope kept his counsel about Waldheim, but did speak about the Holocaust. Significantly, he used the Hebrew term *Shoah* and called it "a Second Exodus" inasmuch as the Jews had been persecuted by Hitler as they had by Pharaoh. Apparently to mollify Jewish apprehension that the Holy See was inclined to universalize the catastrophe, the pope described the Nazi slaughter as a "ruthless and inhuman attempt to exterminate the Jewish people . . . only because they were Jews."[70]

Still, John Paul has repeatedly and staunchly defended the role played by Pacelli vis-à-vis the Jews. He did so at the Castel Gondolfo parley on September 1 and again less than two weeks later in Miami when he recalled the "strong, unequivocal efforts of the popes against anti-Semitism and Nazis at the height of the persecution of the

Jews.''[71] Moreover, he prophesied that history would persuasively disclose ''how deeply Pius XII felt about the tragedy of the Jewish people, and how hard and effectively he worked to assist them during the Second World War.''[72]

At Castel Gondolfo it was announced that a Vatican statement on the Holocaust would be forthcoming. Conceivably, that could help to ascertain just how sincere and effective Pacelli's efforts were. Many Jewish leaders are of the opinion that the Vatican will procrastinate on the document which, they believe, may not be finished for years.[73]

More credible and clearer answers to the heretofore unanswered questions of papal policy during the Holocaust would surely be found in the secret Vatican archives now closed under a restrictive hundred year rule. John Cardinal O'Connor's bold proposal that scholars be given access to those archives is a sound one, but is unlikely to win the Vatican's favor. There is more than a slim chance that the information contained therein might aggravate rather than mitigate Catholic-Jewish tensions attributable to the Holocaust.

A second meeting between John Paul II and Waldheim occurred when the pontiff paid a five day visit to Austria in June 1988, in the fiftieth anniversary year of the Anschluss incorporating Austria into the Third Reich. Waldheim was still being given the cold shoulder by most Western leaders so that it was inevitable that the pope's tour would elicit protests from Jews and others. Nor was the protesters' ire assuaged when John Paul visited Mauthausen. In fact, his failure to mention Jews murdered at that concentration camp—Jesus was the only Jew specifically cited there—miffed Jews who were already distressed that the pope did not admonish Waldheim or allude to Austria's complicity with Nazi Germany. Speaking at Mauthausen, John Paul did name several Catholic victims whose martyrdom at the hands of the Nazis had led to their beatification.

Holocaust survivor and Nobel laureate Elie Wiesel is convinced that John Paul II has a Jewish problem. Wiesel is persuaded that the pope would like to ''dejudaize'' the *Shoah*, for not only did he omit the Jews when he spoke at Mauthausen, but he ignored the Jewish martyrs when he first visited Auschwitz. On the occasion of his second visit, the pontiff again failed to acknowledge the Jewishness of most of those who perished in that killing factory located near his native Cracow.

Wiesel has commented that instead of a general mass for all the victims, a rabbi should have been invited to say *kaddish*, the Hebrew prayer for the dead as John Paul offered Catholic prayers. Did the holy father wish (subconsciously) "to convert the Jewish dead posthumously?" Wiesel asked rhetorically.[74]

At a meeting with Austrian Jews, His Holiness did refer to the pain and suffering of the children of Israel, but added defensively that "it would be unjust and not truthful to charge Christianity with these unspeakable crimes." Tensions ran high, and a performance of Hochhuth's *The Deputy* was disrupted in Vienna by pro-papal demonstrators who found it unseemly to stage the play condemning Pius XII while the reigning holy father was in the country.

When John Paul told thousands of the faithful at a prayer service in the Austrian city of Lorch that the suffering of the Jews was "a gift to the world," the chasm between Jewish and Vatican perceptions of the Holocaust was widened still further. Jews who have suffered because of their Jewishness see little nobility in their suffering "as a communal sacrifice for the sins of Christian anti-Semitism," as one American rabbi put it.

In this connection, Wiesel has pointed out that "Jews have never considered the death of anyone a gift to anyone."[75] For Wiesel and for most Jews, the "murder of one million Jewish children was a moral scandal, a catastrophe of universal dimensions, not a gift."[76] Furthermore, describing the martyrdom of Jews as a gift served to exculpate the murderers and the silent bystanders whose silence made them accomplices to murder. Wiesel did not explicitly identify Pius XII as one of the bystanders, but the implication was there.

Within days of Pius XII's death in 1958, his last will and testament was discovered in a safe in his private study. In that document, which was made public, Pacelli begged the Almighty's mercy for his unspecified failures during the grave epoch when he was supreme pontiff. Forgiveness was also asked of anybody he might have offended by word or by deed.[77] Chief Rabbi Zolli to the contrary notwithstanding, posterity will long speculate about the real possibility that his greatest offense was his repeated failure to speak words and to carry out deeds that might have saved some of the six million Jewish men, women, and children immolated by the Nazis.

Notes

1. Chaim Bermant, "Rome Report," *Present Tense* (Winter 1978), p. 17.
2. "The Catholic Church and Judaism: The Bonds That Unite," Text of remarks delivered by John Paul II at the Rome synagogue, 13 April 1986.
3. Eugene J. Fisher and Leon Klenicki (eds.), *Pope John Paul II On Jews and Judaism 1979–1986* (Washington D.C.: NCCB Committee for Ecumenical and Interreligious Affairs and the Anti-Defamation League of B'nai B'rith, 1987), p. 82.
4. *New York Times*, 7 December 1986.
5. Ibid., 16 April 1986.
6. Ibid.
7. M. Keller, "The Case of the Finaly Orphans," *Congress Weekly*, 23 March 1953, p. 8. Keller, who played an important role in the case, was vice-chairman of the Grenoble committee of the World Jewish Congress. Also see Nicolas Baudy, "The Affair Of The Finaly Children: France Debates a Drama of Faith and the Family," *Commentary*, 15 No. 6 (June 1953), p. 548. Both the mayor and a Mr. Ettinger acknowledged that Dr. Finaly wished the boys to be raised by his sister in New Zealand.
8. Quoted in Baudy, p. 554.
9. Ibid., p. 555.
10. *The Jerusalem Post*, 15 March 1953.
11. S. J. Goldsmith, "The Finaly Drama," *World Jewish Affairs News and Feature Service*, 8 June 1953, pp. 1–2.
12. *The Jerusalem Post*, 28 June 1953.
13. Edward H. Flannery, "The Finaly Case," *The Bridge*, 1 (1955), p. 309.
14. Ibid.
15. "Il Gattopardo e il rabbino Mosé'," *Shalom* No. 8 (Settembre 1987), p. 13.
16. Ibid.
17. Susanne M. Batzdorff, "A Martyr of Auschwitz," *The New York Times Magazine*, 12 April 1987, p. 54.
18. Edith Stein, *Life In A Jewish Family 1891–1916: An Autobiography*. tran. Josephine Koeppel. (Washington D.C.: ICS Publications, 1986), p. 425.
19. Ibid., p. 428.
20. Ibid., pp 429, 431.
21. Ibid., p. 432.
22. See *Time*, 4 May 1987. Also see Jeannette Kupferman, "From Tragedy To Travesty," *Jewish Chronicle*, 23 May 1987.
23. Susanne M. Batzdorff, "Watching Tante Edith Become Teresa, Blessed Martyr of the Church," *Moment*, 12 No. 6 (September, 1987), p. 53. Also see Judith Hershcopf Banki, "The Beatification of Edith Stein: Ramifications for Catholic-Jewish Relations," Unpublished paper. The source of the idea that Stein offered her life to God "for the atonement of the unbelief of the Jewish people" is her last spiritual will and testament. See Woodward, *Making Saints*, pp. 136–137.
24. Batzdorff, "Watching," p. 47 and Banki, pp. 2–3. The idea that the Nazi action against Edith Stein was actuated by *odium fidei*, hatred of the faith, has been promoted by the Rev. Ambrogio Eszer, who spearheaded her beatification cause.

25. Eugene J. Fisher, ''Advisory on the Implications for Catholic-Jewish Relations of the Beatification of Edith Stein,'' unpublished statement of 24 April 1987.
26. *New York Times*, 18 October 1971.
27. *Jewish Post and Opinion*, 29 October 1982.
28. There is no dearth of Kolbe defenders. See ''American Defenders of a Polish Saint,'' *America* (30 April 1983); ''Saint Maximilian Kolbe: An Interdisciplinary, Interfaith Learning Project,'' (St. Louis: St. Louis Center for Holocaust Studies, 1983); and Patricia Treece, *A Man For Others: Maximilian Kolbe, Saint of Auschwitz, in the Words of Those Who Knew Him* (New York: Harper and Row, 1982.) There is irony in the fact that Hochhuth dedicated his *Deputy* to both Provost Bernhard Lichtenberg and to ''Father Maximilian Kolbe - Inmate No. 16670 in Auschwitz.'' Hochhuth may not have been aware of the anti-Semitic skeletons in Father Kolbe's closet.
29. Christopher Hitchens, ''Holy Men,'' *The Nation*, 15 January 1983, p. 37.
30. See George E. Irani, *The Papacy and the Middle East: The Role of the Holy See in the Arab-Israeli Conflict 1962–1984* (Notre Dame, Indiana: University of Notre Dame Press, 1986), p. 42.
31. John T. Pawlikowski, ''Recent Controversies Over The Auschwitz Convent and 'Shoah'.'' Unpublished paper prepared for the 1987 Meeting of the Polish American Historical Association (Washington, D.C., 28 December 1987), pp. 8–9. Pawlikowski argues that ''there is an equal need to recognize Auschwitz as the symbol of the Nazi attack against the Polish nation.'' Several years before he became Pope John Paul II, Cardinal Wojtyla expressed the opinion that the Catholic Church in his native Poland required a place at Auschwitz to mark its sacrifice. See Karen Adler, ''Controversy over the Carmelite Convent at Auschwitz 1988–1989: A Narrative of Events.'' A Research Report of the Institute of Jewish Affairs, London, No. 7, 1989, p. 14.
32. Judith H. Banki, ''The Convent Crisis,'' *American Jewish Committee Journal* (Spring 1987), p. 5.
33. Ibid.
34. Asher Wallfish, ''Church 'annexation of the camps' '', *Jerusalem Post International Edition*, Week ending 16 August 1986, p. 11.
35. Pawlikowski, p. 7.
36. *Jerusalem Post International Edition*, Week ending, 1 October 1988, p. 11.
37. George L. Spectre, ''The Challenge of Catholic-Jewish Dialogue,'' *The Star* (August-September 1988), p. 5. In 1989 the Mother Superior, Sister Teresa, told a journalist working for a Polish-American periodical that prior to the Holocaust ''the Jews were an insignificant minority group in Poland with a majority of privileges.'' There was no anti-Semitism in Poland at that time, she asserted. After the war, Jews were allegedly responsible for the Communist takeover of her homeland and the ensuing economic hardships. See Alan M. Dershowitz, ''A pious anti-Semite,'' *Jerusalem Post International Edition*, Week ending 2 December 1989. p. 8b.
38. Press release, International Jewish Committee on Interreligious Consultations, 23 February 1989. Jewish agencies in the United States did not speak with a single voice on the Auschwitz convent dispute. The Anti-Defamation League felt that ''any organized religious presence on the Auschwitz site disturbs the sanctity and symbolism of Auschwitz for Jews and Christians alike throughout the world and

particularly for Holocaust survivors—and their offspring." The American section of the World Jewish Congress passed a resolution which stated that the "convent controversy is symptomatic of a clear pattern by the Vatican to revise the history of the Holocaust and the role of the church during that terrible period." In sharp contrast, Rabbi Marc Tannenbaum of the American Jewish Committee praised the Pope's good will and sensitivity to Jewish feelings. See *The Star* (April 1989), p. 21; *New York Times*, 2 April 1989; and "WJC Reacts Sharply to Auschwitz Convent," *World Jewish Congress News and Views* (March/April 1989), p. 14.

39. *New York Times*, 21 May 1989.
40. *Jerusalem Post International Edition*, Week ending 13 May 1989; Haim Shapiro, "Survivor's plea to Vatican: Remove shadow of cross," *The Jewish Week*, 12 May 1989, p. 24 and Yossi Lempkowicz, "Auschwitz convent controversy is called 'misunderstanding' ", *The Jewish Week*, 12 May 1989, p. 24. In Cracow, a representative of the Carmelites argued that Birkenau not Auschwitz was the true symbol of the Holocaust for Jews because it was at Birkenau that Jews had been gassed. He added that Auschwitz was important for Poles because Father Kolbe and many of his Christian compatriots had been martyred there. See Lempkowicz, p. 24.
41. *New York Times*, 30 May 1989; *Jerusalem Post International Edition*, Week ending 10 June 1989.
42. The "sit-in" was led by the activist Orthodox rabbi from New York, Avi Weiss. The American Jewish Congress felt that Weiss' tactic was counterproductive. See "The Siegman syndrome," *Jerusalem Post*, 9 July 1990 and Henry Siegman, "Mocking the Messenger," *Jerusalem Post International Edition*, Week ending 21 July 1990.
43. *New York Times*, 11 August 1989 and 27 July 1989; *Jerusalem Post International Edition*, Weeks ending 29 July 1989 and 5 August 1989. According to a publication of the World Jewish Congress, Belgian Jews and Gentiles conducted weekly vigils outside the residence of the papal nuncio in Brussels to dramatize their opposition to the convent. See *Dateline World Jewry*, August 1989, p. 3. The Congress adopted another strongly worded resolution pressing John Paul II to "exercise his authority to assure the removal of the convent" from Auschwitz which it called "hallowed ground" for Jews. See *World Jewish Congress News and Views*, (June/July 1989), p. 12.
44. *New York Times*, 29 August 1989 and 30 August 1989.
45. Ibid., 20 September 1989. In February 1990, ground was finally broken for the center to replace the Carmelite convent. Polish prime minister Tadeusz Mazowiecki told representatives of the World Jewish Congress that he was sorry for "the hurt caused by the Auschwitz convent controversy." See the *World Jewish Congress News and Views*, May/June 1990, p. 3.
46. A. James Rudin, "Catholics and Jews Together," *Hadassah Magazine*, (August/September 1986), p. 13.
47. Banki, Judith and Mittelman, Alan L., "Why the 'Notes' Were Disappointing: Jews and Catholics: taking stock," *Commonweal (6 September 1985), p. 467.*
48. Walter Abbott, M. (ed.), *The Documents of Vatican II* (New York: Guild America, Association Presses, 1966), pp. 664–665.
49. *L'Osservatore Romano*, 3 March 1986.
50. Ibid., 10 March, 1986. This homily was delivered on 23 February 1986. Jews

were outraged again in August 1989 when John Paul II again opined that owing to the Jewish peoples' "infidelity to its God," a new covenant had been established through Christ. See the *New York Times*, 13 August 1989.

51. *Il Sabato*, 24–30 October 1987.
52. Ibid.
53. "Solo divenendo cristiano io divengo un vero ebreo,": *Shalom* N.9 Ottobre 1987, p. 9 and *New York Times*, 18 November 1987.
54. *New York Times*, 18 November 1987.
55. American Jewish Committee files, Rabbi Waxman to Cardinal Willebrands, 18 November 1987.
56. Arthur Hertzberg, "Cardinal Ratzinger Cures Jews of an Illusion," *New York Times*, 22 December 1987.
57. American Jewish Committee files, Agostino Bono, "Cardinal Ratzinger Issues Clarification of Remarks On Jews." Dispatch from Vatican City. American evangelical Protestant theologians are quite open about their goal of converting Jews to Christianity. In a 1989 declaration fifteen such theologians flatly repudiated the idea that Judaism today "contains within itself true knowledge of God's salvation."
58. Archbishop Lefebvre's Sermon at the Priestly Ordination in Econe, 29 June 1987.
59. A Public Statement on the Occasion of the Episcopal Consecration of Several Priests of the Society of St. Pius X, Albano, 19 October 1983.
60. Ibid.
61. Ibid.
62. Tape of an interview with Bishop Richard Williamson of the Society of St. Pius X (undated). Williamson also shares the view of the so-called "revisionists" that the Holocaust never occurred. It was a Jewish invention "so we would prostrate ourselves on our knees before them and approve of their new State of Israel," he told a Quebec audience. See *Dateline - World Jewry* (June 1989), pp. 6–7.
63. *New York Times*, 10 February 1988 and *Providence Journal* 9 February 1988.
64. *New York Times*, 26 June 1987.
65. The United States Justice Department did place Waldheim's name on a watch list of excludable aliens.
66. Protesters also gathered outside the residence of the Apostolic Delegate to Israel on the Mount of Olives. See the *Jerusalem Post International Edition*, week ending 27 June 1987.
67. *New York Times*, 26 June 1987.
68. Reproduced in the *New York Times*, 12 July 1987.
69. *New York Times*, 20 August 1987.
70. Levinson, Burton S. "Catholics and Jews: Another Chapter." *ADL Bulletin* (November 1987), p. 7.

    The question of universalizing the Holocaust has divided Jews. Some prefer to discuss the martyrdom of French resistance fighters, Ukrainian peasants, Polish patriots, Jehovah's Witnesses, Gypsies, and others along with the six million. Others insist on discussing the destruction of European Jewry almost exclusively because only Jews (and perhaps Gypsies) were earmarked for death simply because they were born into a particular ethnic group. See Henryk Greenberg, "Don't Universalize the Holocaust Memorial," *Midstream*, April 1986, pp. 6–7.
71. *New York Times*, 12 September 1987.
72. Ibid.

73. Seymour D. Reich, President of B'nai B'rith, has criticized John Paul II for defending Pacelli before the Vatican statement on the Holocaust is issued. Reich called it ''gratuitous and inappropriate to prejudge'' the statement. See George L. Spectre, ''The Challenge of Catholic-Jewish Dialogue,'' *The Star* (August–September, 1988), p. 44.
74. Elie Wiesel, ''Pope John Paul II and his Jewish Problem,'' *World Jewish Congress: News and Views* (July–August 1988), pp. 8–9.
75. Ibid., p. 9.
76. Ibid. In a similar vein John Cardinal O'Connor of New York once nettled Jews when he commented upon departing the Yad Vashem Holocaust memorial that the *Shoah* might be ''an enormous gift that Judaism has given the world.'' See Joseph Berger, ''The View From St. Patrick's,'' *New York Times Magazine*, 26 March 1989, p. 46.
77. *New York Times*, 11 October 1958.

Bibliography

Books

Abbott, Walter M. (ed.) *The Documents of Vatican II*. New York: Guild, America, Associated Presses, 1966.

Allen, Charles R. Jr. *Nazi War Criminals In America: Facts . . . Action*. New York: Highgate House, 1985.

Almansi, Dante. *Prima Relazione Al Governo Italiano circa le persecuzioni nazi-fasciste degli Ebrei in Roma* (Settembre 1943-guigno 1944). Roma: Unione Delle Comunità' Israelitiche Italiane, 1944.

Almog, Schmuel. (ed.) *Antisemitism Through the Ages*. Oxford: Pergamon Press, 1988.

American Jewish Committee, *The Jewish Communities of Nazi-Occupied Europe*. New York: Howard Fertig, 1982.

American Jewish Year Book, 5707 (1946–1947) Volume 48. Edited by Harry Schneiderman and Julius B. Maller. Philadelphia: The Jewish Publication Society, 1946.

Arieti, Silvano. *The Parnas*. New York: Basic Books, Inc., Publishers, 1979.

Armstrong, John A. *Ukrainian Nationalism 1939–1945*. New York: Columbia University Press, 1955.

Aron, Wellesley. *Wheels In The Storm: The Genesis of the Israeli Defense Forces*. Canberra: Roebuck Society Publication #13, 1974.

Aziz, Philippe. *Doctors of Death*, vol. 4. Geneva: Ferni Publishers, 1976.

Baer, Yitzhak. *A History Of The Jews In Christian Spain*. Philadelphia: The Jewish Publication Society of America, volume 1 and 2, 1961 and 1966.

Bauer, Yehuda. *A History of the Holocaust*. New York: Franklin Watts, 1982.

Bea, Augustin Cardinal. *The Church and the Jewish People: A Commentary on the Second Vatican Council on the Relation of the Church to Non-Christian Religions*. Translated by Philip Loretz. New York: Harper & Row, Publishers, 1966.

Berdoe, Edward. *The Browning Cyclopedia: A Guide To The Study Of The Works of Robert Browning*. London: George Allen and Unwin 1964.
Blanshard, Paul. *Paul Blanshard On Vatican II*. Boston: Beacon Press, 1966.
Blet, Pierre et al. (eds.) *Records and Documents Of The Holy See Relating To The Second World War - The Holy See And The War in Europe March 1939–August 1940*, volume 1. Washington: Corpus Books, 1965.
________. *Actes Et Documents Du Saint Siège Relatifs À La Seconde Guerre Mondiale*, Volumes 2, 8, 9, 10. Vatican City: Libreria Editrice Vaticana, 1966–1980.
Bokun, Branko. *Spy in the Vatican 1941–45*. New York: Praeger Publishers, 1973.
Blied, Benjamin J. *Catholics And the Civil War*. Milwaukee, 1945.
Brockdorff, Werner. *Flucht Vor Nurnberg: Plane und Organisation der Fluchtwege der NS-Prominenz in "Romischen Weg"* Munchen: Verlag Welsermuhl, 1969.
Browne-Olf, Lillian. *Their Name Is Pius: Portraits of Five Great Modern Popes*. Freeport, New York: Books For Libraries Press, 1970.
Browning, Robert. *The Complete Poetic And Dramatic Works of Robert Browning*. Boston: Houghton Mifflin Co., 1895.
Brunacci, D. Aldo. *Ebrei In Assisi durante la guerra-ricordi di un protagonista*. Assisi: Libreria Fonteiviva, 1985.
Bytwerk, Randall L. *Julius Streicher*. New York: Dorset Press, 1983.
Carpi, Daniel; Attilio Milano, Umberto Nahon (eds.) *Scritti in memoria di Enzo Sereni - Saggi sull' ebraismo romano*. Milano e Gerusalemme: Editrice Fondazione Sally Mayer Scuola Superiore Di Studi Ebraici, 1970.
Chadwick, Owen. *Britain and the Vatican during the Second World War*. Cambridge: Cambridge University Press, 1986.
Clancy, John G. *Apostle For Our Time Pope Paul VI*. New York: P. J. Kenedy and Sons, 1963.
Clark, Martin. *Modern Italy 1871–1982*. London: Longman, 1987.
Cohen, Arthur A. *The Myth of the Judeo-Christian Tradition*. New York and Evanston: Harper & Row, Publishers, 1957.
Coles, Robert. *Simone Weil: A Modern Pilgrimage*. Reading, Mass.: Addison-Wesley, 1987.
La Comunità Israelitica di Roma, *Ottobre 1943: Cronaca di un' infamia*. Roma, 1961.
Constantine, Prince of Bavaria, *The Pope: A Portrait From Life*. Translated by Diana Pyke. New York: Roy Publishers, n.d.
Conway, John S. *The Nazi Persecution of the Churches 1933–45*. London: Weidenfeld and Nicolson, 1968.
Cooney, John. *The American Pope: The Life And Times of Francis Cardinal Spellman*. New York: Times Books, 1984.
Debenedetti, Giacomo. *16 ottobre 1943 Otto ebrei*. Roma: Editori Riuniti, 1987.

DeFelice, Renzo. *Storia degli ebrei italiani sotto il fascismo*. Roma: Einaudi, 1961.

Delzell, Charles F. (ed.) *The Papacy and Totalitarianism Between The Two World Wars*. New York: John Wiley and Sons, Inc., 1974.

Documents on German Foreign Policy 1918–1945. Washington D.C.: United States Government Printing Office, 1964. Series D, volume 13.

Dollman, Eugenio. *Roma Nazista*. Milano: Longanesi & C., 1949.

———. *Call Me Coward*. London: William Kimber, 1956.

Endelman, Todd (ed.). *Jewish Apostasy In The Modern World*. New York: Holmes and Meier, 1987.

Falconi, Carlo. *The Silence Of Pius XII*. Translated by Bernard Wall. Boston: Little, Brown and Co., 1970.

Fiorentino, Fiorenza. *La Roma di Charles Poletti*. Roma: Bonacci Editore, 1986.

Fisher, Eugene J. and Leon Klenicki (eds.) *Pope John Paul II On Jews And Judaism 1979–1986*. Washington: United States Catholic Conference, 1987.

———. James A. Rudin, Marc H. Tannenbaum (eds.). *Twenty Years of Jewish-Catholic Relations*. New York: Paulist Press, 1986.

Flannery, Edward H. *The Anguish of the Jews: Twenty-three Centuries of Anti-Semitism*. New York: Paulist Press 1985.

Flusser, David. *Judaism And The Origins Of Christianity*. Jerusalem: The Magnes Press, The Hebrew University, 1988.

Foreign Relations of the United States: Diplomatic Papers, 1942 vol. 3 Europe. Washington, D.C.: United States Government Printing Office, 1961.

———. 1943 vol. 2. Europe. Washington, D.C.: United States Government Printing Office, 1964.

Friedlander, Saul. *Kurt Gerstein: The Ambiguity of Good*. Translated by Charles Fullman. New York: Alfred A. Knopf, 1969.

———. *Pius XII and the Third Reich: A Documentation*. Translated by Charles Fullman. New York: Alfred A. Knopf, 1966.

Gilbert, Arthur. *The Vatican Council and the Jews*. Cleveland and New York: World Publishing Co., 1968.

Gilbert, Martin. *Auschwitz and the Allies*. New York: Holt, Rinehart and Winston, 1982.

Gilman, Richard. *Faith, Sex, Mystery: A Memoir*. New York: Simon and Schuster, 1986.

Giovanetti, Alberto. *Roma città aperta*. Milano: Editrice Ancora Milano, 1962.

Graham, Robert A. *Pius XII's Defense Of Jews and Others: 1944–1945*. Milwaukee: Catholic League For Religious and Civil Rights.

Grayzel, Solomon. *The Church and the Jews in the XIIIth Century*. Edited by Kenneth R. Stow. Detroit: Wayne State University Press, 1989.

Hargrove, Katharine T. (ed.). *The Star and the Cross: Essays On Jewish-Christian Relations*. Milwaukee: The Bruce Publishing Co., 1966.
Hatch, Alden and Seamus Walshe. *Crown Of Glory: The Life Of Pope Pius XII*. New York: Hawthorn Books, Inc., Publishers, 1958.
Hearder, Harry. *Italy in the Age of the Risorgimento 1790–1870*. London: Longman, 1983.
Hebblethwaite, Peter. *In The Vatican*. London: Sidgwick & Jackson, 1986.
———. *Pope John XXIII Shepherd of the Modern World*. Garden City, New York: Doubleday and Company, Inc., 1985.
Helmreich, Ernst Christian. *The German Churches under Hitler: Background, Struggle And Epilogue*. Detroit: Wayne State University Press, 1979.
Herzer, Ivo, Klaus Voigt, James Burgwyn. *The Italian Refuge: Rescue of Jews During the Holocaust*. Washington D.C.: The Catholic University of America Press, 1989.
Herzstein, Robert Edwin. *Waldheim: The Missing Years*. New York: Arbor House/William Morrow and Co., 1987.
Hilberg, Raul. *The Destruction Of The European Jews*. New York: Harper and Row, 1979.
Hochhuth, Rolf. *The Deputy*. Translated by Richard and Clara Winston. New York: Grove Press, 1964.
Holmes, Derek, J. *The Papacy in the Modern World*. New York: The Crossroad Publishing Co., 1981.
Hsia, R. Po-Chia. *The Myth of Ritual Murder: Jews and Magic in Reformation Germany*. New Haven: Yale University Press, 1988.
Hudal, Alois. *Die Grundlagen des Nationalsozialismus: Eine ideengeschichtliche Untersuchung*. Leipzig: Johannes Gunther Verlag, 1937.
Hughes, H. Stuart. *Prisoners of Hope: The Silver Age of the Italian Jews 1924–1974*. Cambridge: Harvard University Press, 1983.
Irani, George E. *The Papacy and the Middle East: The Role of the Holy See in the Arab-Israeli Conflict 1962–1984*. Notre Dame, Indiana: University of Notre Dame Press, 1986.
Isaac, Jules. *The Teaching of Contempt: Christian Roots of Anti-Semitism*. New York: Holt, Rinehart and Winston, 1964.
John, Eric (ed.). *The Popes: A Concise Biographical History*. New York: Hawthorn Books, Inc., 1964.
Katz, Robert. *Black Sabbath: A Journey Through A Crime Against Humanity*. Toronto: The Macmillan Co., 1969.
———. *Death In Rome*. New York: The Macmillan Company, 1967.
Kertzer, Morris N. *With an H on my Dog Tag*. New York: Behrman House, Inc., 1947.
Korn, Bertram W. *The American Reaction to the Mortara Case: 1858–1859*. Cincinnati: 1957.

Kuhner, Hans. *Encyclopedia Of The Papacy*. New York: Philosophical Library, 1958.

Kurzman, Dan. *The Race for Rome*. Garden City, NY: Doubleday, 1975.

Lapide, Pinchas E. *The Last Three Popes And The Jews*. London: Souvenir Press, 1967.

Laqueur, Walter. *The Terrible Secret: Suppression of the Truth about Hitler's "Final Solution"*. New York: Penguin Books, 1982.

Leboucher, Fernande. *Incredible Mission*. Translated by J. F. Bernard. Garden City, New York: Doubleday & Company, Inc. 1969.

Lehnert, Pascalina. *Pio XII Il privilegio di servirlo*. Translated by Marola Guarducci Milano: Rusconi, 1984.

Levai, Jeno. *Hungarian Jewry and the Papacy: Pope Pius XII Did Not Remain Silent*. Translated by J. R. Foster. London: Sands & Co. (Publishers) Ltd., 1967.

Levi, Abramo. *Noi ebrei: In risposta a Paolo Orano*. Roma: Casa Editrice Pinciana, 1937.

Levin, Nora. *The Holocaust: The Destruction of European Jewry 1933–1945*. New York: Schocken Books, 1978.

Lewy, Guenter. *The Catholic Church and Nazi Germany*. New York: McGraw-Hill, 1964.

Lifton, Robert Jay. *The Nazi Doctors: Medical Killing and the Psychology of Genocide*. New York: Basic Books, Inc. Publishers, 1986.

Lipman, Sonia and V. D. (eds.). *The Century of Moses Montefiore*. Oxford University Press, 1985.

Littell, Franklin H. and Hubert G. Locke. (eds.). *The German Church Struggle and the Holocaust*. Detroit: Wayne State University Press, 1974.

Lukas, Richard C. *The Forgotten Holocaust: The Poles Under German Occupation 1939–1944*. Lexington: The University Press of Kentucky, 1986.

Manhattan, Avro. *The Vatican In World Politics*. New York: Gaer Associates, 1949.

Mann, Vivian B. (ed.). *Gardens And Ghettos: The Art of Jewish Life in Italy*. Berkeley: University of California Press, 1989.

Markish, Shimon. *Erasmus and the Jews*. Translated by Anthony Olcott. Chicago: The University of Chicago Press, 1986.

Martin, Malachi. *Three Popes and the Cardinal*. New York: Farrar, Straus and Giroux, 1972.

________. *The Jesuits: The Society of Jesus and the Betrayal of the Roman Catholic Church*. New York: Simon and Schuster, 1987.

Mayer, Hans. *Outsiders: A Study in Life and Letters*. Translated by Denis M. Sweet. Cambridge: The M.I.T. Press, 1982.

Medici, Paolo. *Conversione di Sabbato Nachamu: Rabbino Ebreo in Ancona*. Firenze: 1735.

Michaelis, Meir. *Mussolini and the Jews: German-Italian Relations and the*

Jewish Question in Italy 1922–1945. New York: Oxford University Press 1978.

Milano, Attilio. *Storia degli ebrei in Italia*. Turin: Einaudi, 1963.

Minerbi, Sergio Itzhak. *Ha-Vatican, Eretz Ha-Kodesh Veha-Tziyyonut* (The Vatican, the Holy Land and Zionism). Jerusalem: Yad Ben-Zvi Institute.

Modigliani, Piero. *I nazisti a Roma dal diario di un ebreo*. Roma: Città Nuova Editrice, 1984.

Morley, John F. *Vatican Diplomacy and the Jews during the Holocaust 1939–1943*: New York: Ktav Publishing House, 1980.

Morpurgo, Luciano. *Caccia all'Uomo! Vita sofferenze e beffe: Pagine di diario 1938–1944*. Roma: Casa Editrice Dalmatia S. A. Di Luciano Morpurgo, 1946.

Morse, Arthur D. *While Six Million Died: A Chronicle Of American Apathy*. New York: Random House, 1968.

Murphy, Paul I. and R. Rene Arlington. *La Popessa*. New York: Warner Books, 1983.

Namier, Lewis. *In The Nazi Era*. London: Macmillan & Co. Ltd., 1952.

Newman, Louis I. *A "Chief Rabbi" Of Rome Becomes A Catholic - A Study in Fright and Spite*. New York: The Renascence Press, 1945.

Ovazza, Ettore. *Il problema ebraico: Risposta a Paolo Orano*. Roma: Casa Editrice Pinciana, 1938.

Pacifici, Emanuele (ed.). *Commemorazione di Riccardo Pacifici Rabbino Capo di Genova vittima delle persecuzioni naziste*. Genova, 1984.

Pallenberg, Corrado. *The Vatican From Within*. London: George G. Harrap & Co., Ltd., 1961.

Papée, Kazimierz. *Pius XII A Polska 1939–1949*. Roma: Editrice Stadium 1954.

Paladini, Arrigo. *Via Tasso: Carcere nazista*. Roma: Istituto Poligrafico e Zecca dello Stato, 1986.

Picciotto Fargion, Liliana. *La deportazione degli ebrei dall' Italia*. Milano: Capelli, Editore, 1987.

———. *L'occupazione tedesca e gli ebrei di Roma — Documenti e fatti*. Roma: Carucci Editore Roma, 1979.

———. *"La persecuzione antiebraica in Italia"* in *L'Italia Nella Seconda Guerra Mondiale & nella Resistenza*. Edited by Francesca Ferratini Tosi, Gaetano Grassi, and Massimo Legnani. Milano: Franco Angeli, 1988, pp.. 197–217.

Plant, Richard. *The Pink Triangle*. New York: Henry Holt and Company, 1986.

Poliakov, Leon and Jacques Sabille. *Jews Under the Italian Occupation*. New York: Howard Fertig, 1983.

Posner, Gerald L. and John Ware. *Mengele: The Complete Story*. London: MacDonald Queen Anne Press, 1986.

Presser, J. *The Destruction of the Dutch Jews*. Translated by Arnold Pomerans. New York: E. P. Dutton & Co., Inc., 1969.

Prinz, Joachim. *Popes From The Ghetto: A View of Medieval Christendom.* New York: Dorset Press, 1966.
Ramati, Alexander (as told by Padre Rufino Niccacci). *The Assisi Underground: The Priests Who Rescued Jews.* New York: Harcourt Brace Jovanovich, 1978.
Rhodes, Anthony. *The Vatican in the Age of the Dictators 1922–1945.* London: Hodder and Stoughton, 1973.
Robertson, Esmonde M. *Mussolini as Empire-Builder: Europe and Africa 1932–1936.* New York: St. Martin's Press, 1977.
Roth, Cecil. *Gleanings: Essays In Jewish History Letters And Art.* New York: Bloch Publishing Co., 1967.
———. *The History of the Jews of Italy* Philadelphia: Jewish Publication Society, 1946.
———. *A History Of The Marranos.* Philadelphia: The Jewish Publication Society of America, 1932.
———. *Personalities And Events In Jewish History.* Philadelphia: The Jewish Publication Society of America, 1953.
Roche, Georges and Philippe Saint Germain. *Pie XII Devant L'Histoire.* Paris: Editions Robert Laffont, 1973.
Safran, Alexandre. *Resisting The Storm: Romania, 1940–1947 Memoirs.* Edited by Jean Ancel. Jerusalem: Yad Vashem, 1987.
Saint Maximilian Kolbe: An Interdisciplinary, Interfaith Learning Project. St. Louis: St. Louis Center for Holocaust Studies, 1982.
Salvemini, Gaetano and George La Piana. *What to do with Italy.* New York: Duell, Sloan and Pearce, 1943.
Schechtman, Joseph B. *Fighter and Prophet: The Vladimir Jabotinsky Story, The Last Years.* New York: Thomas Yoseloff, 1961.
Schlafke, Jakob. *Edith Stein: Documents Concerning Her Life and Death.* Translated by Susanne M. Batzdorff. New York: Edith Stein Guild, 1984.
Schwarzbaum, Haim. *Studies In Jewish And World Folklore.* Berlin: Walter De Gruyter & Co., 1968.
Scrivener, Jane. *Inside Rome With The Germans.* New York: The Macmillan Co., 1945.
Segre, Dan Vittorio. *Memoirs Of A Fortunate Jew: An Italian Story.* New York: Dell Publishing, 1988.
Shandruk, Pavlo. *Arms of Valor.* Translated by Roman Olesnicki. New York: Robert Speller and Sons, Publishers, Inc., 1959.
Sharkey, Don. *White Smoke Over The Vatican.* Dublin: C. J. Fallon Limited.
Simpson, Christopher. *Blowback: America's Recruitment of Nazis and Its Effects on the Cold War.* New York: Weidenfeld and Nicolson, 1988.
Sereny, Gitta. *Into That Darkness: An Examination of Conscience.* New York: Vintage Books, 1983.
Seven Great Encyclicals. Glen Rock, New Jersey: Paulist Press, 1963.
Sorani, Settimio. *Che cosa chiediamo al nuovo consiglio.* Roma: Tipografia Del Senato, 1945.

Smith, Dennis Mack. *Mussolini's Roman Empire*. New York: The Viking Press, 1976.

Stehlin, Stewart A. *Weimar and the Vatican 1919–1933 German-Vatican Diplomatic Relations in the Interwar Years*. Princeton: Princeton University Press, 1983.

Stein, Edith. *Life In A Jewish Family 1891–1916: An Autobiography*. Translated by Josephine Koeppel. Washington D.C.: ICS Publication, 1986.

Stein, George H. *The Waffen SS-Hitler's Elite Guard at War 1939–1945*. Ithaca: Cornell University Press, 1967.

Steinberg, Jonathan. *All or Nothing: The Axis and the Holocaust 1941–1943*. London: Routledge, 1990.

Stock, Mario. *Nel segno di Geremia: Storia della comunità israelitica di Trieste dal 1200*. Udine: Istituto Per L'Enciclopedia Del Friuli, Venezia Giulia, 1979.

Tas, Luciano. *Storia degli ebrei italiani*. Roma: Newton Compton editori, 1987.

Tec, Nechama. *When Light Pierced The Darkness: Christian Rescue of Jews in Nazi-Occupied Poland*. New York: Oxford University Press, 1986.

Toaff, Elio. *Perfidi giudei fratelli maggiori*. Milano: Arnoldo Mondadori Editore, 1987.

Torres, Tereska. *The Converts*. New York. Alfred A. Knopf, 1970.

Trachtenberg, Joshua. *The Devil And The Jews: The Medieval Conception Of The Jew And Its Relation To Modern Antisemitism*. New Haven: Yale University Press, 1943.

Treece, Patricia. *A Man For Others: Maximilian Kolbe, Saint of Auschwitz, in the Words of Those Who Knew Him*. New York: Harper and Row, 1982.

Trevelyan, Raleigh. *Rome '44: The Battle for the Eternal City*. New York: The Viking Press, 1981.

Troper, Harold and Morton Weinfeld. *Old Wounds: Jews, Ukrainians and the Hunt for Nazi War Criminals in Canada*. Chapel Hill: University of North Carolina Press, 1989.

Waagenaar, Sam. *The Pope's Jews*. La Salle, Illinois: A Library Press Book, 1974.

Weizsäcker, Ernst Von *Memories of Ernst Von Weizsäcker*. Translated by John Andrews. London: Victor Gollancz, 1951.

Wyman, David S. *The Abandonment Of The Jews: America And The Holocaust 1941–1945*. New York: Pantheon Books, 1984.

Zoller, Israele. *La comunità israelitica di Trieste: Studio di demografia storica* Ferrara: Casa Editrice, 1924.

________. *Israele: Studi storico-religiosi*. Udine: 1a delle Ediz. Accademiche, 1935.

________. *In Memoria di Ahad Ha'am*. Trieste: "La Sera", 1927.

________. *Letture ebraiche*. Trieste: Libreria Editrice, Treves Zanichelli, 1922.

_______. *Il nome della lettera "Cadde," Il nome divino Shaddas*. Firenze: La Poligrafica, 1926.
_______. *La vita religiosa ebraica*. Trieste: Tip. Sociale, 1932.
_______. *Tre milleni di storia*. Firenze: Israel, 1924.
Zolli, Eugenio. *Antisemitismo*. Roma: Casa Editrice A.V.E., 1945.
_______. *Before the Dawn*. New York: Sheed and Ward, 1954.
_______. *Christus*. Roma: Casa Editrice A.V.E., 1946.
_______. *L'ebraismo*. Roma: Editrice Studium, 1953.
_______. *Guida all' antico e nuovo testamento*. Milano: Garzanti, 1956.
_______. *Il Nazareno: Studi di esegesi neotestamentaria alla luce dell' aramaico e del pensiero rabbinico*. Udine: Istituto Delle Edizioni Accademiche, 1938.
_______. *Mi Encuentro Con Cristo*. Translated by Jose Maria Gonzalez Ruiz. Madrid: Patmos-Ediciones Rial, 1948.
_______. *The Nazarene: Studies in New Testament Exegesis*. translated by Cyril Vollert. St. Louis: B. Herder Book Co., 1950.
_______. (ed.) *Talmud Babilonese: Trattato delle benedizioni*. Bari: Editori Laterza, 1958.
_______. *Un'iscrizione votiva antico-sinaitica*. Roma: Anoninia romana editoriale, 1926.
_______. *Sinaischrift und greshcisch lateinisches Alphabet: Ursprung und Ideologie*, dargestellt von Dr. I. Zoller. Trieste: Selbstverlag, 1925.
Zuccotti, Susan. *The Italian and the Holocaust: Persecution, Rescue and Survival*. New York: Basic Books, Inc. Publishers, 1987.

Articles

Allen, Charles R. Jr. "U.S. documents attest to clerical involvement." *National Catholic Reporter*, 2 March 1984.
_______. "The Vatican and the Nazis." *Reform Judaism* (Spring/Summer 1983): 4–5.
"American Defenders of a Polish Saint," *America*, 30 April 1983.
Altholz, Josef L. "A Note On The English Catholic Reaction To The Mortara Case." *Jewish Social Studies*, Vol. 23 (April 1961): 111–118.
"Auschwitz Convent Still In Place." *Jerusalem Post International Edition*, week ending 1 October 1988.
Banki, Judith H. "The Convent Crisis." *American Jewish Committee Journal* (Spring, 1987): 5–6.
_______. and Mittelman, Alan L. "Why The 'Notes' Were Disappointing—Jews and Catholics: Taking Stock." *Commonweal* (6 September 1985) p. 463ff.
Barrillot, Bruno. "Defender of the Faith." *Present Tense*, 17 No. 1 (November/December 1989): 32–37.

Batzdorff, Susanne M. "A Martyr Of Auschwitz." *The New York Times Magazine*, 12 April 1987, pp. 52ff.

———. "Watching Tante Edith Become Teresa, Blessed Martyr of the Church," *Moment*, Vol. 12, no. 6 (September 1987): 46–53.

Baudy, Nicolas. "The Affair Of The Finaly Children." *Commentary*, 15 No. 6 (June 1953): 547–557.

Bauer, Yehuda. "The Goldberg Report." *Midstream* (February 1985): 25–28.

Berger, Joseph. "The View From St. Patrick's." *New York Times Magazine*, 26 March 1989, pp. 38ff.

Bermant, Chaim. "Rome Report." *Present Tense* (Winter 1978): 16–17.

Bernstein, Philip S. "Jewish Chaplains In World War II," *The American Jewish Year Book 5706* (1945–46), Vol. 47. Harry Schneiderman and Julius B. Maller, eds. Philadelphia: The Jewish Publication Society of America, 1945: 173–200.

Bertel, Giuseppe. "The Case Of Rabbi Zolli." *Congress Bi-Weekly* 2 March 1945, pp. 11–12.

Bole, William. "Who Helped Nazis Escape to America." *Present Tense* (Summer 1986): 6–10.

Bonfil, Robert. "The Devil and the Jews in the Christian Consciousness of the Middle Ages." *Antisemitism Through The Ages*. Edited by Shmuel Almog. Oxford: Pergamon Press, 1988: 91–98.

Boutwell, Jane. "Letter From Trieste." *The New Yorker*, 26 December 1988, pp. 76–80.

Briskin, Mae. "Rescue Italian Style." *The Jewish Monthly* (May 1986): 20–25.

Brodie, Israel. "British and Palestinian Jews In World War II." *The American Jewish Year Book 5707* (1946–47), Vol. 48. Harry Schneiderman and Julius B. Maller, eds. Philadelphia: The Jewish Publication Society of America, 1946.

Canepa, A. M. "Emancipation and Jewish Response in Mid-19th Century Italy." *European Historical Quarterly*. Vol. 16 No. 4 (October 1986): 403–439.

Cantoni, Raffaele. "Dante Almansi." *Israel* (13 January 1949), p. 1.

Carpi, Daniel. "The Catholic Church and Italian Jewry under the Fascists (to the Death of Pius XI)." *Yad Vashem Studies*, IV (1960): 43–56.

———. "The Rescue of Jews in the Italian Zone of Occupied Croatia." *Rescue Attempts During the Holocaust: Proceedings of the Second Yad Vashem International Historical Conference Jerusalem*, April 8–11, 1974. Jerusalem: Yad Vashem, 1977: 465–525.

Casper, Capt. [Bernard] "Parole fraterne agli Ebrei di Roma." *Israel*, 22 February 1945, pp. 1–2.

Castelli, Jim. "Unpublished encyclical attacked anti-Semitism." *National Catholic Reporter*, 15 December 1972, pp. 1ff.

Cavalli, Fiorello. "La Santa Sede contro le deportazioni degli ebrei dalla Slovacchia durante la Seconda Guerra Mondiale." *La Civilità Cattolica* Vol. 112 No. 3 (1961): 3–18.
"The Challenge of Rabbi Zolli's Conversion." *The Reconstructionist*, No. 2 (12 October 1945): 4–6.
Chadwick, Owen. "Weizsäcker, the Vatican, and the Jews of Rome." *The Journal of Ecclesiastical History* Vol. 28 No. 2 (1977): 179–199.
"The Conversion of the Chief Rabbi of Rome to Catholicism." *Religion* (April 1945): 22–23.
Conway, John S. "Records and Documents of the Holy See Relating to the Second World War." *Yad Vashem Studies* Vol. XV (1983): 327–345.
———. "The Silence of Pope Pius XII." *The Review Of Politics* Vol. 27 No. 1 (January 1965): 105–131.
David, Michael. "Great Jewish Convert." *Integrity* 8 (June 1954), p. 47.
Day, A. F. "The Mortara Case." *The Month*, Vol. 153 (1929): 500–529.
Dershowitz, Alan M. "A pious anti-Semite." *Jerusalem Post International Edition*, Week ending 2 December 1989, p. 8B.
Dezza, P. "Eugenio Zolli: da Gran Rabbino a testimone di Cristo (1881–1956).", *La Civiltà Cattolica*, I, Quaderno 3136 (21 February 1981): 340–349.
DiNola, Alfonso M. "Ma i veri ebrei sono i cristiani?" *Shalom* No. 10 (novembre 1987).
Dmytryshyn, Basil. "The Nazis And The SS Volunteer Division Galicia." *The American Slavic And East European Review*, XV No. 1 (February 1956): 1–10.
Donahue, John W. "Edith Stein's Early Years." *America* 10 January 1987, pp. 7ff.
Dushnyck, Walter. "Archbishop Buchko: Arch-Shepherd Of Ukrainian Refugees." *The Ukrainian Quarterly* (Spring 1975): 32–43.
Fink, Michael. "Marrano No More." *Jewish Monthly*, December 1989, pp. 16–21.
Fisher, Eugene J. "Twenty Years After Vatican II: The Church Is Still Struggling To Define Its Relationship With The Jewish People." *The Jewish Monthly* October 1985, pp. 20–25.
———. "Zionism and Catholic-Jewish Relations." *Jewish Frontier* (July–August 1988), No. 4 (574): 12–14.
———. "The Roman Liturgy and Catholic-Jewish Relations Since the Second Vatican Council." *Twenty Years of Jewish-Catholic Relations*, edited by Eugene J. Fisher, A. James Rudin, and Marc H. Tannenbaum. New York: Paulist Press, 1986: 135–155.
Flannery, Edward H. "The Finaly Case." *The Bridge*, Vol. I (1955): 292–313.
———. "Mortara Case." *New Catholic Encyclopedia* Vol. IX. New York: McGraw Hill Book Company, 1967: 1153.
Frisch, Daniel. "Another Letter by the Layman to His Daughter." *New Palestine*, 36 (12 October 1945): 19–20.

''From out of the Vatican: Tokenism.'' *The Jewish Week*, 17 February 1989, p. 26.

''From Synagogue to Christianity.'' *Journal of Religious Instruction*, 16 (October 1945): 173–174.

Fromm, Joe. ''Cleanup Man for the AMG.'' *Coronet*, November 1944.

''Il Gattopardo e il rabbino Mosè.'' *Shalom*, No. 8 (settembre 1987): p. 13.

Goldsmith, S. J. ''The Finaly Drama.'' *World Jewish Affairs News and Feature Service*, 8 June 1953, pp. 1–2.

Graham, Robert A. ''The 'Right To Kill' In The Third Reich: Prelude To Genocide.'' *The Catholic Historical Review* Vol. LXII (1976): 56–76.

Graubart, Judah L. ''The Vatican and the Jews: Cynicism and Indifference.'' *Judaism* Vol. 24 No. 2 (Spring 1975): 168–180.

Greiner, Franz. ''The Unpublished Encyclical.'' *International Catholic Review ''Communio''* (March/April 1973): p. 120.

Gross, John. ''Life Saving.'' *New York Review of Books*, 17 February 1983, pp. 3ff.

Hennesey, James. ''American Jesuit In Wartime Rome: The Diary of Vincent A. McCormick, S. J., 1942–1945.'' *Mid-America; an Historical Review*. 56 No. 1 (1974): 32–55.

Hertzberg, Arthur. ''Cardinal Ratzinger Cures Jews of an Illusion.'' *New York Times*, 22 December 1987.

_______. ''Doing Unto Others.'' *Present Tense*, 17 No. 1 (November/December 1989): 14–15.

Hill, Leonidas E. ''History and Rolf Hochhuth's The Deputy.'' *Mosaic* Vol. 1 No. 1 (October 1967): 118–131.

_______. ''The Vatican Embassy of Ernst Von Weizsäcker, 1943–1945.'' *The Journal of Modern History* Vol. 39 No. 2 (June 1967): 138–159.

Hitchens, Christopher. ''Holy Men.'' *The Nation*, 15 January 1983, p. 87.

Isser, Natalie. ''The Mortara Affair and Louis Veuillot.'' *Proceedings of the Annual Meeting of the Western Society for French History*. Vol. 7 (1979): 69–78.

Jona, Salvatore. ''Contributo allo studio degli ebrei in Italia durante il fascismo.'' *Gli ebrei in Italia durante il fascismo*. Guido Valabrega (ed.). Quaderni del Centro Di Documentazione Ebraica Contemporanea Sezione Italiana (Milano: 1962): 7–31.

Kahn, Lothar. ''Italy's New Anti-Semitism and the Old: Mussolini's Racial Laws.'' *Jewish Frontier*, No. 5 (September/October 1988): 25–26.

Keller, M. ''The Case of the Finaly Orphans.'' *Congress Weekly* 23 March 1953: 7–11.

Klein, Charlotte. ''Damascus to Kiev: *Civiltà Cattolica* on Ritual Murder.'' *The Wiener Library Bulletin* 27 No. 32 (1974): 18–25.

_______. ''In the Mirror of *Civiltà Cattolica*: Vatican view of Jewry, 1939–1962,'' *Christian attitudes on Jews and Judaism*, Vol. 43 (August 1975): pp. 12–16.

———. "Vatican and Zionism 1897–1967." *Christian attitudes on Jews and Judaism* No. 36–37 (June–August 1967): 11–16.
Klyber, A. B. "The Chief Rabbi's Conversion." *The Catholic Digest* September 1945: pp. 92–96.
Kubovy, Aryeh L. "The Silence of Pope Pius XII and the Beginnings of the 'Jewish Document'." *Yad Vashem Studies* VI (1967): 7–26.
Kupfermann, Jeannette. "From Tragedy To Travesty." *Jewish Chronicle*, 23 May 1986.
Lavi, Theodore. "The Vatican's Endeavors on Behalf of Rumanian Jewry During the Second World War." *Yad Vashem Studies* Vol. 5 (1963): 405–418.
Leiber, R. "Pio XII e gli ebrei di Roma 1943–1944." *La Civiltà Cattolica* 112 Vol. I (4 marzo 1961): 449–458.
———. "Pius XII as I Knew Him." *The Catholic Mind*, 57 (July–August 1959): 292–304.
Lempkowicz, Yossi. "Auschwitz convent controversy is called 'misunderstanding.' " *The Jewish Week*, 12 May 1989, p. 24.
———. "The 'Auschwitz Convent'." *Jerusalem Post International Edition*, Week ending 30 August 1986, p. 21.
Levin, Meyer. "What's Left of the Jews." *The Nation*, 28 July 1945, pp. 74–76.
Levinson, Burton S. "Catholics and Jews: Another Chapter." *ADL Bulletin* (November 1987) pp. 1ff.
Lichten, Joseph L. "Pius XII and the Jews." *The Catholic Mind*, Vol. 57 #1142 (March–April 1959): 159–162.
Lipson, Alfred and Samuel Lipson. "A Reply To The Pope's Request." *New York Times*, 16 July 1988, p. 27.
Littman, Sol. "Canada swallowed U.K. assurances on war crimes." *The Gazette* (Montreal), 21 August 1989.
Longley, Clifford. "Nazi legacy boils up again." *The Times* [London], 19 July 1988.
Marrus, Michael R. "French Churches and The Persecution of Jews in France, 1940–1944." In *Judaism And Christianity Under The Impact Of National Socialism*. Jerusalem: the Historical Society of Israel and the Zalman Shazar Center for Jewish History, 1987: 305–326.
Marx, Patricia. "An Interview With Rolf Hochhuth." *Partisan Review*, XXXI No. 3 (Summer 1964): 363–376.
Mashberg, Michael. "The Unpublished Encyclical of Pope Pius XI." *The National Jewish Monthly*, April 1978 pp. 40ff.
Michael, Robert. "Christian Theology and the Holocaust." *Midstream*, XXX No. 4 (April 1984): 6–9.
Michaelis, Meir. "The Attitude of the Fascist Regime to the Jews in Italy." *Yad Vashem Studies* IV (1960): 7–41.
———."The 'Duce' and the Jews: An Assessment of the Literature on

Italian Jewry under Fascism (1922–1945).'' *Yad Vashem Studies*. Vol. II (1976): 7–32.

Momigliano, Arnaldo. ''The Jews of Italy.'' *The New York Review of Books* 24 October 1985: 22–26.

Montini, Giovanni. ''Pius XII And The Jews.'' *The Tablet* [London] (29 June 1963): Pages unknown.

Morgan, Ted. ''L'Affaire Touvier: Opening Old Wounds.'' *The New York Times Magazine*, 1 October 1989, pp. 32ff.

''The Mortara Case.'' In *Documentary History of the Jews in the United States*. Edited by Morris U. Schappes. New York: The Citadel Press, 1952: 385–392.

O'Brien, Conor Cruise. ''A Lost Chance to Save the Jews?'' *The New York Review of Books*, 27 April 1989, pp. 27ff.

Oesterreicher, John M. ''Accusations not True nor made in good faith.'' *National Catholic Reporter*, 2 March 1984.

_______. Review of *A ''Chief Rabbi'' of Rome Becomes a Catholic: A Study in Fright and Spite* by Louis I. Newman *Catholic World*, vol. 163 (April 1946): 86–87.

''Le parole di Woytila e i silenzi di Pacelli.'' *Shalom* n.5 (maggio 1987): 8.

''Papal Politics.'' *Israel Scene* (November 1985): 10–11.

Pedatella, R. Anthony. ''The Italians Are Looking Better Than Ever.'' *Jewish Frontier* (April, 1985): pp. 10ff.

_______. ''Missing the Forest for the Trees.'' *Jewish Frontier* No. 5 (September/October 1988): 27–28.

_______. ''Reflections on Italian Attitudes Toward Jewry.'' *Jewish Frontier* (February 1984): 12–16.

_______. ''The Thematic Orientation of Major Jewish Italian Writers.'' *Jewish Frontier* (January–February 1987): 23–27.

Picciotto Fargion, Liliana. ''The Anti-Jewish Policy of the Italian Social Republic (1943–1945)'' Reprint from XVII of *Yad Vashem* (Jerusalem 1986).

Piperno, Sergio. ''Si poteva evitare il sabato nero?'' *Shalom* (July–August 1973): 20.

''Pius XII And The Third Reich.'' *Look*, 17 May 1966, pp. 36ff.

''Pius XII Papst der Deutschen.'' *Der Spiegel*, 18 November 1964, pp. 107–124.

''Por Que Se Convirtio El Gran Rabino De Roma.'' *Ecclesia* No. 192 (1945): 18.

''Poletti Slated For AMG Post In Milan, Lombardy.'' *The Stars and Stripes*, 23 February 1945.

Poliakov, Leon. ''The Vatican And The 'Jewish Question.' '' *Commentary* (November 1950): 439–449.

Pope Pius XII. ''Mystici Corporis Christi.'' *The Catholic Mind*, 41 No. 971 (November 1943): 1–44.

Pope Pius XII. ''The Unity of Human Society (Summi Pontificatus),'' *The Catholic Mind*, 37 No. 885 (November 8, 1939): 889–910.

Quinlan, John. ''Prisoner in the Vatican.'' *History Today*, XX No. 9 (September 1970): 620–627.

''Rabbi Becomes A Catholic.'' *Catholic World* 161 No. 81 (April 1945): 81–82.

''Rabbi Zolli Explains.'' *Ave Maria*, 6 October 1945, p. 211.

Rackman, Emanuel. ''Papal Problem.'' *The Jewish Week*, 17 February 1989, p. 31.

Rokeah, David. ''The Church Fathers and The Jews in Writings Designed for Internal and External Use.'' *Antisemitism Through The Ages*. Edited by Shmuel Almog. Oxford: Pergamon Press, 1988: 39–69.

Romano, Giorgio. ''La persecuzione e le deportazioni degli ebrei di Roma e d'Italia nelle opere di scrittori ebrei.'' In *Scritti in Memoria di Enzo Sereni*, edited by Daniel Carpi, Attilio Milano, and Umberto Nahon. Jerusalem and Milan Editrice Fondazione Sally Mayer Scuola Superiore Di Studi Ebraici: 314–339.

Rothkirchen, Livia. ''Vatican Policy and the 'Jewish Problem' in 'Independent' Slovakia (1939–1945).'' *Yad Vashem Studies in the European Jewish Catastrophe and Resistance*. Vol. 6 (1967): 27–53.

Rudin, A. James. ''Catholics and Jews Together.'' *Hadassah Magazine* August–September 1986): 13–14.

''Rund um die Affare Zolli.'' *Aufbau*, 16 March 1945, p. 32.

Sachs, Harvey. ''When Toscanini Went to Palestine.'' *Moment* (June 1989): 44–49.

Schwartz, Barry Dov. ''The Vatican And The Holocaust.'' *Conservative Judaism*, XVIII No. 4 (Summer 1964): 27–50.

Segre, Dan Vittorio. ''My Mother's Conversion.'' *Commentary*. Vol. 83 #2 (February 1987): 27–37.

Shapiro, Haim. ''Survivor's plea to Vatican: Remove shadow of cross.'' *The Jewish Week*, 12 May 1989, p. 24.

Sierra, Sergio J. ''Ma non furono 'Buoni vicini?'' in *Shalom* 5 (maggio 1987): 9.

Spectre, George L. ''The Challenge of Catholic-Jewish Dialogue.'' *The Star* August–September 1988, pp. 5ff.

Stehle, Hansjakob. ''Passe vom Papst?'' *Die Zeit*, 4 May 1984, pp. 9ff.

Stow, Kenneth R. ''Hatred of the Jews or Love of the Church: Papal Policy Toward the Jews in the Middle Ages.'' In *Antisemitism Through The Ages*. Edited by Shmuel Almog. Oxford: Pergamon Press, 1988: 71–89.

Tagliacozzo, Michael. ''La Comunità' di Roma sotto l'incubo della svastica—La grande razzia del 16 ottobre 1943'' in *Gli ebrei in Italia durante il fascismo* a cura di Guido Valabrega Quaderni del Centro di Documentazione Ebraica Contemporanea Sezione Italiana, Milano (novembre 1963): 8–37.

———. ''Le responsabilità di Kappler nella strage degli ebrei di Roma,'' *La*

Rassegna Mensile Di Israel—Volume Speciale In Memoria Di Attilio Milano Vol. XXXVI (July–September 1970): 389–414.

Toaff, Ariel. "Eugenio Zolli e l'oro di Roma." *Shalom*, Vol. 2, no. 9 (ottobre, 1968): pp. 3–4.

Toaff, Elio. "Finchè mi scavai la fossa." *Panorama*, 15 novembre 1987, pp. 290ff.

Toscano, Mario. "Gli ebrei in Italia dall' emancipazione alle persecuzioni." *Storia Contemporanea*, a XVII, m.s., ottobre 1986, pp. 905–954.

Ungar, Andre. "The Deputy." *Conservative Judaism*, XVIII No. 4 (Summer 1964): 51–62.

Varon, Benno Weiser. "The Nazis' Friends in Rome." *Midstream* XXX No. 4 (April 1984): 10–13.

Volli, Gemma. "Trieste 1938–1945." In *Gli ebrei in Italia durante il fascismo* a cura di Guido Valabrega. Quaderni del Centro di Documentazione Ebraica Contemporanea Sezione Italiana, Milano (novembre 1963): 38–50.

Wallfish, Asher. "Church 'annexation of the camps.' " *Jerusalem Post International Edition*, Week ending 16 August 1986, p. 71.

Ward, Leo R., "Conversion Story," *Commonweal*, 59, 26 (April 2, 1954): 652–653.

Wiesel, Elie. "Pope John Paul II and his Jewish Problem." *World Jewish Congress News and Views* (July–August 1988): 8–9.

Wigoder, Geoffrey. "The Pope in the Synagogue." *Midstream* (June–July 1986): 11–14.

"WJC Reacts Sharply to Auschwitz Convent." *World Jewish Congress News and Views* (March/April 1989): pp. 12ff.

Yahuda, A.S.E., "The Conversion of a 'Chief Rabbi.' " *The Jewish Forum* (September 1945): pp. 174–177.

Zahn, Gordon. "The unpublished encyclical: an opportunity missed." *National Catholic Reporter*, 15 December 1972, p. 9.

Zevi, Tullia. "Solo divenendo cristiano io divengo un vero ebreo." *Shalom* no. 9 ottobre 1987:9.

Zoller, Israel. "Il significato delle pitture nelle catacombe guidaiche a Roma." *Studi e materiali di storia delle religioni*, VII (1931): 144–152.

Zolli, Eugenio. "The Status of the State of Israel." *The Catholic World*, Vol. 169 (August 1949): 326–329.

———. "Note di esegesi biblica." In *Miscellanea di studi ebraici in memoria di H.P. Chajes*, publicata da Elia S. Artom et al. Firenze: Casa editrice Israel, 1930.

"Zolli's Apostasy." *Opinion*, XV No. 5 (March 1945): 3–4.

Zuccotti, Susan. "Pope Pius XII and the Holocaust: The Case in Italy." In *The Italian Refuge—Rescue of Jews During the Holocaust*. Edited by Ivo Herzer, Klaus Voigt, and James Burgwyn. Washington D.C.: The Catholic University of America Press, 1989: 254–270.

Newspapers and Periodicals

Avanti, 15 February 1945.
Daily News Bulletin, Jewish Telegraphic Agency, 20 September 1944; 15 February 1945, 20 February 1946.
Dateline World Jewry, June 1989 and August 1989.
The European Jewish Observer, 15 December 1944; 23 February 1945 and 2 March 1945.
Israel, 1 February 1945; 15 February 1945; 22 February 1945; 1 March 1945 and 13 January 1949.
Jerusalem Post, 15 March 1953.
Jerusalem Post International Edition. Week ending, 13 May 1989, 10 June 1989; 29 July 1989; 5 August 1989, 2 December 1989.
Jewish Chronicle, 23 February 1945.
Jewish Post And Opinion, 29 October 1982.
The Jewish Standard, 23 February 1945.
Journal de Genêve, 27 July 1964.
Ma'ariv, 9 June 1950.
London Times, 28 November 1975.
New York World Telegram, 28 November 1938.
New York Times, 1938–1990.
L'Osservatore Romano, 15 February 1945; 3 March 1986; 10 March 1986.
Palestine Post, 18 February 1945.
Il Piccolo Di Trieste, 1934–1936.
Il Popolo, 15 February 1945.
Il Popolo Di Trieste 1934.
Providence Journal, 9 February 1988.
Il Quotidiano, 15 February 1945.
Risorgimento Liberale, 14 February 1945.
Il Sabato, 24–30 October 1987.
Shalom, July–August 1973.
The Star, April, 1989.
The Stars and Stripes, 23 February 1944.
Time, 4 May 1987.
World Jewish Congress News and Views, June/July 1989 and May/June 1990.

Interviews

Almansi, Renato. Telephone interviews, 9 January 1987 and 30 April 1987.
Becker, Fritz. Telephone interview. Rome, 13 June 1985.
Ben-Horin, Nathan. Personal interview. Rome, June 12, 1985.
Berman, Judith. Personal interview. London, 14 June 1987.

deBernart, Maura. Personal interview. Rome, 23 May 1987.
Boccaccio, Father Pietro Paolo. Personal interview. Rome, 22 May 1987.
Burdett, Giorgina. Telephone interview. Rome, 9 June 1987.
Castelbolognese, Nives. Personal interview. Trieste, 24 May 1988.
Cavaletti, Sofia. Personal interviews. Rome, 24 June 1985 and 29 May 1987.
Daniel, Brother. Personal interview. Haifa, 14 October 1980.
Della Seta, Clara. Personal interview. Rome, 1 June 1987.
Dezza, Father Paolo. Personal interview. Vatican City, 22 May 1987.
Erbsen, Laura T. Telephone interview. 9 February 1988 and Personal interview. New York City, 14 March 1988.
Fiorentino, Gino. Personal interview. Rome, 3 June 1987.
Flannery, Edward H. Personal interview. Providence, Rhode Island, 12 March 1985.
Fumagalli, Father Pier Francesco. Personal interview. Vatican City, 25 May 1987.
Gilles, Sister Mireille. Personal interview. Rome, 26 May 1987.
Graham, Father Robert. Personal interviews. Rome, June 12, 1985 and 4 June 1987.
Greenleigh, Arthur. Personal interview. New York City, 12 March 1987.
Ianni, Clementina. Personal interview. Trieste, 26 May 1988.
Katz, Robert. Personal interview. Rome, 21 June 1985.
Kern, Piero. Personal interview. Trieste. 26 May 1988.
Kertzer, Julia. Telephone interview. 6 September 1988.
Landi, Monsignor Andrew P. Telephone interview. 2 May 1990.
Lichten, Joseph. Personal interview. Rome, 23 June 1985.
Littman, Sol. Telephone interview. 24 April 1990.
Margulies, Johanna Pick. Telephone interview. 2 June 1988.
McGrath, Sister Margaret. Personal interview. Rome, 30 May 1987.
Mejia, Msgr. Jorge. Personal interview. Vatican City, 14 June 1985.
Migliao, Bice. Personal interview. Rome, 28 May 1987.
Modigliani, Piero. Personal interview. Rome, 28 May 1987.
Morpurgo, Alma. Personal interview. Trieste, 26 May 1988.
Neufeld, Maurice. Telephone interview. 2 March 1987.
Nunberg, Elena Altri, Personal interview. Rome 26 May 1987.
Oesterreicher, John. Telephone interview. 11 January 1989.
Ottolenghi, Giuseppe. Personal interview. Rome, 3 June 1987.
Ottolenghi-Mortara, Luisa. Telephone interview. 2 June 1987.
Pacifici, Emanuele. Personal interview. Rome, 21 May 1987.
Paperman, Rabbi Aaron. Telephone interview. 23 June 1987.
Pavincello, More Nello. Personal interview. Rome, 27 May 1987.
Perlman, Max S. Telephone interview. 1 April 1987.
Picciotto Fargion, Liliana. Personal interview. Milan, 20 May 1988.
Richetti, Rabbi Elia. Personal interview. Trieste, 25 May 1988.
Rodal, Alti. Telephone interview. 24 April 1990.

Spiegel, Guido. Personal interview. Trieste, 24 May 1988.
Stock, Mario. Personal interview. Trieste, 31 May 1988.
Suadi Volpi, Silvia. Personal interview. Trieste, 30 May 1988.
Tedeschi, Anna Marcella. Personal interview. Milan. 21 May 1988.
Toaff, Rabbi Elio. Personal interview. Rome, 29 May 1987.
Toscano, Prof. Mario. Personal interview. Rome, 25 May 1987.
Voghera, Giorgio. Personal interview. Trieste, 25 May 1988.
Waagenaar, Sam. Personal interview. Rome, 5 June 1987.
Zaccaria, Nilda. Personal interview. Trieste, 27 May 1988.
Zolli-deBernart, Miriam. Personal interview. Rome, 23 May 1987.

Manuscript Collections

American Jewish Joint Distribution Committee Papers (New York City), File 716.
American Jewish Committee Files.
Father Edward Stanton Papers, Boston College, Boxes 1–3.
Italian State Archives, Interior Ministry, 1944.
Jacob Hochman Papers.
Maurice Neufeld Papers, Library of Congress (Washington D.C.).
Meyer Berman Papers.
National Archives, Suitland, Md. Rg 84, Records of the Foreign Service Posts of the Department of State, Rome Embassy and Consulate, General Records 1944 and 1945.
National Archives, Washington D.C. RG 59, General Records of the Department of State.
Public Record Office (London), Foreign Office, 371/16727/5452(1933) and 371/37255(1943).
Tempio Maggiore (Rome) Modern Archives, Israele Zolli File.
Trieste Synagogue Files.

Other Unpublished Sources

Adler, Karen. ''Controversy over the Carmelite Convent at Auschwitz 1988–1989: A Narrative of Events.'' A Research Report of the Institute of Jewish Affairs, London, No. 7, 1989.
Almansi, Renato J. ''Dante Almansi-President of the Union of Italian Jewish Communities November 13, 1939 to October 1, 1944.'' Unpublished manuscript (1971).
Archbishop Lefebvre's Sermon at the Priestly Ordination in Econe, 29 June 1987.
Banki, Judith Hershcopf. ''The Beatification of Edith Stein: Ramifications for Catholic-Jewish Relations.'' Unpublished paper prepared for the American Jewish Committee.

Canepa, Andrew. ''Christian-Jewish Relations in Italy from Unification to Fascism.'' Unpublished paper presented to the Conference on ''Italians and Jews: Rescue And Aid During The Holocaust.'' Boston University, 6 and 7 November 1986.
''The Catholic Church and Judaism: The Bonds That Unite.'' Text of remarks delivered by John Paul II at the Rome synagogue, 13 April 1986.
———. ''Controversy over the Carmelite Convent at Auschwitz 1988–89: A Narrative of Events.'' Unpublished research report No. 7 of the Institute of Jewish Affairs (London), 1989.
Fisher, Eugene J. ''Advisory on the Implications for Catholic-Jewish Relations of the Beatification of Edith Stein.'' Unpublished statement 24 April 1987.
———. ''The Holocaust And The State of Israel: A Catholic Perspective.'' Unpublished paper (n.d.)
La Vista, Vincent. ''Illegal Emigration Movements In And Through Italy.'' Unpublished report, 15 May 1947.
Matrimonial Records of the Jewish Community of Trieste 1913–1925.
Michaelis, Meir. ''Rabbi Eugenio Zolli and Italian Jewry.'' Unpublished manuscript (in Hebrew).
Mittleman, Alan. ''Declaration on the Relation of the Church to Non-Christian Religions (Nostra Aetate): A Synopsis and Commentary.'' Unpublished paper prepared for the American Jewish Committee.
———. ''Issues in the Jewish-Christian Dialogue: A Syllabus for Adult Education.'' Unpublished paper prepared for the American Jewish Committee.
———. ''John Paul II and the Jews: A Paradoxical Relationship.'' Unpublished paper prepared for the American Jewish Committee.
———. ''Landmark Statements in Catholic-Jewish Relations 1967–1986—A Synopsis and Commentary.'' Unpublished paper prepared for the American Jewish Committee.
———. ''Origins of Contemporary Catholic-Jewish Relations: The Second Vatican Council and the Statement on the Jews.'' Unpublished paper prepared for the American Jewish Committee.
Pawlikowski, John T. ''Recent Controversies Over the Auschwitz Convent and 'Shoah'.'' Unpublished paper prepared for the 1987 Meeting of the Polish American Historical Association, Washington D.C., 28 December 1987.
———. ''Jews and Christians: The Road Ahead.'' Unpublished paper prepared for the National Institute for Catholic-Jewish Education.
Perlman, Max S. ''Address Given At Southern Regional Meeting of the American Jewish Joint Distribution Committee Meeting.'' 14 January 1945, Atlanta, Ga.
Pontifical Commission ''Iustitia et Pax''. ''The Church and Racism: Towards A More Fraternal Society.'' Vatican City: 1988.

''Present Memory: Jews and the City of Rome During the Nazi Occupation.'' 1983 film (Italian).

Press Release of the National Catholic News Service, 12 December 1972.

A Public Statement on the Occasion of the Episcopal Consecration of Several Priests of the Society of St. Pius X, Albano, 19 October 1983.

Raiskin, Gerald. ''Story Of A Convert.'' Unpublished sermon delivered at Stephen Wise Free Synagogue, New York City, 9 April 1954.

Rodal, Alti. ''Nazi War Criminals In Canada: The Historical and Policy Setting From The 1940's To The Present.'' Unpublished report prepared as an annex to the Deschenes Commission Report (1985).

Rudin, A. James. ''The Worship of Good Friday: Jewish Concerns.'' Unpublished paper prepared for the National Institute For Catholic-Jewish Education.

''Summary of Facts and Documents: Simon Wiesenthal Center Investigations on Rauff and the Church.''

Tape of an interview with Bishop Richard Williamson of the Society of St. Pius X (undated).

Index